Poor Children and Welfare Reform

Poor Children and Welfare Reform

OLIVIA GOLDEN

Foreword by Lisbeth Schorr

Auburn House
Westport, Connecticut • London

HV
699
.G64
1992

Library of Congress Cataloging-in-Publication Data

Golden, Olivia Ann.
  Poor children and welfare reform / Olivia Golden ; foreword
by Lisbeth Schorr.
    p.   cm.
  Includes bibliographical references and index.
  ISBN 0-86569-045-6 (alk. paper)
  1. Family services—United States. 2. Child welfare—United
States. 3. Poor children—United States. I. Title.
HV699.G64 1992
362.7'1'0973—dc20   92-886

British Library Cataloguing in Publication Data is available.

Library of Congress Catalog Card Number: 92-886
ISBN: 0-86569-045-6

First published in 1992

Auburn House, 88 Post Road West, Westport, CT 06881
An imprint of Greenwood Publishing Group, Inc.

Printed in the United States of America

The paper used in this book complies with the
Permanent Paper Standard issued by the National
Information Standards Organization (Z39.48-1984).

10 9 8 7 6 5 4 3 2 1

Research funded by the Foundation for Child Development, New York City

The Foundation for Child Development is a private foundation that makes grants to educational and charitable institutions. Its main interests are in research, advocacy, and public
information projects, and service experiments in New York City that help translate theoretical
knowledge about children at risk into policies and practices that affect their daily lives.

To my parents, Morris and Hilda Golden

Contents

Foreword

Olivia Golden's thorough analysis of the potential of welfare reform to improve the lives of children comes at just the right time. The country is in a great ferment, trying to rethink and reshape an outmoded welfare system. We are in the midst of a crisis of confidence about whether American institutions can be made to work to assure our survival as a decent, competitive, and prosperous nation. Policymakers, administrators, and the public desperately need exactly the kind of information this excellent book provides.

The part of the "welfare system" that is provoking so much concern today originally became law as the "Aid to Dependent Children" provisions of the 1935 Social Security Act, designed primarily to provide support to the children of mothers who had been widowed. By the time the Family Support Act of 1988 was passed, the beneficiary population consisted predominantly of families headed by women who were separated or divorced or had never been married. Reflecting the rapid social and economic changes of the previous two decades, including the rapidly rising proportion of mothers in the work force, its primary purpose was no longer to provide mothers with income to enable them to stay home to care for their children. Rather it was to help the recipients of welfare move toward economic self-sufficiency, by providing them with education, training, and other services which would result in their employability and employment.

The language of the Family Support Act reflects some, but not much, concern with the impact of the new provisions on the children of welfare recipients. Like much of America's social policy, it responded primarily to short-term agendas (reduce the costs of welfare, and get "those women'' into the labor market). It recognized that single mothers needed someone to care for their children if they were to be able to take advantage of training and employment opportunities, but if there was a long-term agenda, it was limited to the vague hope that children would benefit when the source of family income is the mother's employment rather than a welfare check. The legislation did not clearly reflect either the well-established finding that children's chances of success at school and in life improve significantly when their needs for health care, early education, and child care are well met, or the possibility that the welfare system could play a significant role in assuring that this is done.

This is the potential of welfare reform that Olivia Golden addresses in this book. She and her colleagues visited seven welfare agencies that had organized themselves to respond to the needs of children as well as to the jobs-related needs of their mothers, even before the Family Support Act became law. She has come to understand the ingredients of their success, and is now in a position to provide advice based on real-world experience. Policymakers and administrators who recognize the need to harness welfare reform to improve the prospects of two generations will find in this book the essential guidelines they need.

In supporting this work, the Foundation for Child Development was particularly enthusiastic about its potential to highlight the ways the Family Support Act could meet the needs of two generations at once. The population of children who could be helped in this context is among the most vulnerable in the society, and their families' access to quality child care, health care, support services and schooling has been severely constrained. For too long, the employment needs of adults have been dealt with in isolation from the needs for quality child care and support for parenting, and the results of these piecemeal efforts have often been disappointing. Welfare agencies that are able to take on the combined tasks of supporting adult economic self-sufficiency and healthy child development will become part of the new movement in human services, away from fragmented, disconnected and episodic efforts to help, and towards a more responsive, family-focused, prevention oriented system of services.

The observations, analyses and conclusions of this study will be particularly useful because they reflect Olivia Golden's rich background as an academic, policy and budget analyst, manager, administrator and child advocate. These varied perspectives give her unique insight into the challenges inherent in efforts to connect the sharp realities of service delivery and public management with difficult policy and political choices.

The reader will find in the pages to follow no attempt to minimize the difficulties of the task. Organizations that have been instructed over the years that their achievements will be measured exclusively by their success in getting checks out on time, but only to those who can provide proof that they meet detailed and rigid eligibility criteria, are being asked to take on a new mission that requires a totally different relationship between worker and client. Welfare workers who have been undervalued, underpaid, and overworked are being asked to form warm, trusting, and supporting relationships with a dispirited, depressed, and despairing clientele. Welfare agencies that have been isolated from social services, schools, and other community agencies working with children are being asked to mobilize a narrow, specialized, fragmented service system on behalf of children and families with complex, multiple needs.

Dr. Golden's "cautiously optimistic" conclusions about the potential of welfare agencies to meet the needs of welfare recipients *and* their children are based on solid evidence of programs that have overcome these difficulties. They have done so by systematically paying attention to the needs of children, by providing workers with low caseloads to permit intensive, personal work with families, and by actually altering the ways that health, child care, and other agencies deal with high risk children. Successful agencies have articulated and promulgated a new and coherent mission that focuses on lifting families out of poverty in this generation and the next; they have developed collaborative relationships with child-serving agencies; they have chosen and supported staff who could respond to family needs; and they have found ways of reconciling the need to be responsive (to families) with the need to be accountable (in the expenditure of public funds).

The role for the welfare agencies of tomorrow that is mapped out in this book is a difficult one. But if the nation is to provide ladders out of poverty for the families that are now stuck at the bottom, then welfare agencies must be able to play the broader role that Dr. Golden envisions, and that she demonstrates is possible.

Lisbeth Schorr

Acknowledgments

I would like to express my appreciation to the Foundation for Child Development for its support of this research. At a personal level, I am deeply grateful to Barbara Blum, President of the foundation, and to Susan Blank, Project Officer, for their unwavering enthusiasm for the project. I would also like to express enormous gratitude to Mary Skinner, Project Director, and Ruth Baker, Research Assistant, for their talent, commitment, and wisdom at every stage of the research design and execution. As Project Director, Mary Skinner collaborated on the research design, supervised the site selection and site visit process, conducted three site visits, and participated in two others. Her creativity, careful judgment, and original insights have deeply influenced the study report. Ruth Baker assisted impeccably in the research design and the site selection, provided invaluable help in organizing information and logistics for the site visits, participated in two of the visits, and wrote thoughtful initial drafts of two of the case studies. In addition, I want to thank William Clark, who provided valuable assistance in site visit preparation and information collection as an undergraduate assistant to the project.

The members of the Project Advisory Board deserve special thanks for their willingness to read drafts and answer questions. The members are: Dr. J. Lawrence Aber, Columbia University; Dr. Jerome Kagan, Harvard University; Dr. Sharon Lynn Kagan, Yale University; Allen Kraus, former Deputy Commissioner for Income Maintenance of the New York City Human Resources Administration; Gwen Morgan, Work/Family Directions; Dr. Julius Richmond, Harvard University; Lucy Williams, Northeastern University.

For extraordinarily thoughtful and helpful comments on the many drafts of this study, I would like to thank Mary Jo Bane, Susan Blank, Mark

Greenberg, Toby Herr, James Riccio, Sheila Smith, the site administrators, and the Project Advisory Board. In particular, the study could not have been completed without Mary Jo Bane's wisdom and encouragement. Of course, any remaining mistakes of fact and errors in judgment are the author's alone. For professional, patient, and enthusiastic assistance in typing and preparation of the study's many drafts, I would like to thank Jesselynn Opie. Thanks also go to Sharie Brown, who ably took over the final draft with its many details.

Finally, I want to thank the program administrators, workers, and clients at the eight study sites, for time, help, and enthusiasm, which were graciously and generously given.

1

Introduction

In a scene that is repeated many times every day all over the country, a young woman walks into a state office that offers benefits under Aid to Families with Dependent Children (AFDC), the major benefit program in the United States for families in poverty. She is there for a routine eligibility review, but she is also worried about a landlord who is threatening eviction, about the health of her younger child, and about her older child, who is not doing well in school. With her younger son always crying from ear infections and her older child skipping school, she feels at her wits' end about how to cope with them—let alone how to find a new apartment that she can afford on the $400-a-month AFDC check. She may have to move the whole family into one room in her mother's apartment, but she and her mother always fight about child rearing and she does not trust her mother's boyfriend anywhere near the kids after her own experiences of his sexual advances.

What will happen to this young woman in the welfare office? One state welfare eligibility worker reports on how she conducts eligibility interviews:

[The clients] would get a packet which they had filled out when they came in. . . . [We] make sure they have no changes. . . . Then we have the computer forms that we have to do.

Interviewer: Does it ever come up . . . problems that the client has?

A: Yeah. . . . We have a lot that sometimes don't have the money to pay their rent. We don't basically handle that here, but we have different agencies that we can refer them to. . . . Some of them will just call afraid of their husband or the father of the child. We really can't do anything here, but we can give

them the number for one of our other agencies where they can call for
protection. . . .

Interviewer: What if you have concerns, say, about whether or not the child is
getting to a doctor, or something like that? Do you make referrals to health care—is
that part of your job?

A: It's not part of my job. . . .

Interviewer: What do you find most rewarding about your job?

A: Being able to help the client. . . .

Interviewer: And how do you know when you are doing a good job?

A: Well, I guess when the end of the year report comes back, and the quality
control [the audit of accuracy in eligibility determinations] comes back and I have
no errors.

In short, what is most likely to happen at the welfare department is
that the young woman will fill out the proper forms without mentioning
any of her concerns. If she does manage to break the format of the interview and raise them, she is likely to be brushed off by a busy worker
who is concerned about accuracy and "quality control," rather than other
needs which are "not part of [the] job."

This particular young woman's story is imaginary, though it draws on
both interview and statistical evidence about frequent experiences of
AFDC families. However, the welfare eligibility worker's description of
her job is real. And, as the remainder of this book documents, while the
description is not universal, it is certainly neither rare nor a worst case.
It omits unpleasant and demeaning features of the welfare experience
that recipients and advocates sometimes cite: discrimination and outright
hostility, for example. However, even without these additional features,
and even when the welfare worker genuinely wants to help, the example suggests that our large public welfare agencies (despite employing
some hundred thousand workers to assist several million poor families
with children) too often play little positive role in the lives of those
children.[1]

At one level, this book is intended to explain why this is the case—why
welfare agencies have played so small a role on behalf of poor children—
and to propose solutions and new directions. It aims to assist policymakers,
advocates, community members, and state and local welfare administrators
who are working to do better on behalf of children. With the explosion of
research knowledge about children's development and early interventions
that can help disadvantaged children, it seems natural to consider how the
welfare department can make a positive difference in the lives of the many
children whose families pass through its door.

At a more specific level, the research described in this book is designed
to answer the following question: How might states and localities use

the opportunities available through the Family Support Act of 1988 to meet the needs of *children* in welfare families? The Family Support Act, the most recent congressional legislation to reform the welfare system, embodies a new conception of the role of welfare for parents (generally, mothers): Rather than simply providing financial support, the welfare system ought to assist and require mothers to move toward economic self-sufficiency through education, training, and employment. This shift offers both opportunities and risks for the children in welfare families, opportunities and risks that formed the starting point for this study.

Finally, at the most general level, this book grew out of the interest of researchers, policymakers, and advocates in applying the growing knowledge of child development and family functioning to the large existing service systems that affect children and families: not only to welfare agencies, but also to the public schools, the child protective agencies, and the health system. Seen in this broad context, the fundamental theme of the study is that even in agencies like these whose mandate and resources are sharply constrained, committed and skillful administrators can rethink and refocus their services in ways that will be much more helpful to needy children and their families. In particular, they can reconceive their programs as two-generational, in the sense that they identify and take seriously the needs of both children and adults.

At all these levels, the study findings are cautiously optimistic. Drawing on examples of welfare agencies that have effectively served children, the study found that these agencies have faced certain predictable challenges in expanding their service focus beyond the traditional limits. It also found that their approaches to these challenges have diverged from each other in order to respond to each agency's unique setting, but that it is nonetheless possible to identify practical tools that help them meet the challenges. Moreover, the study found that welfare agencies, under the right circumstances, can act as catalysts for change in the delivery of services to poor families and children.

WHY THE QUESTION MATTERS

In 1988, Congress passed the Family Support Act (FSA), a set of amendments to the AFDC welfare program that is informally known as "welfare reform." The central question that prompted this study was: How might welfare agencies implement the Family Support Act in a way that meets the needs of *children* in welfare families?

The question matters for four reasons:

- Children are not doing well in the United States today according to many measures of income and well-being. Any program that affects so many families with children—and particularly, vulnerable, low-income families with children— needs to pay attention to its effects on children, and not only on adults.

- Researchers have accumulated considerable knowledge about the kinds of services that can help poor children grow up successfully, avoiding what Lisbeth and Daniel Schorr called "rotten outcomes."[2] A program that affects families with children on a large scale might offer opportunities to link more of them to effective services.

- The welfare department sees the families of about half of all poor children during the course of a year. Thus, it appears to offer substantial opportunities as a source of services or referral.

- The Family Support Act, as it tries to redirect the energies of welfare departments across the nation, offers both opportunities for improving *and* risks of damaging the well-being of young children.

Child Poverty and the Experiences of Poor Children

As many people have noted recently, the United States is not doing well by its children. In the mid-1970s, children overtook the elderly as the age group most likely to be living in poverty—and the younger the child, the more likely he or she is to be poor. In 1990, about one in five children under age 18 (more than 13 million children) lived in a family with income below the government-defined poverty line, a threshold set in 1990 at $10,419 for a family of three and $13,359 for a family of four. For the youngest children (under age three), the poverty rate was one in four.[3]

A variety of recent research largely confirms the commonsense view that living in poverty is bad for children. While the causal links are complex and not fully understood, research suggests that poor children are more likely to have health, nutritional, and developmental problems when they are young and more likely to experience "rotten outcomes" such as early childbearing, delinquency, school dropout, and unemployment as teenagers and young adults.[4]

Among poor children, some experience poverty only temporarily, while others experience it for long periods of time. A recent estimate suggested that about 30 percent of children are poor at some time during their childhood, with about half of them experiencing poverty for a relatively brief period (one or two years). However, about 9 percent of children are poor for three to six years, and about 8 percent, for seven years or more— that is, most of childhood.[5] Long-lasting poverty is particularly likely for children who spend part of their childhood in single-parent families.[6]

The limited research available on children's experiences over time again seems to confirm the commonsense view that being poor for a long time is worse for children than being poor for a shorter time. For example, a recent study based on a national data base that follows families for 20 years concluded that, while many poor children go on to succeed in school and adulthood, ["The longer children are poor, the smaller their chance of on-time high school completion, and the greater their chance of early child-bearing."] About two-thirds of children in this study who were persistently poor during their childhoods (defined as seven or more years in poverty) did not complete high school on time, compared to less than one-third of children who were never poor. Moreover, girls who were persistently poor were 10 times as likely to bear a child before age 18 as girls who were never poor—34 percent of persistently poor young women, compared to 3.5 percent of those who were never poor.[8]

Programs That Can Help Poor Children

At the same time that there is reason to worry about children in poverty, researchers have also learned a great deal about programs that dramatically improve outcomes for poor children, if they are reached early enough. A wide variety of preventive programs targeted at pregnant mothers or children in their early months and years have demonstrated their effect on children's healthy development and later success. Frequently cited examples are intensive approaches to prenatal care; the Woman, Infants, Children (WIC) nutrition program; Head Start and other early childhood programs; and home visit programs to mothers with infants.[9]

The Opportunity Offered by the Welfare Department

An estimated half of poor children live in families that receive AFDC benefits in a given year.[10] This half probably includes disproportionate numbers of the children whose futures are most endangered: children who experience poverty not for one or two years, but for most of their childhood. While there is no direct evidence on this point, many children on AFDC fit the profile of children who are at risk of long-term poverty. For example, half the children in AFDC families live with single mothers who have never been married and another 36 percent live in families that are single-parent due to divorce, separation, or death. About 40 percent of the parents in AFDC households are black, 40 percent are white, and 15 percent are Hispanic.[11] While mothers on AFDC at any given time are typically in their twenties rather than their teens, more than half had their first child as a teenager, according to a recent estimate.[12]

It is natural to ask whether the welfare department can help connect these mothers and their children to one or another of the services that can make a difference to their future. Because of the urgency of financial support, mothers who might never know about or be able to gain access to other service programs will find the doorway to the welfare department;

it is the closest thing there is to a universal intake point for poor families.

The welfare department also seems to be a particularly natural entry point for preventive services aimed at *young* children because it sees many families before school-based service deliverers make contact with the family. About 41 percent of the children in AFDC families in 1989 were under six years old, and about half those children were under age three.[13] Since almost three-quarters of the children lived in small families with only one or two children, we cannot always count on older siblings to bring a family to the attention of school services.

The Family Support Act

The Family Support Act makes it even more important to think about how the welfare department affects, and ought to affect, the lives of children. This is true for two reasons: The FSA offers new opportunities, and it creates new risks. The central purpose of the legislation is to shift the focus of the AFDC program, and of welfare departments nationally, from delivering benefits accurately to promoting the self-sufficiency of welfare recipients. Under the legislation, welfare agencies are to provide recipients with opportunities for education, training, and other activities leading to employment, and they are to pay for child care and other support services. Mothers with children age three or above (or age one or above, at state option) are required to take part if the state has the resources to offer them a program slot. The law requires states to assess the mothers' situations in order to develop a plan for their employment-related activities, and it permits (but does not require) the states to provide case management services, which will be partially reimbursed by the federal government.

The law offers several potentially important opportunities to the children in welfare families. First, if the services do lead to improvements in mothers' education and incomes, such improvements could translate into improvements in children's lives, especially if the family income rises well above the poverty level and remains there. Second, the provisions for assessment and case management make it possible for states to pay much greater attention to the individual situations of families on welfare, attention that could be (but may not be) directed to the needs and experiences of children as well as adults. Third, the funding for child care could offer the opportunity for AFDC children to gain access to high-quality programs.

On the other hand, the law poses real risks. Most important are the unknown effects of its mandate for training or work outside the home for mothers of young children. The new mandate will undoubtedly create stresses on the family as mothers try to juggle additional obligations in their lives, and it will change the way in which children are cared for and who cares for them. If a child is bounced around from one unsatisfactory and temporary child care arrangement to another, recent research on child development suggests that the effects will not be good.[14]

Therefore, because of both the opportunities we should take advantage of and the damage we must avoid doing, this is an opportune time to determine how welfare agencies might best meet the needs of children and families. Could welfare agencies identify child and family needs and connect children to services? Could they build relationships with particular service providers, such as Head Start programs? Could they offer assessment and case management that are oriented to the special needs of the child and the family? Finally, how might they go about all these tasks? For example, should they try to provide key services directly—say, excellent, developmentally oriented child care—or should they try to stimulate, or perhaps fund, the provision of services by other agencies?

APPROACH OF THE STUDY

To answer these questions, this study examined programs that already had experience successfully providing services to children and families in conjunction with the welfare department *before* the enactment of the Family Support Act. Two assumptions lay behind this study design.

First, the study emphasized sites with successful *operational* experience—experience in actually providing services and not just planning or developing policy—because of the assumption that programs have to succeed at the service delivery level (where workers and families interact) if they are to make a difference in children's lives. For example, a well-intentioned policy to assess the developmental progress of children in welfare families might or might not help families in practice, depending on whether families found out about the screening programs, whether workers were skilled enough to carry it out effectively and sensitive enough to family and cultural differences to avoid identifying children as "failures," and whether families were able to find outside services or make changes in their own lives that would help their children develop in a more healthy way.

Second, the study starts from the assumption (which is common in the "strategic management" literature about public and private organizations) that there is not likely to be a single best way of reforming a large and complex organization like a welfare agency.[15] Instead, the best reform depends on characteristics of the organization's environment—its political setting, the skills of its staff, and so forth—and on the particular problems to be solved. Therefore, the analysis does not attempt to force the activities of the study sites into a single framework or a single program model. Rather, it identifies the major challenges that faced the programs—

which do, in fact, turn out to be common across programs—and the multiple approaches taken by the sites to meeting those challenges—which turn out to be more varied.

The more typical research design in studies based on successful or exemplary programs is to identify practices or characteristics that all the programs have in common and to argue that since the programs are all successful, any practice they have in common is likely to be a good thing. Such a design relies very heavily on the researcher's ability to prove that the programs are, in fact, successful, since otherwise the inference about the value of any practice will be weak. In contrast, the approach used in this study requires good evidence that a particular component of a program is successfully responding to a particular challenge—for example, that a program's referral system successfully brings targeted families into the program—but it does *not* require that the programs be exemplary on every dimension. Chapter 2 below provides a fuller account of the meaning and dimensions of success in this study.

With these background assumptions, the study sites were selected based on three criteria:

1. Success in delivering high-quality services to families and children on welfare, preferably during at least a year of actual operating experience (as discussed further in Chapter 2).

2. Provision of services to the dependent children in AFDC families, and not only to the head of the household. For example, the teen programs selected as sites all served the teen's child as well as the teen herself.

3. A close relationship between the services and the welfare system, although the welfare agency did not have to be the service provider. (In fact, we looked for variation in the actual service provider.) This criterion excluded programs that simply happened to serve some welfare families but did not have strong links to the welfare department.

Appendix A describes in full the seven sites selected through these criteria. The sites all serve children in some welfare families successfully, but they provide quite different kinds of programs that are targeted to different kinds of families, as shown in Table 1. In addition to the programs shown in Table 1, a supplemental site without an explicit child focus (the Massachusetts ET CHOICES program of adult case management) was included to allow comparison of the child-oriented sites with a fully developed model of adult case management for welfare recipients.

Table 1
The Seven Study Sites

Teen Parent Programs

Chemung and Schuyler Counties, New York: TASA Next Step Program

San Diego, California: GAIN Teen Parent Project

San Francisco, California: TAPP/GAIN Collaboration

Services to School-Age Children

Detroit, Michigan: Earhart—Fort Wayne—Jackson—Conner-Warren Dropout Prevention Program

Services to Young Children

Massachusetts: ET CHOICES/Voucher Child Care Program

Kentucky: Parent and Child Education (PACE)

Services to Multineed Families

Oklahoma: Integrated Family Services System (IFS)

Note: TASA = Teenage Services Act; GAIN = Greater Avenues for Independence; TAPP = Teen-Age Pregnancy and Parenting; ET CHOICES = Employment and Training Choices.

The case studies of the sites drew on telephone interviews, document review, and site visits in order to explore the goals of service deliverers and administrators, the nature of service delivery to children and families, the relationships among organizations involved in service delivery, and the bureaucratic and political context. In general, each site visit lasted at least two days and included interviews with about 15 to 20 people, including service delivery workers for the program being visited, welfare eligibility workers, other service deliverers who collaborate with the special program (such as child protective services workers or public health nurses), program administrators, and program clients.

The most important gap in the stories gathered through the site visits is probably the limited representation of the client perspective. While in every program we spoke with some families receiving services, we never spoke with more than about five. As a result, the client conversations suggested interpretations or insights different from those of workers and provided a reality check on worker views, but they were not numerous enough to let us develop a generalizable client perspective. Appendix B provides full details on the site selection process, the content of the site visits, and the limits, as well as the strengths, of the approach.

STRUCTURE AND THEMES OF THE STUDY

While the approach of the study was to examine programs that serve children successfully through the welfare system in order to identify lessons for other jurisdictions, the experience of the study sites soon made clear that simply identifying lessons from success was too simple. Rather, understanding a site successfully enough to derive lessons from it required first understanding the challenges and obstacles it had overcome to become successful. The approaches of the successful sites did not follow from a single program model, and none could really be described as a total overhaul of existing program designs or agency mandates. Rather, they exemplified thoughtful approaches to the delicate balance between the mission and accountability of the welfare agency, the nature of family needs, and the available capacity, both in the welfare agency and outside, to deliver needed services.

Therefore, after a discussion in Chapter 2 of the key methodological question faced by the study—What is success?—Chapter 3 goes on to discuss not the successful approaches but rather the barriers that welfare agencies encounter in reforming services to meet children's needs. Both the search for successful sites and the experience of the sites selected illustrate the power of these barriers. For example, the site selection process revealed that few programs were actually operating to link state early childhood services with welfare agencies, despite an active interest in early childhood services for disadvantaged children at the state level. Chapter 3 concludes that serving families with complex and interrelated needs is no easy task for an agency like the welfare department, which is urgently accountable for a narrow mandate; staffed by workers whose job too often leads to frustration, anger, and cynicism; and isolated from other agencies that serve families and children.

The fourth and fifth chapters, however, present evidence that, despite the difficulty of the task, welfare agencies are overcoming these barriers and playing a valuable role in the lives of families and children. Chapter 4 describes the services offered by the successful programs, which range from nurse home visits and early childhood education to advocacy on behalf of welfare families with other community agencies. In addition to specific, functionally defined services, most of the programs offer individualized attention and informal counseling from a case manager who gets to know the family well.

Chapter 5 analyzes the strategies that enable these programs to succeed and overcome the barriers. The evidence suggests that these successful programs addressed a common set of tasks but developed quite divergent approaches to them, in order to respond to each agency's unique circumstances. For example, all the agencies had to develop a conception of their mission toward families and children: What were they trying to do for families and children and why was it the welfare department's job to do it, as opposed to the job of the schools, the child protective services, or someone else? Without such a conception, overburdened welfare staff are unlikely to keep children at the top of their list of tasks, a problem that seems to have contributed to the ending of services in two sites since our site visit. Without a clear conception of mission, public and political support may wane as well.

Welfare administrators at the sites therefore addressed this common task, but they came up with quite different answers. In the ET CHOICES/ Voucher Child Care program, welfare department staff saw attention to child care quality as intimately bound up with the broader goal of self-sufficiency: The purpose of the agency's attention to children was to support the mother in her pursuit of self-sufficiency, to ensure her peace of mind while she made a transition to work, and (at least in the specific site visited, though perhaps not statewide) to assist her with her own transition from parent to provider.

In other agencies, on the other hand, the welfare agency's mission was seen as much broader. Administrators argued, for example, that the welfare agency should work to strengthen family life for preventive reasons: It should provide comprehensive services to teen parents in order to avert foster care placements, and it should help educate children in order to prevent them from falling back into the cycle of poverty. Moreover, these administrators often argued that the welfare department needs to assist families with motivation and with a healthy family life—through what some called "old-fashioned social work"—in order to make possible true and long-term self-sufficiency. Perhaps the most comprehensive argument for why families are simultaneously the job of the welfare department, the schools, *and* the health care system came from Richard Jacobsen, director of the San Diego County Department of Social Services, which is represented in this report by the GAIN Teen Parent Program:

Economics are going to drive it. They will force people to get together. Everyone around the country has overwhelming caseloads and too few resources. The federal deficit won't be resolved, taxes won't be enough to keep up with health and social problems. So collaboration makes sense from an economic point of view. And it makes sense from a program point of view—it's going back to what social workers did pre-1969, before we split eligibility and social work.

As agencies realize that they share a common client, Jacobsen thinks, they will come to agree with San Diego's definition of purpose: "We wanted to eliminate patients, clients, offenders and increase the number of leaders, parents, students."

Chapter 6, the concluding chapter, draws from this analysis to provide recommendations for advocates, policymakers, administrators, and others who are committed to the needs of poor children and families. The chapter argues that in order for the nation's large public welfare agencies to play a fuller role for young children in poverty, a role attuned to what we know about children's development and family functioning, they need to achieve a balance between the agency's own mission and capacity, on the one hand, and the needs of children and families, on the other. The study evidence suggests that the way in which a particular agency achieves this balance needs to fit the agency's circumstances and purposes in three important ways: The approach needs to fit a mission that the agency can sustain on behalf of children and families, the opportunities it has to collaborate with other service deliverers, and the capacity of its staff and bureaucratic structure to serve families and not merely process them.

To illustrate this idea of multiple approaches more concretely, Chapter 6 offers two scenarios, loosely based on the experience of the sites, to show how agencies with quite different purposes and circumstances might serve children and families more fully. The chapter then goes on to suggest guiding principles for serving children through welfare agencies and to apply these principles specifically to the implementation of the Family Support Act. The chapter concludes with possible extensions of these principles to other large public agencies that serve disadvantaged children and families.

2

What Is a Successful Program?

rationale

In any study of the operation of public programs, an important but difficult question is whether the programs under study are ultimately effective. The question is difficult because results in many public programs are likely to be hard to measure, discernible only over the long term, and produced by the interaction of the program itself with a great many other influences. Therefore, convincing answers about the effect of the program itself are likely to require experimental or quasi-experimental studies carried out over long periods of time and across many outcome dimensions, studies that are rarely conducted for any program and certainly beyond the scope of this project.

However, even if it is hard to measure, program effectiveness matters a great deal, especially in a study that draws lessons for public policy from the experience of particular programs. What if these programs are really not good examples? What if they do not serve families effectively or change children's lives in the long run? As noted in Chapter 1, this study does not go as far as do some studies based on model programs—it does not assume that everything about the study sites works well—but it does assume that the sites offer operational practices that are effective enough in their circumstances to be worth studying. Even this more limited assumption clearly requires both a definition and evidence of operational effectiveness. Moreover, if the study is to be truly useful to policymakers, it also requires at least some evidence of success in a broader outcome sense as well: evidence that the programs are reasonably likely to improve the lives of poor children and families. Unless the program approaches and practices are at least consistent with the research evidence about changing life chances, there is no reason for policymakers to care about their operational effectiveness.

To address these issues, this chapter therefore divides the idea of program success into two parts: operational effectiveness, meaning the ability of a program to do what it intends to do, and outcome success, meaning the ability of a program approach to change life outcomes for children and families. Operational effectiveness includes, for example, a program's ability to reach targeted families and enroll them in services, to deliver the intended services, to deliver services of high quality (as judged by relevant professional standards), and to carry out other key activities (such as influencing the actions of other service systems, like the public schools, that lie outside the scope of the program itself). Outcome success might mean, for example, reduced infant mortality, improved cognitive test scores and school success for young children, or reduced rates of child abuse and neglect.

The chapter concludes that the site programs show considerable evidence of success on both dimensions, and the evidence is sufficiently strong that policymakers should pay them close attention. The programs are operationally effective overall, though no single program is perfectly exemplary across all the operational challenges, and the evidence on outcome success suggests that all seven site programs are promising in their approaches. While only one program has its own evaluation, the others are generally consistent with the evaluation evidence about approaches that work to change life chances.

OPERATIONAL EFFECTIVENESS

The sites were selected for study based primarily on the judgment of professionals in the field. This judgment generally addressed both the programs' operational effectiveness (discussed in this section) and their consistency with available knowledge about what program models lead to *outcome* success (discussed in the next section). The site selection process explicitly tried to weed out programs that fit only the second criterion: that is, ideal models that had not been effectively implemented.

The reason for this emphasis on operational success was the study's focus on actual service delivery rather than plans or policy. For a program to work in service delivery terms, it has to reach the people it means to reach and actually carry out actions that affect them either directly, through the delivery of specific services, or indirectly, through changes in larger service delivery systems that will lead those systems to treat clients in a different way. A program's success at this basic level of implementation can be judged by its ability to:

- Reach targeted clients, bring them into the program, and keep them there;
- Deliver promised services to targeted children and families;

- Deliver services that are of high quality, as judged by relevant professional standards; and
- Influence the delivery of services in large public systems outside the scope of the program itself (for example, the public school system).

In addition, because many of the programs were new and were clearly not in final form, a final dimension of implementation success is the ability to:

- Adapt over time to new evidence about what works for families and what does not.

Only some of these dimensions may be relevant to a particular program, depending on its purposes. For example, one program may intend only to deliver one service of high quality to its clients, while another may intend to deliver a comprehensive service package, and yet another to change the operation of large service delivery organizations such as the welfare eligibility agency or the school system.

Even though we chose programs for their reputation and track record in operations, the site visits provided evidence that not all the programs were equally successful across all these dimensions. More specifically, the site evidence suggested the following conclusions about operational effectiveness on each of the five criteria:[1]

- Five of the programs were particularly strong at the first two criteria: bringing in targeted clients and delivering services to them. For example, the TASA Next Step program regularly enrolls 90 percent or more of all AFDC teens, despite the fact that it is a voluntary program. It also shows high rates of effective referrals (meaning that teens actually get the services to which they are referred) and actual client contact through home visits. The other two of the seven programs, PACE and the TAPP/GAIN collaboration, had difficulties in collaboration between the welfare agency and the service agency, which meant that welfare families sometimes were not smoothly referred into the excellent services that were available. As explained in the individual cases, the PACE program has moved to a different kind of collaboration since the visit, and the TAPP/GAIN collaboration has ended, at least for now.
- On the other hand, PACE and TAPP were among the programs with the strongest evidence on the third criterion, quality services (as well as the strongest evidence on outcome effects). Other programs with strong evidence about program quality, as assessed by client evaluations and professional reputation, included the TASA Next Step

program, the ET CHOICES/Voucher Child Care site, and Oklahoma's Integrated Family Services.

• Not all programs had systems change as a goal, but for those that did, we looked for evidence of specific, identifiable changes in the operation of the larger service delivery system as a result of the program. The San Diego GAIN Teen Parent Program, the Oklahoma Integrated Family Services System, and the Detroit dropout prevention program had evidence of success along this dimension.

• All the programs showed evidence of change and development in response to success and failure, the final dimension of program success. We were particularly struck by this feature in the GAIN Teen Parent Program and the Detroit dropout prevention program, which are both seen by their founders as being still in an early stage of development, where learning is part of the goal. Similarly, learning and adaptation to local needs are explicit aims of each new Oklahoma IFS office, and we found considerable evidence of this process in operation.

Overall, then, the programs are operationally impressive, but no single program is perfectly exemplary across all dimensions. The finding is not surprising, given the newness of the programs and the difficulty of the task. Instead, the programs have developed very successful components and creative solutions to difficult dilemmas, and it is in these terms that the book discusses program success.

OUTCOME SUCCESS

Even though operational effectiveness clearly matters—and it is central to the research questions for this study—it is not the only way in which to think about success. To change families' lives, a program not only needs to deliver high-quality services effectively but also to deliver the *right* services to make a difference. To capture this dimension of success, a policymaker might ask about the long-run effect of the program on the life chances of the children and families it serves. Such outcomes may be measured at various points after program completion: For example, does the Kentucky PACE program increase the likelihood that the children it serves at age four will start school better prepared, do well in the elementary grades, complete high school, and avoid poverty as adults?

As this example suggests, there are many difficulties involved in measuring success in these terms: Such measurement generally requires long-term follow-up; comparison groups, so that we can understand what would have happened without the program; measurement across a wide range of outcome dimensions, so that we do not omit important results about which we care; and a stable, rather than constantly developing, program, so that the "treatment" to be measured can be held constant. In addition, measuring outcomes for individual families does not cover program goals that are expressed at the level of service systems, as in the previously mentioned examples of the Detroit, Oklahoma, and San Diego programs.

Unfortunately, therefore, it was far beyond the scope of this study to obtain direct evidence about outcome effectiveness for the site programs. An alternative approach, limiting the sites studied to those with their own, previously completed, outcome evaluation, was also impossible. Only one site (TAPP) could have met this standard, which is unappealing for an underlying theoretical reason as well: Such a standard would probably bias the group of sites away from programs with ambitious or multidimensional goals because it is much easier to evaluate programs with easily quantified or short-term outcome dimensions (for example, low birth weight).

However, despite the difficulties, it seemed critical to somehow assess whether the programs looked sensible in the light of professional and research knowledge about successful outcomes. Without such evidence, limited though it may be, there would be no reason for policymakers to pay attention to the programs or to care about their considerable operational success. Therefore, the study chose to assemble evidence from a range of sources about whether these programs have a reasonable likelihood of outcome success. Important sources of evidence included an existing evaluation of one site program, the evaluation literature on related programs, the expertise of the advisory board for this study, and the expert judgments of other professionals in the field.[2]

What does all this evidence add up to? First, one program *has* been formally evaluated. An evaluation found that the San Francisco TAPP program was successful at increasing the birth weights of babies born to teens in the program: Participation in TAPP was associated with an increased birth weight of 114 grams.[3] None of the other programs has yet had a published outcome evaluation, although the PACE program has been evaluated in one Ph.D. dissertation, and a second dissertation is in progress.

Second, evaluation evidence about outcomes does exist for programs that are analogous to some of the programs examined here. In particular, evidence exists for programs that serve teen parents and their children, early childhood education programs, programs across a range of substantive areas that are effective for very disadvantaged children and families, and welfare-to-work programs. The study sites generally offer programs that make sense in the light of these evaluations.

Teen Parent Programs

A variety of programs to serve teen parents and their children have been formally evaluated. In addition to the TAPP evaluation, a multisite demonstration project for young teenagers, called Project Redirection, was evaluated by the Manpower Demonstration Research Corporation (MDRC) with a quasi-experimental design (a comparison group consisting of teens in cities not offering the Project Redirection program) and a five-year follow-up.[4] In Elmira, New York, the same community that houses one of our study sites, David Olds operated and evaluated the Prenatal and Early Infancy Project (PEIP), a program intended to prevent abuse and enhance maternal and child functioning among high-risk pregnant women with no previous live births, including, but not limited to, teenagers. The evaluation involved a randomized control group and a two-year follow-up period.[5] In addition, two recent literature reviews have looked at the evidence on what program models work for pregnant and parenting teens[6] and what support services help AFDC mothers, including young mothers.[7]

All three evaluated programs reported positive results for the teenager and the child. Among the good results for the child were improved birth weight outcomes (TAPP); prevention of substandard care, including abuse and neglect (PEIP); and improved child development, as measured on several dimensions (PEIP and Project Redirection). The young mothers benefited through increased employment (Project Redirection and PEIP), an effect that was concentrated among the most disadvantaged young women; in the early months, they also appeared to benefit through increased educational attainment, but in both Project Redirection and PEIP, comparison mothers caught up to the experimental group over time. Finally, both PEIP and TAPP reported success in delaying subsequent pregnancy, but Project Redirection reported no success and, in fact, reported that five years after program entry, the experimental group had, on average, slightly more children than the control group.

All three of the evaluated programs provided a one-on-one relationship with a key service provider (case manager, nurse home visitor, social worker, or volunteer mentor) and comprehensive service delivery beyond this central relationship through brokered services. All reported an emphasis on the warmth and compassion of the service provider, and TAPP and Project Redirection also reported an ethos that emphasizes the teen's own worth as a person and the value of her own goals. TAPP and PEIP reported low caseloads (20–35) for the individual service providers. Consistent with these findings, Denise Polit and Joseph O'Hara have suggested that the evidence on teen parent programs supports case management as an approach.[8] The MDRC review of evidence (for the purpose of developing the Project New Chance program model) identified five elements of successful teen parent programs that seem to be supported by experience: comprehensive services, substantial duration, on-site services (which were *not* characteristic of the three evaluated programs, though the TAPP evaluation did find the strongest effects for teens who attended a school where they could get many services on-site), warm and caring staff, and an emphasis on accountability and achievement.[9]

Both TASA Next Step and the San Diego GAIN Teen Parent Project share important program elements with these formally evaluated models, and therefore it seems reasonable to anticipate that they might be having positive effects. TASA Next Step looks most like the models, with its low caseloads and intensive mentoring relationship. On the other hand, it differs from the models in its even longer-term approach and perhaps in its program ethos, which emphasizes building the teen's self-esteem even more than do the other programs and emphasizes challenging her to achieve particular outcomes (such as completing high school) somewhat less than the others.[10] The evaluation evidence offers no basis for judging whether these differences increase, decrease, or have no effect on the program's impact on teens and their children. The GAIN Teen Parent Project, with much higher caseloads per worker, might be expected to have a less intensive effect on teens if taken by itself, but since one of its aims is to supplement the effect of other community programs through gap-filling resources, it may be working very effectively in that role. Thus, of the three teen parent programs, TAPP has been evaluated as successful at least in producing good birth-weight outcomes, and the other models are generally consistent with what we know about effective programs.

Early Childhood Programs

While the ongoing evaluations of PACE itself are not yet conclusive, its curriculum and program design are consistent with the large body of evaluation evidence about what works in early childhood development programs. The program uses a well-known, developmentally oriented curriculum and emphasizes parent involvement and small group sizes, program elements that have been identified by professionals and researchers in early childhood development as contributing to effectiveness.[11]

In addition, the judgment of professionals in the field is that working on education with parents and children together makes sense given the research evidence about child development and family interactions. A recent study of the experiences of poor children over time concluded that "the importance of parents' education as a predictor of children's education supports the efficacy of programs that serve two generations at once," such as PACE.[12] Thus, while no full outcome evaluation yet exists, the PACE program, too, seems promising, based on existing evidence.

Programs That Work for Disadvantaged Children and Families

A third type of evidence about outcome success comes from Lisbeth and Daniel Schorr's book, *Within Our Reach: Breaking the Cycle of Disadvantage*, which identified a large group of programs whose evaluations demonstrated effective outcomes for disadvantaged children and families. The authors concluded that these programs share common attributes, including flexible staff that see the family as a whole and operate across bureaucratic boundaries, warm and trusting relationships between staff and clients, and low caseload-to-staff ratios.[13] Such programs as Oklahoma's Integrated Family Services and Detroit's dropout prevention program fit this set of characteristics, though each is different in other ways from Schorr and Schorr's model programs. Again, we cannot conclude that these programs are certain to have effective outcomes for children and families but, based on currently available evidence, they are at least promising.

Welfare to Work Programs

A large body of evaluations, primarily by MDRC, has found that overall, training and education programs for welfare recipients have positive (though small) effects on their income and employment. To date, however, none of these evaluations has looked at program effects on children in welfare families, and none has looked at the effect of programs such as ET CHOICES/Voucher Child Care, which assists with child care selection as well as financing care, on either mothers or children. A limited body of evidence on the effect of *financing* child care for welfare mothers does exist; Polit and O'Hara concluded that this evidence ''does lend support to the argument that child care services help to remove an important barrier to employment among welfare-dependent mothers of young children.''[14]

Thus, there is no outcome evidence that is fully relevant to the ET CHOICES/Voucher Child Care Program, though there is reason to believe that its services may be needed. As for the effect on children, we can only say that if the program does succeed in linking children to high-quality care, the research strongly suggests that such care will lead to improved long-term outcomes.[15]

Overall, then, the outcome evidence argues that these programs are promising and worth paying attention to. While only TAPP (which no longer operates in conjunction with the welfare department) has its own complete evaluation, the other programs generally appear consistent with the evaluation evidence about what works to change life chances. We cannot say whether specific elements of the program models (such as the long-term philosophy of TASA Next Step) are successful in terms of outcomes, but we would not encourage other jurisdictions to copy details of program models in any case. Rather, as the remainder of this book argues, other jurisdictions should find in the impressive implementation success of these programs the insights they need to develop their *own* approach to serving welfare families and children more richly and responsively.

3

Serving Children and Families through the Welfare System: Challenges and Opportunities

Suppose a welfare agency decides to take up the challenge described in the first chapter: to do better for children and families on welfare. In order to meet that challenge, the agency has to figure out what its staff are capable of, what resources are available, and what political support or controversy might arise from a new role. That is, the agency has to assess its own organizational capacity and political environment in order to decide what kinds of services it can, in fact, provide or arrange. Second, the agency will probably have to learn about the capacity of other agencies in the community to cooperate in providing services to children and families. The reason is that few welfare agencies have staff who are expert in the range of services that families and children might need. Third, the agency has to learn about the needs of the children and families who make up its caseload and assess the implications of those needs for service provision.

This chapter analyzes evidence from a variety of sources about all three of these issues: the capacity and limits of the welfare agency, the capacity and limits of the rest of the service system for children, and the needs of families and children on welfare. It argues that important common circumstances across welfare agencies lead to five predictable challenges for those agencies when they try to deliver high-quality services to families and children. For example, the job of the welfare agency (dispensing large amounts of money in accordance with detailed regulations) and the job of the welfare eligibility worker (determining, under great time pressure, whether a family's circumstances are consistent with the regulations) are difficult to reconcile with a broad, responsive, and flexible family services mission. The challenge is particularly great because the needs of some, at least, of the families and children on welfare demand extremely cross-cutting, responsive, and flexible treatment.

The first three sections of the chapter follow the order mapped out above: first analyzing the welfare agency itself, then the surrounding network of services to children, and then the needs of children and families on welfare. The fourth section builds on the third to develop much more fully the implications of child and family needs for high-quality service delivery, while the fifth and final section draws from the whole analysis five key barriers that welfare agencies face in delivering high-quality family services.

CAPACITY AND LIMITS OF THE WELFARE DEPARTMENT

Welfare agencies in the 50 states have some common structures and functions, along with some variation. All the agencies have as a central function determining eligibility for Aid to Families with Dependent Children (AFDC), the major federal-state income support program. Federal statute and regulations set the key features of the program, federal funds pay for 50 to 80 percent of the benefits, and federal audits to identify ineligible or overpaid clients provide a common incentive for the states to focus on controlling access to the programs. However, at the same time, the states control key features such as benefit levels and income levels for eligibility. States may either operate the program themselves or supervise county operation of the program; while the majority of the states operate AFDC themselves, several large states, such as New York and California, have state-supervised, county-operated systems.

Whatever the organizational structure of the program, a family's contact with the system is likely to occur through one or more eligibility workers (or financial assistance workers, eligibility technicians, or any of a variety of other job titles). These workers are responsible for collecting information bearing on eligibility—such as family income, bank accounts or property owned by the family, age of the children, household living arrangements, and (to aid in the collection of child support) the name and whereabouts of the father of each child—from families applying for AFDC and from ongoing recipients. They are required to verify this information through documents collected by the recipient and interviewing techniques, keep up with policy changes about how to apply the information to determine benefits, and, at the same time, get the benefit check out quickly to recipients who are truly in need. With caseloads sometimes in the range of several hundred, it is not surprising that the eligibility worker's interactions with recipients are often hurried (after the recipient has waited, perhaps for hours, in a run-down, dirty, and noisy waiting room), narrowly focused on the paperwork, and felt by the recipient as demeaning.

The AFDC eligibility function, along with eligibility for other income-tested programs such as state General Assistance programs and the national Food Stamps program, may be organizationally located in a single-purpose Department of Public Welfare. On the other hand, it may be located in a broader agency (often with a title such as Department of Social Services or Department of Human Services) that also provides child protective services (investigation of child abuse and neglect, foster care, and other child and family social services) and perhaps other human services such as rehabilitation services to the disabled or home care for the elderly. The worker that a family sees on applying for AFDC, however, will almost certainly work only on eligibility and not on other social services.

The Limits of the Welfare Department as a Focal Point for Family and Children's Services

As this account of welfare agency operation suggests, the welfare department has major limits as a focal point for services to families and children. Three limits are particularly important: the overall mission and accountability of welfare agencies; the current role, capacity, and culture of eligibility workers; and the isolation of the welfare system from child-serving agencies.

Mission and Accountability. The welfare department's function of providing income maintenance to families in need is very costly to state and local governments. It is also crucial to the well-being of families that may well be without income, running short on food, or facing eviction at the time they apply for aid. Not surprisingly, therefore, welfare departments are generally held accountable for controlling spending—which is likely to mean spending as little money as possible and spending it accurately, as measured by federally determined error rates—and for sending out benefit checks quickly. Accuracy in terms of error rates means preventing ineligible recipients from receiving aid, paying eligible recipients the correct amount, and following procedural rules correctly.

The department's success in responding to each of these demands is easily measured in quantitative terms. Thus, eligibility workers (or units) are commonly evaluated by the timeliness of check issuance and the accuracy of eligibility and benefit determination. Not surprisingly, these standards for evaluation encourage eligibility workers to emphasize verification and procedural correctness and can easily drive out other goals that are measured in less quantitative terms.

The director of one local welfare office made clear how this central mandate affects his capacity for broader programs: "Right now our sole purpose is to provide timely and correct benefits. . . . One of the major problems that we have [in going beyond that] is that in the short time that we have with a client, one of the major things that we are doing is just getting eligibility information." Similarly, the eligibility mandate has shaped the culture of his office: "Our attitude right now is that we just got to get them their benefits. Hopefully, ten years from now, it will be that we have to get them into a job. . . . Our problem is that someone [an eligibility worker] that's been here three months, they are walking around like zombies and with the same attitude as someone who has been here three years."

A welfare director in another county who is eagerly experimenting with new approaches nonetheless commented that the Family Support Act is meaningless as long as accountability continues to be measured only on one dimension, accuracy ("quality control"). He argued that local and state welfare directors will continue to focus on quality control rather than implementing the FSA, because "Where I'm going to get hurt is where I'm going to spend my time."

The Eligibility Worker's Role. Driven by accountability for these limited results, the eligibility worker's role is, in several respects, difficult to reconcile with the delivery of services to families and children. First, the eligibility worker's function of investigating misstatements and ensuring accuracy can promote cynicism and distrust on both sides of the client-worker relationship, despite the best of intentions. One supervisor of eligibility underscored this problem when he urged avoiding programs that "make the client seem like a crook to the worker and the worker a fool to the client." A community case manager who used to work in the welfare system said that her eligibility job taught her to deal with people but also to wonder, "What's the con game? Should I double check?" Moreover, while many eligibility workers with whom we spoke reported talking with clients about their problems, one worker, when asked about the content of her conversations with clients, said that she looked for misstatements or violations of eligibility rules: "I have busted so many clients just talking."

Second, at the same time that eligibility workers have this crucial investigative function, they cope with high caseloads, low pay, computer systems that seem to drive rather than work for them, and the crucial function of getting checks out on time. The local office director quoted above continued his description of the effect of the office culture on individual workers: "We have workers out there who have a hard time dealing with their fellow employees, let alone their clients. Sometimes we have people blowing up at their clients,and I get complaints, and I have to say, 'The reason we are here is for the clients.'" An eligibility worker in another state provided the worker's view of this kind of setting: "I've been in this job since 1975, and I'm tired, angry and burned out. I'm sick of lonely, desperate women. I want a new job."

Third, to cope with this setting, workers often try to emphasize fairness and adherence to the rules, virtues that may not be completely consistent with the flexibility required by service-oriented approaches. One eligibility worker, when asked if he could play a case management role, first said that it would be impossible because of his caseload, time pressures, and client attitudes to workers, but then reconsidered, with the proviso that the rules would have to be explicit: Case management would be possible, he said, if workers were very clear with clients that "this is what you gotta do."

A recent study of the implementation of California's welfare-to-work program, GAIN, provided evidence on a broader scale to support these observations from the sites. Eligibility workers tended to see being on welfare as more the individual's fault than the consequence of broad social and situational factors, in contrast to GAIN specialized workers, and they were much less likely than the GAIN workers to report that their morale was high (29 percent of eligibility workers compared to 72 percent of GAIN workers).[1] Welfare administrators in California, when explaining their choice to hire specialized GAIN workers rather than rely heavily on eligibility workers, described the latter as "prone to taking a legalistic approach in dealing with welfare recipients."[2]

Isolation from Other Agencies. There are two main reasons why welfare agencies are frequently isolated from other agencies that have the capacity to serve children and families. First, and not surprisingly, the eligibility system may well have a bad reputation with other service providers. In one state, service providers who had not previously worked closely with the welfare department reported on what it looked like to them: an incompetent bureaucratic jungle with a six-month backup in the computer system and a demeaning attitude on the part of staff toward recipients. Said one outside service provider, "I never realized how badly or poorly [clients] were treated." Another provider, when asked if working with AFDC families was any different from working with non-AFDC families, said, "I don't think the people are any different. It's just working with the bureaucracy that makes it so hard." In another state, a community case manager described a situation in which an eligibility worker said he did not have time to provide an emergency Medicaid card to cover emergency surgery for the baby of a teen client and instead asked her: "Why are you here pregnant? Where is your boyfriend? Why doesn't he have a job?" The case manager intervened with the supervisor and had the emergency Medicaid card issued, but her assessment of the experience was that the eligibility worker was prejudiced against the client because "She was young, she was Hispanic, she was pregnant, and she was undocumented." Clearly, this kind of experience can leave outside service providers eager to avoid connections with the welfare system whenever possible.

The second reason is simply that the welfare department, with its traditional adult focus, has few contacts with child-serving agencies such as the schools. Workers in the two kinds of services have different backgrounds and professional histories and may not know each other or have worked together. Moreover, in many jurisdictions they operate at different levels of government: the welfare department works at the state (or county) level and the schools (and early childhood programs, among other community-based child and family services), at the local level.

Evidence for this gap came from both the study's site selection process and the history of the successful sites. For example, as noted in Chapter 1, the site selection process turned up very few programs that linked early childhood programs or schools, on the one hand, with welfare agencies, on the other, at the service delivery level. One program that had been reported as a promising collaboration turned out, on further examination, to be known only to early childhood advocates and not to the welfare agency. Another turned out to have become stuck between the Department of Public Health, which had the expertise on childhood and child health, and the welfare agency, which was trying to get the Health Department to respond to a request for services.

In the successful sites, administrators reported that they had to pay considerable attention over an extended period of time to overcoming this isolation in order to build the links that made their programs work. For example, in San Diego County, where the welfare department and the San Diego Unified School District have the advantage of covering roughly similar geographical areas, the administrator of the Department of Social Services reported that his call to introduce himself to the school superintendent was the first time the latter had ever had a call from the county. In Wayne County, Michigan (Detroit), the welfare office director reported a long and painstaking process of going to every meeting she could find in order to meet school board members and school administrators and offer her ideas for collaboration.

At the same time, this very isolation means that the welfare department itself is unlikely to have the capacity to directly provide services to children and families. Few welfare agencies have on hand the staff expertise to provide medical care to premature or chronically ill babies, assess and serve toddlers with developmental disabilities, or help preschoolers learn through play. While some welfare agencies may have the in-house capacity to provide counseling and case management, virtually all other services will need to be provided to welfare families by other agencies in the service network—or else the welfare agency itself will have to develop a completely new capacity.

Advantages of the Welfare Department as a Focal Point for Family and Children's Services

Given this picture of the welfare agency's limitations, which is not universally, but widely, accurate, why would we even consider it for a role in services to families and children? What advantages or capacities does it have for such a role? Four potential answers come to mind: its role as a broad-based intake point for poor families, its history of connection to a social work mission, its large staff of frontline workers, and the possible effect of the Family Support Act in changing both mission and operations.

The Intake Point for Poor Families. Because money, food, and housing are so crucial to survival, poor families are probably more likely to find their way to the welfare department than to a typical social services program for families. As noted in the Introduction, in fact, an estimated half of poor children live in families that receive AFDC. Further, as the Introduction argued in detail, the welfare department probably sees disproportionately those children whose future is most endangered: children who live in poverty for a long time. In addition, it sees many children who are young, in the early preschool years, a time when available evidence suggests that intervention can be most helpful—yet when no other institution is yet involved with the family.

Thus, the nature of the welfare department's caseload suggests a powerful rationale for considering its possible role as an intake point for services to children and their families. Children on welfare are disproportionately at risk for a whole range of ills and "rotten outcomes," and no other agency has as good an opportunity to link them to early help.[3]

Historical Connection to a Broader Mission. While eligibility workers currently are limited to a technical ("bank teller") role in most state systems and the administrative structures for eligibility and social services are clearly separated, the functions and the workers used to be linked. This history is very much alive in the memories of some welfare administrators in the programs we visited and in those visited by other recent investigators.[4] The separation of the functions was justified at the time on grounds of both cost-effectiveness and civil liberties: The worker who holds the family income should not also have power over custody of the children and be able to exercise discretionary judgment on the fitness or morals of the parents. However, several site administrators saw the link between social work and financial assistance as representing the best tradition of welfare agencies and remembered back to that tradition in justifying their current programs.

According to the director of a teen parent program located in a welfare agency who was explaining her emphasis on counseling: "Years ago, the system used to provide more supportive counseling, being there for people. Over the years, as money has dried up, we have had to do just the bare minimum." Another program director, describing the "social work" component of her new program, said, "This program is really nothing that we didn't used to do."

In addition, in more than half the study sites, welfare eligibility functions are housed within a broader umbrella agency that also includes child protective services and other social services. In welfare agencies with this organizational structure, a broader mission that encompasses some conception of social work and of services to children and families is not only historical, it is also current at the level of the agency as a whole. Thus, the agency as a whole may focus on family issues, particularly if a family-related crisis (such as increasing foster care caseloads) is catching administrators' attention, at the same time that the welfare eligibility subagency focuses on its own, more limited mission. In an agency with this structure, top administrators may eventually come to see the eligibility subagency as a potential tool for addressing broader, agencywide concerns about families.

A Large Staff of Frontline Workers. Despite the limitations of eligibility workers as family services providers, they nonetheless make up a large group of frontline workers who have direct contact with families and, in at least some cases, would welcome a broader role in solving family problems. Adding other welfare agency workers, such as specialists in employment and training services, into the pool of possible providers creates an even larger network.

While a number of eligibility workers said in interviews that they now feel overwhelmed, they also frequently reported that they would like to do more if their workload permitted. One eligibility supervisor, for example, thought that eligibility workers currently resent service functions that are added onto eligibility at the same caseload level but would "love it" if such functions went with lower caseloads and more pay, because "most workers want to help." The director of a community-based case management program provided indirect support for this judgment when she noted that eligibility workers often ask her case managers, "Whatever happened to that kid with the hard-luck story?"

The Impact of the Family Support Act. Finally, the Family Support Act is intended to push welfare agencies to rethink their mission and operations, if they have not done so already, in order to focus on self-sufficiency and employability. Agencies will have to move from simple eligibility determination toward a more complex and individualized process of identifying barriers to employment and possible services, staff will have to be added or retrained, and welfare offices will have to develop links, however rudimentary, with education and training services. While this is a simpler and smaller step than moving toward a focus on the full range of child and family needs, it is nonetheless a step that may provide an opportunity for change.

THE SERVICE SYSTEM FOR CHILDREN AND FAMILIES

The welfare department's limitations as a service provider to children and families mean that it must rely on other agencies in the community service system if it is to expand its role. In the seven sites under study, in fact, welfare agencies relied on a wide variety of other agencies to provide services: state or county agencies for public health, mental health, developmental disability, and child protective services; local or county school systems (sometimes funded or trained by a state Department of Education); city hospitals and clinics; and a host of nonprofit agencies, including child care and Head Start providers, child care resource and referral agencies, Visiting Nurse Associations, counseling agencies of various kinds, community health centers, and teen parent programs. This section briefly notes several features of this broader system that shape the nature and possibility of collaboration on behalf of children and families.

First, as a simple listing of the agencies suggests, there are many agencies and programs already involved in services to children and families. In San Francisco, for example, the TAPP teen parent program has formal arrangements with some 50 public and nonprofit agencies for services to the teen mothers and their children. In some jurisdictions, these existing programs are of very high quality: For example, among the sites, Chemung County, New York, is nationally known for its maternal and child health services, including a nurse home visiting program and an infant registry that screens all newborns for developmental needs. Thus, a welfare agency choosing to get involved in services to families and children is entering an arena that may already be very full.

Second, the array and quality of services vary considerably from place to place, with almost every jurisdiction identifying some key needs for children and families that are not met. For example, local school districts might be unable to respond effectively to teens with infants or teens who speak only Spanish.

Third, the available services, even where relatively comprehensive and of high quality, are generally offered in a fragmented form that makes them extremely hard for families to use. As the listing of programs suggests, the service system for children, and particularly poor children, is often not a system at all but rather a confusing jumble of jurisdictions and providers.

The sites provided examples of this fragmentation and rigidity from the point of view of poor families and children. These examples are consistent with a number of recent analyses that criticize these features of the service system, identifying several key problems.[5]

Categorical Organization of Services

Most providers offer services that are defined "categorically": that is, education, health care, early childhood education, mental health, and so forth. The categories are often defined by funding sources and come with specific accountability requirements. For example, a child protective services agency has one stream of funds to pay for foster care and is accountable to the federal government for appropriate placement and review of children in foster care. To give an idea of the level of complexity in categorical funding and services, Charles Bruner reported that in Iowa's experiment with collaboration in child welfare, the state combined what had originally been 30 different funding streams.[6]

Professional Education and Traditions, Organizational Missions, and Organizational Loyalties

At the same time, the categorical provision of services goes even deeper than the funding streams. The professional education, experiences, outlook, and political accountability of each categorical provider are too often limited to the single service provided, whether that service is education, health, or child protective services. For example, one young woman interviewed for this study when she was in a teen parent program described her experiences with the school system in her county:

"Sandra," age 16 and the mother of a three-year-old son, told the story of her determination to return to school after a long interval and a move between cities. She had last gone to school before her son's birth when she lived with her father in one city, left his home to live with her mother in another city, and was then kicked out of her mother's home. When she went to the school system to enroll, she was told that she could not do so because she did not have her parents' permission and was not an Emancipated Minor. After she went through the judicial process herself, the school system accepted her into a "continuation school" program for young people having trouble in the regular school; after completing one year there, she was hoping to transfer to a regular high school program. In retrospect, she wonders why it was so hard for her to enroll when the school system expends so much effort to bring in "kids who *don't* want to go to school" by "sending the truant officer after them."

Although Sandra was involved with the school system and on AFDC throughout this period, she did not encounter administrators or teachers in the school system or staff in the welfare eligibility system who considered how her estrangement from her parents or her uncertain living situation might affect her education or her child's well-being. As she searched for resources that might help her pay the transportation and child care costs associated with returning to school, she was eventually referred to the teen parent program by a friend. She now has a case manager from that program with whom she can discuss issues that cross specific agency boundaries.

Limited and Illogical Entry Points

Entry points to the service systems are as fragmented as the services themselves, which adds a further complication for families who do not know how to work the system. Each service system allows families to enter for specific, limited reasons: For example, health symptoms allow entry to the emergency room of a big city hospital, while a report of child abuse or neglect leads to entry to the child protective services system. For a family with multiple needs, it may be an almost random process that determines which door the family enters—but, once in, the family may be unable to gain access to services beyond the narrow categorical mandate. Sandra's experience represents an extreme point of this limited entry: To gain access to a high school education, she had to meet the demanding procedural requirement of going to court to be declared an Emancipated Minor. It seems unlikely that many youngsters who are estranged from their parents and living with friends, relatives, or on the streets would have Sandra's ability to take their cases through the judicial system.

For the welfare agency hoping to affect services to children and families, these characteristics of the system offer a mixed message. On the one hand, they suggest that there will be no simple way to ensure high-quality service to children and families and that reconciling multiple conceptions of mission and professional turf will be a considerable part of the task. On the other hand, they suggest that despite the richness of available services in some jurisdictions, there may be a key role available for an agency intending not to offer its own services but to help the most needy and least sophisticated families find a way through the bureaucratic maze.

Fourth, and finally, many of the services for poor families and children are offered in the context of limited funding and staff. Again, the implications for a welfare agency that wants to improve services may be mixed. On the one hand, in many settings this limitation on resources may make collaboration to serve families even more difficult, as staff find themselves unable even to accomplish their core functions, let alone to reach out to other agencies. For example, one response to Sandra's problems might have been attention from a school guidance counselor; however, when we asked in site interviews what role guidance counselors might play as a link to students' family lives, we were commonly told that with caseloads of several hundred, counselors cannot do more than process paper and get to know a handful of students well. To take another example, when child welfare workers are stretched to their limit to investigate emergency cases, even simple collaborative activities like explaining to school personnel why they are unable to take on less critical abuse and neglect referrals seem impossible, and more demanding activities, such as meeting with teachers to discuss common concerns, cannot even be contemplated.[7]

On the other hand, where resources are scarce in the system, there may be an opportunity for the welfare agency to influence services through its own access to money or staff. As Chapter 5 suggests, several of the sites took advantage of such an opportunity to play the role of a catalyst in community service provision.

NEEDS OF CHILDREN AND FAMILIES

An earlier section of this chapter argued that the welfare department could play an important role as an intake point for poor children. The argument drew on aggregate evidence suggesting that children in poor families risk bad outcomes later on, that children in welfare families are probably particularly at risk of long-term poverty, and that children on welfare are typically young, meaning that the welfare agency may be able to identify service needs before the schools.

However, to understand in more detail what kinds of services children and families might need or want and how those services should be delivered, we must go beyond the aggregate statistics and draw on interview evidence to flesh out the picture. Drawing a richer picture of child and family needs is the task of this section.

Before going on to mine the richness of the interview evidence, however, it is important to note its limits. First, this evidence does not describe *typical* families on welfare but rather those families who are served in a variety of intensive services programs. Second, most of the evidence comes from interviews with service providers rather than families, because of the design of the case studies.[8] Therefore, these descriptions of family needs are impressionistic, likely to apply only to the most needy and isolated families rather than to all families on welfare, and probably affected by the nature of the service delivery interaction. Nonetheless, the findings from these interviews are broadly consistent with those of other recent studies of isolated and multineed families, and they raise important issues for effective service delivery.

Before focusing on the characteristics of particularly isolated and needy families, it is important to reemphasize that families on welfare are diverse. While some families may need complex assistance to deal with multiple social problems, many may need only a period of financial assistance or help in overcoming barriers of financial access and discrimination in various service delivery systems. While some children in poor families, whether or not they receive AFDC, suffer from a "clustering of disadvantages," others suffer only from low income.[9] The statistics on the length of stay of families on welfare suggest this variety: About half the new entrants on AFDC will be off welfare in less than 2 years, while almost one in five will stay on for 8 or more years.[10]

The ability of some mothers on AFDC to cope on their own, even with multiple and complex needs, is illustrated by two stories told by women receiving AFDC in Massachusetts:

"Susanna" has three children. The youngest, who is now 4, had many illnesses during his childhood and required surgery at Children's Hospital in Boston. The middle child was sexually abused when he was young; he is now in counseling for school difficulties related to the abuse. The oldest child, now 11, has a hearing problem, but she is doing extremely well academically. "Susanna" has been hearing about training programs from the workers at the Welfare Department since she came on welfare but was not interested when her children were young, especially given the health problems of her youngest. However, once her youngest child was 4, and, in her view, old enough to attend child care, she sought out a training opportunity through the ET CHOICES program and is now about to graduate from a medical paraprofessional training program. Asked how she balances her family and work obligations, she says, "If you want to do something, you just do it."

"Diana" came to the United States from Puerto Rico. Unable to find work here, she went on welfare briefly but responded as soon as she got a mailing from an ET training program in the mail. When we spoke with her, she had just completed training to be a bilingual day care worker. She emphasizes her own role in moving toward employment: "I was on welfare for only three months before I went to ET. I got their advertisements in the mail. . . . They didn't tell me about this place [the training program]—I found it myself."

Acknowledging the impressive abilities and strengths of many women on AFDC, however, should not lead us to understate the problems that they and their children face. They face problems related to poverty itself— for example, constant moves in search of safe and affordable shelter— and problems related to their own life experiences and lack of family and community supports. At the same time, their encounters with the many service systems that ought to be providing help—the schools, the health care system, child and family social services, and the welfare system itself—may exacerbate the problems rather than resolve them.

In the study sites, three characteristics of the personal qualities and past experiences of families are particularly important to the provision of services:

- Some families and children on welfare have emotional needs that are not well matched to any of the official service systems. They may be depressed, lacking in self-esteem, isolated, mistrustful of all professionals, or lacking in the skills to gain access to complicated bureaucratic systems.

- Some families and children on welfare have multiple needs that cross service boundaries and yet must be addressed together.

- The needs of children in particular are often family-related in the sense that they cannot be addressed through individual services. Instead, these needs are intimately related to the needs of adults and the functioning of the family.

Emotional Needs That Are Poorly Matched
to the Service System

Many of the family needs identified by the service providers and families in the sites were emotional needs that were not well matched to any part of the existing service systems. Parents and children may be isolated, depressed (often because of experiences of violence and abuse), angry, or characterized by low self-esteem. In addition, they may well distrust anyone offering help, particularly professional service providers:

This population has a broken spirit. (director of a program for teen mothers)
The most important thing we give them is ourselves. Real trust in a relationship. (case manager in a program for multi-need families)
[The most important thing PACE does for families is] improving their self-esteem, parent and child. Improving their relationship. (teacher in PACE)
One of the most important things that we do is to give the kids personal attention. Because they don't get it from the school, their parents, their relatives or anybody. (caseworker in a dropout prevention program)

In one teen parent program, for example, a case manager reported, "I spend a lot of time defusing anger" because the teens that she works with have been "pawns" and "have been molested and raped most of their lives." Her supervisor, commenting on the case manager's success with young women who everyone else thought were unreachable, identified the cause as the case manager's deep-seated respect for the teens: "For many [teens], this is the first time anyone has seen them as a human being." Another case manager said, "The key is self-esteem"; this theme was repeated in programs that we visited all over the country.

In addition to building self-esteem, program staff emphasized the importance of addressing families' experiences of abuse and violence as a prerequisite to delivering other kinds of services. A teacher in Kentucky's PACE (Parent and Child Education) program reported: "All of our parents have had violence in their lives. They've either been abused as children or had abusive boyfriends. . . . You address all of that in everything you do."

Finally, service deliverers reported that many poor families do not trust the service system, and often for very good reasons. For example, teen case managers in one site reported that in their view, the teens get "talked down to," "discriminated against," victimized by myths about their promiscuity, and demoralized by responses that lead them to think they are stupid—all in their interactions with the people who are supposed to provide them with services.

To reach families who are affected by these emotions and experiences, service deliverers believe, requires a warm and trusting personal relationship; a conclusion supported by recent reviews of the experience of excellent programs. The section on implications of family needs for service delivery develops this link in detail.

Multiple and Complex Needs

Second, many of the families and children on welfare who are served by programs in our sites had multiple and complex service needs. Since the service system is often narrow and fragmented—with health needs met in one place and educational needs in another—these multiple needs placed extraordinary burdens on families, often on those with the least capacity to cope with them. For example, a case manager in a San Diego program for teen parents, many of whom were on AFDC, reported on the difficulties that the teens' lack of education posed for their dealings with the health system, in the case (which, she reported, was not rare) where they had babies with chronic illnesses: "The one I have now without a bladder—this baby will have multiple surgery, and the mother has been tested at third grade and she doesn't understand what is going on. So I have to go along to interpret what the nurses are saying." Similarly, a child protective worker added his example of the interaction between poverty and the health system:

I got a [child protective] referral the other day—two-pound twins at the hospital, mom not coming to visit the twins, pretty sick kids . . . in incubators. But when I went to see mom, she had just had a C-section, was recovering from that, no money, no transportation, two other kids at home. [There's] no way to get from Southeast to Mercy Hospital on a regular basis . . . and to go look at babies in an incubator, not even to interact.

When children and families with such linked needs confront a service system that is divided by categorical specialty, they may be misclassified, as in the example described by the child protective services worker, or they may simply receive inadequate services. For example, a pediatrician commented on the limits of a medical perspective (even one informed by considerable attention to the needs of inner-city youth) for assessing and meeting the needs of a baby affected by a wide range of economic and social ills in the family: "If the baby is in trouble medically, we notice . . . [but] we don't know if he's developing emotionally and socially[,] . . . if he's being stimulated[, or] . . . if they're reading to him."

As these examples illustrate, the most needy families typically face the most difficult tasks in negotiating the service system precisely because no one takes account of all the needs in one place. The most fragile or isolated families may be most likely to be lost in the system. The same pediatrician, reflecting on her experience as the head of a high-risk infant clinic, noted that those families who most need the continuity of one provider to trust and "bond with"—and who will be lost to the service system if they fail to get it—are most likely to encounter the impersonality and fragmentation of hospital emergency rooms, not to mention welfare offices, child protective agencies, and urban school systems.

The implication of these characteristics of families and the service system, as judged by the practice and observations of service deliverers at the study sites, is that to effectively reach the most needy families, a single worker needs to be prepared to offer assistance with multiple needs, working across bureaucratic and functional boundaries. Again, this is an observation that has been recently reported in several reviews of literature and experience and is more fully developed in the section on implications of family needs.

Interrelated Child and Family Needs

While many service bureaucracies focus on a single family member as the client or patient, our site visits suggested that the needs of children in particular (and probably other family members as well) may be impossible to solve, and perhaps even to diagnose, if a program's focus is on the individual child rather than the family. In fact, programs may need to learn a great deal about the family as a whole if they are to diagnose and solve the problems of children. At the simplest level, an example is a problem for a baby that is caused by interaction between a teen mother and her own mother, the baby's grandmother: [One caseworker:] "Most of the grandparents will tell them, "Don't hold the baby, you're going to spoil it." . . . I spend a lot of time trying to talk to grandparents." [Another caseworker:] "[You] have to go back to the grandparents. These kids [the teens]—all they hear is 'You're stupid. I didn't do it that way.' So after a while they figure, 'If I touch this baby, it's wrong.' So, 'Here, momma, take it.'"

Two stories illustrate more fully the way in which children's needs are nested in a family context and intimately connected with the parents' and other family members' own personal well-being. The first example comes from Oklahoma's Integrated Family Services (IFS) System, which serves multiproblem families:

A seven-year-old boy came to the attention of a school principal because of both physical and emotional health problems. The boy had long been prone to seizures and self-destructive behavior and was just starting to threaten other children. When the principal called IFS, he found that IFS was already working with the family because the mother was on AFDC and herself had multiple problems. The

IFS worker called a meeting of all of the agencies who had contact with the family to talk about the child's needs. As a result, the boy was admitted and sent to a diagnostic center for several months of testing and treatment; the mother received needed services such as mental health treatment and literacy training; and the Child Protective Services worker changed her mind about the possible outcomes for the case and concluded that the mother had the potential to be an adequate parent.

In this example, the needs of the child turned out to be related to the needs of the mother—and, perhaps more important for the service delivery system, part of the solution to the child's needs lay in providing services to the mother so that she could help him. According to an IFS case worker, "What the child really [may] need is a mother who can cope."

In the second example, in which meeting a child's needs again depends on an adult's well-being, serving the child depends critically on the service deliverer's relationship with the adult. The illustration comes from a site visitor who accompanied a case manager on a home visit:

The case manager made a home visit to a young (18-year-old) mother who had suffered physical and sexual abuse as a child. During the visit, the case manager picked up and played with the young woman's 8-month-old child and observed how the child responded. Then she asked the mother a specific question about her experience with the child: Did she ever feel as though she were "climbing the walls" and just had to get out of the house when the baby was crying? The young woman said yes, and the case manager asked what she did at such times: Was there anyone she could leave the child with so that she could go on a walk? The teen responded that either she left the baby with her friend downstairs and went for a walk, or she put the child in the crib, closed the door partway, and went into another room. The case manager seemed satisfied with these responses, and she later told the interviewer that, while she has no reason to suspect any abuse or neglect in this case, she realizes that the teen is somewhat unstable and under great stress, so she likes to keep close watch on what is going on.

In this example, the case manager's key contribution to the child's well-being comes through her attention to and friendship with the mother. Only the case manager's strong personal relationship with the teen enabled her to keep a constant eye on the case while not being perceived by the teenager as intrusive, only the strong relationship permitted her diagnosis that the child was doing fine, and only the relationship permitted her to provide preventive services in the form of low-key advice.

These links between a child's needs and the well-being of the family as a whole reinforce the conclusion that effective family service deliverers need a trusting relationship with the family and an ability to reach out across systems. In particular, the links between child and family well-being suggest that serving children in multiproblem families requires that the service deliverer know both child *and* family well and be able to reach out across the service system to help all family members. The next section develops more fully these implications about high-quality service delivery.

IMPLICATIONS OF FAMILY NEEDS FOR THE NATURE OF SERVICE DELIVERY

What are the implications of these family experiences and characteristics for a welfare department hoping to provide child and family services? This section argues that high-quality service delivery to isolated families with multiple needs requires that a worker both develop a trusting personal relationship with family members and reach out across professional and bureaucratic boundaries to gain access to services. The argument draws for evidence on the experience of the study sites, several recent reviews of program evaluations and experience, and recent writing on case management and social services practice.

The Role of the Personal Relationship

The evidence from all the sites suggests that workers see the development of a trusting personal relationship with families as critical to service delivery. While the role of the relationship is least pronounced in the adult case management offered by eligibility workers in ET CHOICES, even those workers emphasized learning about the client and building a relationship in ways that seem different from the eligibility worker's job in other settings. In the intensive, low-caseload programs (TAPP in San Francisco, TASA Next Step in New York, the San Diego Adolescent Pregnancy and Parenting or SANDAPP component of teen parent services in San Diego, PACE in Kentucky, and the dropout prevention program in Detroit), staff see the personal relationship as central to their jobs:

The most important thing we give to them [clients] is ourselves. (IFS case manager)

We are like an extended family. (Detroit dropout prevention worker)

We feel like social workers. . . . We are working real hard to find the right niche. It's different than being a classroom teacher. (PACE teachers)

[SANDAPP case managers describe their job as:] advocate, helper, friend, systems broacher and spanner. . . . I see myself as trying to help them become self-sufficient, sometimes a role model. . . . My role shifts from day to day: mentor back to teaching back to being a counselor. . . . Role model, mentor, and being a father—so many don't have a father. They [the teens] take a lot of pictures, mental pictures of what a father is—a gentleman who opens the door, listens to what they have to say, gives them the male side. . . . You can be [in] the shopping center, food market, gas station—kids know you, walk up to you, and say "I've got a problem." . . . That's what makes SANDAPP work, what makes them take us as family—they call us most of the time before they call their parents. (SAN-DAPP case managers)

[The teens] have basically given up. And so it's a real job for the counselor to infuse them with hope. . . . It's not easy. It's really tough. I think the ones you can reach are the ones who have just a spark of motivation. It's kind of like a plant that looks like it's dead but if you water it and tend to it long enough, it will come back to life. (TAPP counselor)

As the last speaker suggested, staff see the role of the personal relationship as closely linked to the family characteristics described above: the isolation, discouragement, hopelessness, and suspicion of some of the families and children to be served. A successful personal connection with a service deliverer provides the only basis that these staff can see for overcoming such obstacles. For example, the IFS case manager quoted above went on to explain the reason why she believes giving families "ourselves" and "real trust in a relationship" is so important: "These people don't trust police. They don't trust landlords. They don't trust teachers in school. They don't trust social workers. . . . If they can make a relationship with just one professional person, a close relationship that helps them meet their needs, then they can do it with another professional."

Further, there are several reasons why the personal relationship may be particularly important when it comes to family and children's services. First, needs related to child rearing and child development feel more private than, for example, job training, and families fear (often legitimately) that intrusion into their child rearing could lead to the children being taken away. For example, a case manager in TASA Next Step, when asked how she handles concerns she might have about a teen's children, says that she relies on a strong relationship built on mutual honesty and explains to her clients, "I will tell you what I think if you do the same." If the worst happens and she has to "hotline" the teen (report her concerns to Child Protective Services), she finds that "the teen may be mad for a while," but she can maintain the relationship because she makes clear that she still believes in the teen.

Second, children's needs are often personal in the sense that they are closely connected with parents' and other family members' own personal well-being. As a result, the case manager's relationship with the family is especially key to diagnosing and meeting children's needs. This is particularly true when the children's needs include effective parenting, as in the observation cited above in which the case manager was able to provide a teen mother with low-key support and advice that benefited her baby. In the view of case managers in at least two of the programs, building a supportive personal relationship with a young woman is the most crucial contribution they can make to her ability to be a good parent.

Thus, the evidence from the study sites suggests that developing a strong personal relationship with families is part of providing successful, high-quality services to children and families on welfare. In particular, the evidence suggests that the importance of a personal relationship with service deliverers may grow out of the particular needs of the families being served and the sensitivity and subtlety of the issues concerning children's wellbeing and family functioning.

Services That Cross Boundaries

The evidence from the sites also suggests that service deliverers must be able to gain access to services of many different types, working across bureaucratic boundaries, if they are to help families with multiple and complex needs cope with a fragmented delivery system. It was not surprising to find this kind of boundary-crossing service at the sites that explicitly offered case management, since coordinating multiple services is generally part of case management's definition. However, it was more surprising that the three sites that emphasized partnership with a *single* outside service (the Detroit dropout prevention program, the ET CHOICES/Voucher Child Care program, and PACE), programs that we chose because we believed that they did not offer case management, in fact respond to multiple needs as well. The voucher child care program probably does the least service brokering across boundaries since it is nested in a larger system of case management through ET CHOICES, but the parent counselors do make some connections to services beyond child care for related needs, such as parenting skills.

In the other two programs, which stand alone, workers have been pulled much more extensively into responding to the multiple needs of families. In fact, the Detroit program, at least in one of the two schools, involved such extensive connections to multiple services that it is best described as a case management model. Workers in Detroit reported assisting families in getting extra benefits from the eligibility system (for example, payment for utility bills) and setting up appointments with eligibility workers, trying to arrange guardianship for a 14-year-old whose mother was on drugs, making a Child Protective Services referral for a 12-year-old who was in her eighth month of pregnancy and had had no prenatal care (and taking her in for care), referring parents for GED (General Educational Development, or high school equivalency) classes and job training, referring a mother and her two daughters for family counseling, referring a younger sibling to a Head Start program, and trying to respond to frequent requests from students for drug rehabilitation help for their mothers.

Kentucky's PACE program falls somewhere in the middle—with much more case management going on than we had expected when we selected it but less than in Detroit or in the sites selected because they offered case management. The PACE teachers reported that their personal commitment to their students and the students' multiple needs meant that they too paid considerable attention to needs outside education. While the list of services they offered was quite long, however, they tried hard to find a role as more teacher than social worker, lending a hand when they needed to (for example, chopping wood when a family has an illness) and from time to time getting involved with outside agencies such as the welfare department, but keeping those functions at the margin of their jobs rather than the center. Thus, while one teacher reported that "it's frustrating sometimes not to have a social worker background," others noted that "the job is about 50% social work but social services don't come from me" and that the role is "more of a go-between than getters."

Why have these sites, which were selected because they illustrated an approach *other* than case management, moved so far in the case management direction? The comments of service providers supported the analysis offered earlier: Serving families with multiple needs, at least in the context of a service system that is too fragmented for them to work with alone, requires the ability to cross boundaries. As a result, workers found themselves performing a bridging role almost inadvertently if they cared about the success of the families they served. Some emphasized the families and some the system as the reason for this complex task: A PACE administrator working with welfare families found that "there are just so many outside needs," while one of the teachers in the same program said that "I don't think the people [on AFDC] are any different. It's just working with the bureaucracy that makes it so hard." A PACE administrator gave an example of her teachers' commitment to the families, which also illustrates how the service broker role evolves: "One day, it was the end of the month and [a client] didn't have her money. They were waiting for their money. They were eating beans. . . . She [the teacher] went to [a social worker at the school] and the two of them went over to Brighton Center. By the end of the day, they had food in the house."

Thus, the sites suggest that successful and high-quality programs serving a poor, multiproblem clientele need to develop ways to help clients solve more than the single problem the program may originally have been designed for. Helping children stay in school may mean a GED referral for a mother, a Head Start referral for a younger sibling, money to keep the utilities from being shut off, or counseling or guardianship to deal with intolerable conflict within the family. Working on family literacy may require assisting with food in the house, pointing the way to medical care, and easing family conflict. Service deliverers may be able to limit this role somewhat, particularly if they are part of a network that includes case management services close by, but they cannot expect to close it off completely.

Evidence from the Literature: Responsive and Wide-Ranging Services

The picture that emerges from the sites, then, is one in which workers aiming to provide child and family services to families receiving welfare need, in many cases, to be able to provide responsive, personal services—services offered in the context of a trusting relationship—and to go beyond any single service system to provide help with many different kinds of needs. This is an ambitious agenda, but it is consistent with the findings of a number of recent reviews of program experience.

Most notably, Lisbeth Schorr and Daniel Schorr found the same characteristics (along with several others) in their review of programs that have been proven to be effective for disadvantaged children and families:

What is perhaps most striking about programs that work for the children and families in the shadows is that all of them find ways to *adapt or circumvent traditional professional and bureaucratic limitations when necessary to meet the needs of those they serve.* . . . The programs that succeed in helping the children and families in the shadows are intensive, comprehensive, and flexible. They also share an extra dimension, more difficult to capture: Their climate is created by skilled, committed professionals who establish respectful and trusting relationships and respond to the individual needs of those they serve. [emphasis in original][11]

As in the site examples, Schorr linked this finding to the needs of the families being served.

Other evaluation evidence in related fields suggests similar conclusions. A review of the evidence about services to teen mothers, conducted by MDRC in the development of the New Chance program model, concluded that "interventions aimed at the New Chance target group [low-income young mothers] should be comprehensive and of substantial duration, and that services should be delivered on-site by staff who are warm and caring and who emphasize accountability and achievement."[12] Again, this list includes the two elements identified above—comprehensive services across problem areas and staff who develop a strong personal relationship ("warm and caring")—along with additional factors that are not universally true of the study sites (on-site services, for example).

A review of the implementation experience of California's welfare-to-work programs reported that teachers serving AFDC families found that they had to change their roles to respond to recipients' multiple needs, like the PACE teachers and Detroit dropout prevention workers. James A. Riccio and Kay F. Sherwood reported that:

Basic education teachers indicated that the GAIN registrants [that is, AFDC recipients enrolled in GAIN] attending their classes had more personal, health, child care, and transportation problems, and lower expectations of their own abilities, than the other students they taught. . . . In their efforts to help GAIN students overcome these problems, the teachers found themselves filling more of a counselor role than they had in the past.[13]

Finally, a review by Denise Polit and Joseph O'Hara of evidence regarding support services and the transition from welfare to work defined case management to include the elements described above: "an ongoing relationship" with clients, "planning and delivering" assistance from multiple sources, and a role as an "instructor" and model, at least in relation to younger clients. They found that while the evidence is limited, it does support the view that such a role is valuable:

Although the effectiveness of using case managers to orchestrate the delivery of support and training-educational services has not been rigorously evaluated, there is some modest evidence in support of this model of service delivery. In the organizational analysis of [Work Incentive] WIN programs[,] . . . (Mitchell et al., 1980), the high-performing offices emphasized personal counseling, referral to a range of needed support services, and individualized approaches toward job placement. . . . Similarly, a recent analysis of successful employment programs for teenage parents concluded that case management was a salient characteristic of exemplary programs.[14]

As the study sites suggest, Polit and O'Hara linked the current appeal of case management to the fragmentation of the human services system. They also noted the multiple needs of families, though they did not link this finding to the role of case management: At least some low-income mothers "have complex and difficult lives with numerous problems, including abusive family situations, alcohol and drug problems, relationships with men involved in criminal activities, and depression and mental illness."[15]

Thus, the two elements of service delivery highlighted by the sites are consistent with the findings of other evaluation studies. Given the particularly complex and private nature of family and child issues, it is not surprising that personally responsive service deliverers seem most important for family services and teen parent programs and less clearly necessary for programs aimed at economic self-sufficiency.

Evidence from the Literature: Case Management

The literature on effective case management in various settings also addresses the nature of high-quality service delivery for needy families. Case management is a service that is provided in many different human services settings for clients with multiple needs, and definitions usually emphasize brokering or linking multiple services. A typical list of the basic elements of case management would include: (1) assessing needs, (2) developing a service plan, (3) arranging and coordinating services, and (4) monitoring service provision.[16] Nothing in this definition requires the kind of personal relationship described above, and the term *case manager* is sometimes used to describe a fairly limited and impersonal role, as when workers with the title of case manager in a welfare-to-employment program are responsible for taking a client through a relatively limited set of services. However, several recent documents on case management have provided a conception of service delivery very much like the one offered above and have argued that the ability of the worker to build a relationship with the client—a relationship generally based on identifying and meeting needs that the client sees as important—is the central element in the process of brokering services.[17]

For example, the authors of "A Framework for Child Welfare Reform" (prepared for the Annie E. Casey Foundation by the Center for the Study of Social Policy) argued, consistent with the evidence from the sites, that the personal relationship makes service delivery to children and family possible.

We use *case management* to denote the primary relationship a worker establishes with a family in order to assess the family's situation and that of its children; develop a course of action, or service plan, appropriate to the situation; secure the resources necessary to implement the plan; and oversee the situation to ensure that the family's needs are actually met. Importantly, these functions are performed in the context of a relationship between the worker carrying out these tasks and an individual or family, which helps motivate family members and enables them to take responsibility for necessary changes. . . . Experience indicates that it is often the nature of this relationship—its accessibility, its intensity, and its empowering relationship to a family—that results in more effective use of services and produces the major benefits.[18]

Consistent with this picture of a personal role, Julius Ballew and George Mink, in *Case Management in the Human Services* (1986), supported the impression of workers at our study sites that developing the motivation and competence of clients is a key role for service deliverers. They argued that case management is appropriate for people who have multiple needs and who cannot work their way through existing channels to meet those needs—characteristics that apply, at least in the view of the service deliverers we interviewed, to many families that a welfare agency might serve:

Case management is a process for helping people whose lives are unsatisfying or unproductive due to the presence of many problems which require assistance from several helpers at once. Case management has a dual emphasis. On the one hand, it concentrates on developing or enhancing a resource network. . . . On the other hand, case management concentrates on strengthening the personal competence of the client to obtain resources and to use the resource network.[19]

As a result of this explicit emphasis on the particular needs of case management clients, and therefore on the case manager's relationship to them, Ballew and Mink added two more stages to the traditional four elements of case management: "engaging" at the beginning, and "disengaging" at the end.[20] The first of these stages fits the experience of workers at the study sites particularly well: As described in the section on strategies for intake in Chapter 5, many of them devote considerable time to "engaging," reaching out to families to overcome mistrust and isolation and bring them into services. For some programs, but not all, "disengaging," or developing other support services and preparing a client for case closing, is also a major focus of attention.

For many families that a welfare agency might see, then, the case management literature provides insights that are consistent with the view from our sites: Delivering services is much more complicated than simply providing a service slot or even filling out an assessment form. The primary service deliverer, whether or not he or she is called a case manager, probably needs to pay careful attention to the relationship with the client as well as to seek out, somehow, the community resources that will meet a range of client needs.

THE MAJOR BARRIERS TO SERVING CHILDREN AND FAMILIES THROUGH THE WELFARE SYSTEM

This evidence about the capacity and limits of the welfare department, the characteristics of the service system for children and families, and the needs of families suggests three conclusions. First, there are important reasons for strengthening the role of the welfare department in serving children and families. The welfare department's capacity as an intake point for poor families and as a large organization with a large staff of frontline workers who see poor children and their families is too important to waste. The system of service delivery that exists now in most jurisdictions includes many high-quality services but also has important gaps that a welfare agency might fill through roles as case manager, catalyst for services, or funding source. And family needs are not well matched to the existing service system, suggesting that there is room for substantial improvement in services.

Second, however, it clearly will not be easy to use the welfare department as a focal point in serving children and families. Such a commitment seems likely to require a major investment of managerial attention and time in order to change existing organizational capacity and political alignments. And moving welfare departments to focus on children and families looks considerably more difficult than moving them from a focus on accurate check writing to a focus on self-sufficiency, as mandated by the Family Support Act. Moving to a focus on children and families looks more difficult because the issues raised by child and family needs are more private, subtle, and complex; because children and families are further from the traditional mission of the welfare department; and because the network of agencies providing services is even more intricate than the already complex network offering job training, job search, and remedial education.

Third, the analysis in this chapter suggests five particularly important barriers to high-quality services by a welfare agency for children and families:

1. Welfare agencies are accountable for spending large sums of money accurately and for controlling the amount spent. This mission and accountability may be hard to reconcile with a broader role in family services.

2. Line workers in welfare agencies (eligibility workers) must determine accuracy and enforce rules. This job is frequently frustrating and demoralizing, it can lead to considerable conflict with clients, and it may be hard to reconcile with a more flexible and responsive services approach.

3. Welfare agencies are isolated from agencies that serve children, yet they do not have the in-house expertise to do without them.

4. At least some families on welfare are isolated, mistrustful of professionals, depressed or lacking in self-esteem, characterized by multiple and complex service needs, and without the skills to gain access to the complicated bureaucratic systems that are available to meet those needs. High-quality service delivery to these families requires that staff build trusting relationships and reach out to provide services across bureaucratic and professional boundaries.

5. The needs of children are often intimately linked with the needs of adults and the functioning of the family as a whole. As a result, meeting children's needs often requires that staff build trusting relationships not only with a child, but with the family as a whole.

The consequence of these barriers, taken together, is that in order to provide services to children, the welfare agency must sustain a broad mission in the face of pressure for narrow accountability; deliver services in a responsive and flexible way in the face of political and organizational pressures for rigidity; support service deliverers who are capable of such responsiveness and flexibility despite the presence of a core of workers whose job is defined as the opposite; and either develop completely new service capacities or build links to other providers who may initially be skeptical or indifferent. The next two chapters report on the evidence that some welfare agencies are meeting these challenges, extraordinary as such an accomplishment may seem. Chapter 4 summarizes the services offered by successful programs, and Chapter 5 analyzes the strategies that make it possible for them to succeed.

4

Sites and Services: Programs That Meet the Challenges

Chapter 3 identified a range of reasons why it is difficult for welfare agencies to offer services that take children's needs seriously into account: the current mission and job structure of welfare agencies, the isolation of welfare agencies from many services to children, the nature of family needs, and the quality of service delivery required to respond successfully to those needs. At the same time, however, the chapter identified clear opportunities for welfare agencies to respond to those needs more effectively than most now do. Specifically, welfare agencies seem a natural intake point for families, they employ large numbers of workers who know quite a bit about family circumstances and may well want to do more for recipients than their current jobs allow, and their administrators are currently rethinking their agency mandate as a consequence of the Family Support Act.

The sites support the conjecture that despite all the difficulties, it is nonetheless possible for a welfare agency to pay attention to the needs of children in welfare families and provide services that meet those needs. Despite the many difficulties, the sites generally succeeded at providing high-quality services to families and children in a wide variety of urban and rural settings, in both state- and county-operated welfare systems, and for different AFDC populations.

This chapter offers brief descriptions of the services offered to children by the study sites in order to provide a sense of the options currently being explored within the welfare system. The descriptions use the present tense to offer a snapshot of the sites as they were when we visited in the summer and fall of 1989, even though services and programs have been changed, added, and eliminated since that time. (For more detail, see the site case studies in Appendix A.) After this account of what successful programs look like, Chapter 5 goes on to ask *how* these programs succeed: In particular, how do they succeed in overcoming the barriers to effective services through the welfare system that were described in Chapter 3?

The seven sites (plus one supplemental site) deliver a wide range of services to an equally wide range of target groups: intensive case management for teen parents and their children, GED education paired with early childhood education, and dropout prevention plus family services for middle-school children, to take only a few examples. The common feature of the programs is that they pay attention to children in the context of the welfare agency. Thus, the teen parent programs pay attention to the teen's child as well as the teen herself, and the child care resource and referral agency focuses on child development in its parent counseling and provider training.

CAPSULE SUMMARIES OF THE SITES

Oklahoma: Integrated Family Services (IFS)

Operated by the Oklahoma Department of Human Services in nine counties across the state, the Integrated Family Services system provides intense, short-run (three- to six-month) case management to families in crisis, many of whom are AFDC families. Through "team staffings" with other service deliverers, IFS case managers link families to a wide variety of needed services in the community. At the same time, the case managers and the program serve a second function: to build community capacity for family-oriented services through such activities as convening a regular working group of service deliverers and developing a community resource directory.

San Diego, California: The Gain Teen Parent Project

Operated by the county of San Diego Department of Social Services, the project assigns selected caseworkers from GAIN (Greater Avenues to Independence), California's welfare-to-work program, to work with pregnant and parenting AFDC teenagers. The GAIN teen specialists try to develop personal relationships with the teens that will enable them to address underlying issues of self-esteem at the same time that they assist teens toward the specific goals of school completion and self-sufficiency. The teen specialists operate as part of a community network to serve teens, which also includes a community-based program that offers more intensive case management and a program offering health care services tailored to teens.

Detroit, Michigan: Earhart—Fort Wayne—Jackson— Conner-Warren Dropout Prevention Program

Since June 1988, the Wayne County (Detroit) Department of Social Services (DSS) has operated a dropout prevention program in two middle schools for AFDC children who are identified by the schools as being in danger of dropping out. The program expanded to two more schools in the fall of 1990. Under the program, DSS workers assigned to the schools provide activities for the children such as field trips, counseling, and tutoring; make home visits to talk with parents; refer children and parents to various services; and work with teachers and counselors at the schools on behalf of children.

Elmira, New York: The TASA Next Step Program

Next Step, which is operated by a community action agency and funded by the New York State Department of Social Services, began as a pilot site for New York State's Teenage Services Act (TASA) in 1986 and is now part of a statewide network of TASA-funded programs. We chose it as a site because it has a particularly strong reputation among TASA programs for attention to the teen's family, including her children. Next Step case managers offer AFDC and other Medicaid-eligible teens a long-term relationship based on extensive informal contact in the teen's home and a philosophy of "unconditional acceptance." Next Step also offers its teens an extensive program of Family Life Education groups, which include parenting education, parent-child time, and colocated child care. In addition, Next Step serves teens and their children through referral to a rich network of local maternal-child health services, Head Start, other child care resources, and other social and mental health services.

San Francisco, California: The TAPP/GAIN Collaboration

In this collaboration, the San Francisco Department of Social Services, which operates GAIN, teamed up with a community-based organization called the Teen-Age Pregnancy and Parenting Program (TAPP), which has been providing services to pregnant and parenting teens in San Francisco since 1988. Under the collaboration, TAPP was to provide case management services to pregnant and parenting teens who were on AFDC and therefore eligible for GAIN. TAPP's extensive network of interagency agreements gives teens and their children access to a wide range of health, social services, mental health, and child development programs, among others. The collaboration began in the spring of 1989, a few months before our site visit, and ended in the summer of 1990.

Massachusetts: ET CHOICES/Voucher Child Care Program

The ET CHOICES/Voucher Child Care program is a partnership between the Massachusetts Department of Public Welfare and local nonprofit agencies called Voucher Management Agencies (VMAs), that specialize in child care resource and referral for AFDC recipients. The VMAs provide AFDC families who are participating in education, training, or employment with assistance in selecting child care from available community programs. In addition, we selected the particular VMA site we visited for its reputation for paying attention to the needs of the child as well as the employment of the parent in counseling parents about child care settings. (See also the supplemental site visit described below.)

Kentucky: Parent and Child Education (PACE)

Kentucky's Parent and Child Education (PACE) family literacy program aims to break the intergenerational cycle of educational failure through a school-based program that allows parents to pursue adult education while their children attend a high-quality preschool in the same building. The program also includes time for parents and children to be together and learn through play, and it includes opportunities for parents to discuss issues such as discipline and child development. PACE programs are open to all parents without a high school diploma or GED and with preschool-age youngsters. At the time of our site visit, the state had just begun operating two PACE programs reserved for AFDC recipients and funded through a federal WIN demonstration grant, in addition to the regular sites funded by the Kentucky legislature through the Department of Education. As of fall 1990, however, the two programs are no longer funded separately through welfare funds, and they are no longer reserved for AFDC recipients.

Supplemental Site Visit: Massachusetts: ET CHOICES Adult Case Management

We visited the case management portion of ET CHOICES, at the time the Massachusetts welfare-to-employment program, in order to observe a large, statewide case management program operated by eligibility workers serving as case managers. (It was a supplemental site because it did not meet our site selection criterion of emphasizing services to children.) At the time when we visited, eligibility workers were expected to play a role in assisting a family toward independence, which included referring the parent to appropriate education and training activities or to a specialist worker who could help with such activities, encouraging the parent to talk with the specialist about employment opportunities and about child care, and making sure that the family had access to health care. During the months after our visit, eligibility caseloads rose considerably from the level of 130–140 cases per worker at the time we visited, and administrators feared that workers' attention had been forced back to basic eligibility and away from case management.

Despite this variety, the services offered to children by these programs fall into three main categories. First, all the programs offer some specific, functionally defined services—such as high-quality child care, child health services, or education—to at least some children and families in the program. Second, most of the programs offer families a personal link to a worker who can offer counsel and support in the context of a relationship as well as connect the family to multiple services. Children receive "services" through this individual link every time a case manager offers support for a mother's affectionate play with her baby, notices a toddler's possible developmental problem for follow-up, or helps a mother gain the confidence to speak with her child's teacher about a plan for improving his or her schoolwork. Third, some programs affect children's lives by altering the way in which other agencies (such as the schools) serve children or by developing new services through advocacy and community organizing.

SPECIFIC FUNCTIONAL SERVICES AVAILABLE TO CHILDREN

Child Health

Many of the programs consciously aim to improve children's access to physical health care, and to mental health care and developmental services where needed. These links are most systematic in the TAPP/GAIN collaboration, the TASA Next Step program, and the GAIN Teen Parent Project, with a range of services also being available to families with particular needs through the Oklahoma Intensive Family Services (IFS) System. Workers in the Detroit dropout prevention program, the PACE program, and ET CHOICES/Voucher Child Care program also reported examples in which they connected families to health care.

The three teen parent programs provide considerable access to health care for mothers and their infants. In San Diego, for example, the network of programs accessible to the AFDC teens includes a Teen OB (obstetrics) clinic at the University of California at San Diego Hospital. At the time of our visit, the clinic provided case management and follow-up health care to a study group of 168 pregnant teens and their infants for two years. After the teen's two years were up, the program continued to provide pediatric care for as long as the mother and child kept coming in for appointments. In New York State's TASA Next Step program, all pregnant teens who are enrolled in the program receive home visits from a nurse throughout pregnancy and early infancy, as well as ongoing health care and transportation for Medicaid-eligible children. Each teen's Next Step case manager works closely with the teen's nurse home visitor throughout pregnancy and infancy. San Francisco's TAPP/GAIN collaboration also offers all enrolled teens the opportunity to have a public health nurse visit at home during pregnancy and for the first few months after the birth. In addition, TAPP case managers can refer teens to the clinic for high-risk infants at San Francisco General Hospital, which is staffed by a team that includes a pediatrician, a nurse practitioner, a psychiatrist, several nutritionists, and a social worker. A TAPP case manager attends the weekly case conferences at the clinic to ensure that TAPP teens are linked into services and to improve communication between case managers and health care providers. Similarly, a worker from the Golden Gate Regional Center for developmentally disabled children attends the TAPP weekly intake meeting in which pregnant teens are assigned to case managers and flags high-risk cases (for example, those with a history of drug abuse) for follow-up.

In Oklahoma's Intensive Family Services system, which works with multineed families that may often be in crisis, case managers often mentioned a role in connection with health and nutrition services, such as referral to the WIC nutrition program or to a physician, as well as family mental health services. In some cases, a family served by IFS is already in contact with a mental health provider and the role of the IFS case manager is to bring that provider into a team setting in which the whole family's needs can be reviewed. In other cases, the IFS case manager may arrange mental health services or help adults in the family realize that a child might benefit from psychological counseling.

Child Care and Early Childhood Education

As in the case of child health, attention to child care and early childhood education is quite widespread in the sites, although at several of the sites the services available probably vary widely for individual families. We saw two approaches to child care that attends to the needs of the child. One approach links welfare families with special programs targeted to the developmental needs of children. For example, in the collaboration between Kentucky's PACE program and the welfare agency, mothers on welfare have the opportunity to enroll in a two-generational program that couples a high-quality, developmentally oriented preschool program for the child with a GED program for the mother. The three teen parent programs also link some families with particular high-quality programs, though capacity in all cases is limited. TASA Next Step is in the same building as a Head Start center and tries to arrange for the teens' children to attend when they are old enough (often at just about the point that the mothers leave TASA); the TAPP/GAIN program is colocated with a high-quality child care program that is available to teens who enroll in the high school that is also in the same building; and the GAIN Teen Parent Project is able to place some teens in high schools within the San Diego Unified School District that have on-site infant care.

The second approach provides parents on welfare with counseling, referral, support, and financing so that they can select and gain access to the community child care settings that they prefer for their children. This strategy is the central element of the ET CHOICES/Voucher Child Care Program and is also available to some families in the GAIN Teen Parent Project, TAPP/GAIN collaboration, and TASA Next Step program. In the ET CHOICES/Voucher Child Care site that we visited—the Child Care Circuit in Lawrence, Massachusetts—parent counselors with a background in child development educate parents about the nature of high-quality child care, help them think about the needs of their child, and try to "empower" them so that they feel able to question and assess the child care provider. At the same time, provider counselors at the same agency aim to encourage new providers and improve the quality of existing ones through workshops, informal consultation, and a lending library of toys and child development materials.

Parenting Education and the Prevention of Child Abuse and Neglect

Many of the "preventive services" offered by the sites—parenting education and support for parents' ability to nurture their children—occur not through formal services but through the relationship between the family and the case manager. However, several of the sites also provide more formal services, such as support groups, classes, or workshops.

For example, all three of the teen parent programs provide teen support groups that touch on parenting issues as well as other topics such as self-esteem, health and nutrition, and family planning. In addition to knowledge about parenting, these programs generally emphasize providing mothers with the warmth and support that they are seen to need in order to be warm and supportive, in turn, to their children. Some of the programs also emphasize the actual practice of new attitudes and skills in interacting with children. For example, in the TASA Next Step program, teen parent support groups are paired with on-site child care, and the sessions are planned so that mothers meet without their children for the first portion of the visit and with the children for the second.

Kentucky's PACE program also offers a well-developed parent education component, again in the context of a program in which parents and

children learn separately for part of the day and then come together for
a joint activities period. One important purpose of this period is to help
parents learn how to be part of their children's education. In addition,
some PACE sites offer parent discussion groups or speakers on topics
including child rearing.[1]

Finally, the Lawrence Child Care Circuit offers an interesting variation
on parent education services. The circuit provides workshops and programs, such as a workshop on discipline, that are open to both parents
and child care providers. The aim is for both groups to benefit from ideas
about interacting better with children and also to learn about each other's
experiences.

While both formal and informal services at the sites are geared to
preventing child abuse and neglect, program case managers sometimes
find that they need to take stronger, more drastic measures to ensure a
child's safety and well-being. Case managers in a number of the programs
call on child protective services workers for informal consultation and help
when they are worried about a family, and several said that they had
made child protective referrals (hotlined a family) at least once. The informal consultation appears to go both ways: Child protective services
workers in several locations reportedly ask the site case managers to keep
an eye on families which they worry about but cannot serve themselves,
given their caseload of even more urgent crises.

Education

Only one of the programs, Detroit's dropout prevention program for
AFDC children, emphasizes educational services for school-age children,
such as tutoring. Workers in the dropout prevention program also
reported working with teachers on educational practices that might help
the children (such as more frequent feedback on performance), advocating
for the children within the educational system, and encouraging parental support for education and parental advocacy for children. One other
program, Oklahoma's IFS, reported working closely with school personnel when children in the families they serve have educational problems.
(The teen parent programs have all developed links to the school system
and alternative education programs on behalf of the teens but not their
children, who are not yet of school age.)

SERVICES TO CHILDREN THROUGH THE CASE
MANAGEMENT RELATIONSHIP

The last chapter argued that delivering high-quality services to families
and children on welfare may often require a personal relationship between
the family and a program worker. The worker must be able to cross

professional boundaries to meet a wide variety of family needs. In order to serve the child, he or she must also develop a relationship with the whole family, since the child's well-being is often intimately bound up with the well-being of other family members.

What exactly does it mean to serve children through this case management relationship? What does the relationship offer *besides* referral to specific, functional services like those already discussed? The previous chapter offered one example in which a case manager observed a teen's baby at play, asked the teen about tensions she might be experiencing as a young parent, and provided support and encouragement for the solutions to those tensions that the young mother had already developed. More generally, the family-oriented case managers in the site programs serve children by:

- Keeping an eye on children themselves and helping families gauge how their children are doing;
- Providing parents with support and friendship, assistance in improving important family relationships and in dealing differently with their children, and information about parenting or children;
- Providing friendship, support, and role models for a child directly; and
- Encouraging other service deliverers to respond more effectively to a child's needs.

The specific examples below illustrate both the scope of what can be accomplished by skilled case managers and the fragility of their successes. In particular, in several programs, case managers struggle to bring together their role in relation to a single client, such as a teen mother or a school age child, with their role in relation to the family as a whole. In these successful examples, case managers reported integrating those roles to see the child in a family context rather than advocating for one family member against another, but not all experiences were as successful. In addition, case managers operated with quite different levels of training in child development and family functioning; again, the examples illustrate what is possible with training and, in several cases, expert backup support.

Assessment: Keeping an Eye on Children

In several programs, the case managers noted that keeping an eye on the well-being, development, and happiness of children on their caseload was part of their job. Case managers in the SANDAPP community-based case management program in San Diego (which is available to some of the teens in the GAIN Teen Parent Project there), both public health nurses and case managers associated with the TAPP program in San Francisco, case managers in the TASA Next Step Teen Parent program, and case managers in Oklahoma's IFS all reported that they would normally see children in the families that were part of their caseloads, note how they were doing, and try to provide or arrange help for developmental problems and other needs. Case managers also reported that educating parents on developmental stages so that they could make their own judgments about children was part of their job.

These observations of children ranged from quite structured to quite informal. For example:

- The public health nurses in San Francisco reported that their home visit schedule includes observing a young mother carry out a routine task like bathing or feeding her baby. One nurse commented that she makes a point of looking for warmth and interaction between mother and child as well as facility with the task itself; she finds that the teen mothers on her caseload may not interact with their babies in a way she feels comfortable with for several months after birth. Besides observing, in these visits the nurse models both interaction with the baby and performance of the task.

- SANDAPP case managers find that "we case manage the family," including not only the teen parent and her child but her parents and, sometimes, siblings. They report that they have been trained in structured ways of observing children and their development and that they aim to help parents understand child development as well. In one example, a case manager noticed that a baby's development did not seem right and brought the infant in to be diagnosed; it turned out to have cerebral palsy. In another example, a case manager reported on helping a mother understand child development: "Our job is to help mother understand child development—no, your baby will not walk at four months, no you cannot give her table food for her to put in her mouth, even if your mother says that."

- A TASA Next Step case manager said, "I pay attention to every child, at least visually." TASA case managers reported that they will see every child over the course of a case management relationship, though they might not ask to see the child on the first visit because that would seem too intimidating. Rather than perform a formal assessment of the child's well-being or needs, they look for information to emerge over the course of visits, conversations, and observation, as in the example in the last chapter. They also meet monthly with the nurse home visitors who see the mothers and infants.

- For TASA teens who are enrolled in the teen parent support group, another provider in addition to the case manager looks out for the children. The caregivers who provide child care during the support groups keep track of how the children are doing, including cleanliness, signs of abuse, and changes in behavior, and they talk over what they have learned with the support group leader and the case manager.

- A TAPP case manager reported working closely with professional staff from the Golden Gate Regional Center (GGRC) who specialize in developmental disability when she has a concern about a child. A nurse from GGRC will go out on a joint home visit with her and perform a developmental assessment of a child or assist her in providing advice to a parent. She too reported an example of a baby who did not seem to be developing normally and who was referred for a more extensive workup and diagnosis.

- Oklahoma's IFS case managers, who focus from the first visit on the whole family, include several aspects of the children's well-being and relations to their parents in their initial assessment. One county, for example, assesses a family's "coping skills, life styles, child rearing patterns, relationship patterns, peer supports, [and] medical care." As in TASA and SANDAPP, case managers reported that assessment is not a one-time event: They gain an initial sense of the key information in three or four visits, but even after that, "The assessment goes on and on." One case manager, for example, noted that he is keeping an eye on the 10-year-old sister of a very disturbed 7-year-old boy: She seems fine, but given the severe problems in the family, he is concerned that the appearance might be misleading.

- In the Lawrence Child Care Circuit, parent counselors do not usually see the child, but they do emphasize helping the parent think about the child's personality and needs. In the initial conversation about child care, counselors ask what a child is like, whether he or she is quiet, whether he or she would feel lost in a large day care center, and so forth. They also ask about health—for example, a counselor reported looking for a day care home with no pets for a child with asthma—and about behavioral problems, but they find that parents are reluctant to talk about the latter.

Helping Children through Their Parents

As suggested in the last chapter, case managers are able to respond to some of the needs they identify in children or in family relationships through their relationships with the parents. At the simplest level, the case managers respond by offering information, though their experience is consistent with expert opinion suggesting that information by itself is frequently not sufficient to improve parenting.[2] More important, in their view, case managers model alternative behavior and skills, provide a sounding board and source of advice on other family relationships that may be affecting relationships with the children, and provide warmth and support to the parents—which case managers see as crucial to the parents' ability to nurture their children. While it is clearly difficult in the course of a brief relationship to affect behavior formed over as long a time as parenting, a number of the case managers bring considerable thought and sophistication to the task.[3]

For example, TASA case managers and support group leaders (known as family life educators) emphasize that the teens with whom they work often have not known warm and nurturing care themselves. To nurture the teens so they, in turn, can nurture their children, TASA staff use several strategies: support groups for both teens and their mothers, in order to work on that relationship from both ends; warmth and personal support from the case manager; and direct modeling of behavior with the teens' infants and children. For example, one case manager pointed out that when a child acts out on a home visit and the mother becomes upset, the case manager can say, "This is what two-year-olds do." Another case manager noted that when she holds and talks to an infant on a home visit, she is also modeling behavior.

In the SANDAPP program as well, one of the goals for case managers is to "teach nonabusive parenting skills." As in TASA, SANDAPP case managers believe that the teens themselves need nurturing in order to nurture their children. As one case manager put it: "[We] always help mother to understand: Baby is one thing, you're another, and together you're going to be a family. But we're gonna first see what we can do for you." The SANDAPP case managers also work with both teens and their parents (the baby's grandparents). They emphasize that the teens really want to be good parents—having often fought social ostracism to have their babies—but "may not have the equipment," whether intellectual, social, or financial, to be good parents without considerable support.

To help the teens become better parents, SANDAPP case managers report spending a lot of time talking with teens and grandparents, explaining appropriate expectations for children, suggesting new ways of responding to them, and trying to improve the mother-grandmother relationship (because the baby may become caught in the middle). For example:

- "One of my clients was saying 'I know she wants to walk . . . —it's just that my mother-in-law won't let her walk.' And I said, 'The baby is 3 1/2 months old.' I told her it wasn't good for a baby—[the mother] was doing all kinds of things to get her [baby] to walk before 4 months."

- "You go and make a home visit to mother and grandmother on a two-week-old baby, and they say, 'This baby is bad. . . . It doesn't behave.' [They're] starting to spank it at two weeks old. . . . It hurts [to hear them say that]—we have to help them understand that that's what little babies do."

- "Most of the grandparents will tell [the teens], 'Don't hold the baby, you're going to spoil it.'" Another case manager interjects, "So you have to say there's no such thing as a spoiled baby." First case manager: "I spend a lot of time trying to talk to grandparents."

- One case manager reported that the teens may be afraid to take their babies in for medical visits, particularly when the baby is very ill and the procedures required seem incomprehensible or painful. She tries to support the mother as needed—for example, going along to the doctor's office to interpret the instructions or diagnosis.

Providing Direct Support to the Child

Case managers may also provide informal services to children through a direct relationship with them. That is, they may be mentors and friends to children as well as parents in the families they serve. Among the study sites, the Detroit dropout prevention workers provided the clearest example. They took children on field trips and tried to offer warmth, support, and "coping skills": "One of the most important things that we do is to give the kids personal attention. Because they don't get it from the school, their parents, their relatives or anybody."

One challenge that the Detroit workers sometimes encounter, and that could also arise in other programs in which a worker's primary relationship is with the child rather than the parent, is uncertainty about the workers' role in serving families that do not initially seem supportive of their children. Workers reported mixed feelings in this regard: Some did not see a way in which to help parents become more supportive of their children and therefore concentrated their energy on the children, while others were firmly committed to working with the parents as well.

Encouraging Effective, Family-Oriented Response by Other Service Deliverers

A fourth way in which family-oriented case managers provide services to children is through their conversations with other service deliverers, who may know only one member of the family and only one narrow slice of that family member's circumstances (for example, a mother's thoughts about suicide but not her desire to go back to school). The roles that case managers play in relation to these outside service deliverers go far beyond simply referring clients and even beyond negotiating individual arrangements for client access. Rather, case managers work to change existing services to fit a family better; create new services to fit a particular family's needs, often by developing informal helping networks; pull together teams of service deliverers in order to improve the quality and coordination of services; and advocate for families in order to change the perspectives of other service deliverers about what the families can achieve.

Two examples illustrate these roles:

- The Next Step program director reported creating a new service when she needed to find a place for a mentally retarded teen mother to live with her child. After finding no formal services, she asked the local church to make an announcement and a volunteer came forward to take the mother and child into her home.
- SANDAPP case managers advocate on behalf of individual clients by knowing the eligibility rules of other programs, articulating what fair treatment means and protesting its violation, and going to supervisors or program administrators when necessary. In one example, a case manager succeeded in getting a welfare supervisor to overrule an eligibility worker who had delayed an authorization for emergency medical care and had, in the case manager's view, treated her client disrespectfully. After winning the point, the case manager used the experience to teach her teenage client a lesson about self-esteem by telling her, "No one ever has the right to talk to you that way"—that is, the way in which the eligibility worker had spoken to her.

However, while case managers in a range of programs described this function of influencing other service deliverers, it is most fully developed and institutionalized in Oklahoma's IFS. A key function of IFS case managers is to coordinate a family's multiple service providers, generally by convening a "team staffing": a meeting in which the family and the workers put their information together and develop a joint course of action. In an example cited in the previous chapter, a team staffing assisted a child who was engaging in violent and self-destructive behavior in three ways: It identified direct services that would be valuable for him, it gained services for his mother to enable her to care for him, and it changed the Child Protective Services worker's view of the family from one in which the mother was "sleazy" to one in which she could possibly be a capable parent. Another example makes the role of the IFS case manager even more vivid:

I had one lady who had lost her children through child welfare and just gotten them back, and . . . the court ordered her to get parenting classes for herself, counseling at one place for one kid, counseling at another place for another kid, school counseling for all of them together. They had physical health needs, they have a child welfare worker, AFDC worker. . . . And we all sat down together. We literally made a pie, and everybody got a piece of a pie, and I mean a cut-up piece of paper. It was something she understood, and it was something they understood. And the plan that they were involved in was on their piece.

Despite the creativity of case managers' work with other service systems, however, they are not always successful. First, as might be expected, case managers sometimes cannot meet families' needs through other systems because there are no slots available. Somewhat surprisingly, a major problem in this regard is the schools: For example, the schools may have no program available to take a 16-year-old who speaks only Spanish, tests at a fifth-grade level, and has a 2-year-old toddler. Other gaps noted by various sites include a lack of residential programs for drug abuse, mental health, and mental retardation that will take a mother with children and insufficient infant and toddler child care.

Second, in addition to a simple lack of slots, case managers sometimes encounter policy conflicts that they are unable to resolve at the service delivery level. Staff at one community-based program offered a sad example of a pregnant teenager who was seriously involved with drugs but who seemed, with enormous time and attention from two case managers, to pull her life together in the late stages of her pregnancy. When her drug screening test in the hospital came out negative, her case managers considered it a major victory. All went well until the teen's mother was incarcerated and the teen and her child were put into foster care. The teen did well in her first placement with a foster family, but it was an emergency placement, a temporary setting that cost the Department of Social Services more than regular foster care. Therefore, she was moved to a second family and then to two more, none of which worked out. Eventually the teen left the system for the streets, and the caseworkers have completely lost sight of her and her child. The caseworkers said they had "begged [and] pleaded" with DSS to keep the teen in the first, successful placement, but they observed that sometimes they could not alter "policies and procedures."

Precisely because case managers are not always able to compensate for service gaps and conflicts through their activities on behalf of individual clients, some of the sites go beyond these individual interactions with other service systems to try to change policy or attitudes systemwide.

SERVICES THROUGH SYSTEMS CHANGE, COMMUNITY ORGANIZING, AND ADVOCACY

A final way in which these programs serve children is through efforts to change systems of service delivery *outside* the program as well as to develop new, broadly available services. While case managers in virtually all the programs work to develop new services or packages of services for specific clients, four programs particularly emphasize this broader role of influencing other systems and developing communitywide services: the Lawrence Child Care Circuit, the Detroit dropout prevention program, San Diego's Teen Parent Project, and Oklahoma's IFS. In Detroit, for example, program case managers reported some evidence that their approach to serving children is beginning to influence school procedures for at-risk youngsters. Caseworkers reported on a school principal who decided to work with all the sixth-graders who were at risk of failing because she thought that the group approach and special attention offered by the caseworkers to youngsters on their caseloads were working well. At a broader policy level, caseworkers reported that one school was changing its policy from suspension to in-school detention as a disciplinary measure; while they had not suggested this change, they thought that their experiences with children who never came back after they left school for a suspension might have influenced the decision.

In San Diego, the county DSS director described the Teen Parent Project as one example of a broader system collaboration called New Beginnings, which brings together San Diego County, the city of San Diego, the community college district, and the San Diego Unified School District to focus on the needs of disadvantaged families. With this support from above, the Teen Parent Project manager is able to work on a number of activities to influence the way in which the schools deliver services: For example, she is currently meeting with both the schools and the Private Industry Council to set up an alternative school with on-site child care.

The GAIN Teen Parent Project and the other teen programs also aim to change public and service deliverer attitudes toward teen parents in their communities. Case managers and administrators regularly speak to various audiences about the teens, and a couple of the programs have gone further by putting together celebrations or events that bring a broader cross-section of the community into contact with teen participants and their children.

Oklahoma's IFS system is again the program that is most explicit about its role in community and systems change. In IFS, community organizing and system development are part of the job of every case manager rather than that of the program administrators. In fact, the IFS manual says that case managers are "obligated" to identify community service gaps and try to fill them. Consistent with this obligation, IFS staff have created or lobbied successfully for a wide range of spin-off programs that help children: for example, MATCH (Mothers Affirming, Teaching, Caring and Helping), a program of volunteer parent aides for teen mothers; Families First, a program of intensive, in-home mental health services to prevent placement of a child; and a community-based tutoring center for youth.

CONCLUSION

The seven sites illustrate that despite the difficulties enumerated in the last chapter, welfare agencies can pay attention to the lives of children and serve both children and families much more richly than most agencies do now. The nature of these services is quite varied, and perhaps surprisingly so: Specific, traditional services such as health care or parenting education are frequently backed up by more informal services provided by the case manager through his or her relationship of trust with the family. And both of these services may, in turn, be supported by an active program role in community organizing and advocacy.

In fact, however, given the needs of families and the characteristics of the system described in the last chapter, this array of different kinds of services should not be surprising. Serving children and families with these needs who are trapped in this service system may well require a mix of specific services, ongoing personal connection, and a head-on attack on the rest of the service system. What *is* surprising, however, is the success of these programs at delivering complex and high-quality services in the face of the challenges described in Chapter 3. Chapter 5 goes on to analyze the strategies that have made possible their success.

5

Strategies for Meeting the Challenges

Chapter 3 explained that welfare agencies are in many ways not well suited to serving families and children. However, Chapter 4 identified a range of programs that do serve families and children by way of the welfare system, offering case management for troubled families, health care for mothers and infants, care and education for young children, tutoring for children on the verge of dropping out, and a wide variety of other assistance. How did these programs achieve this success in the light of all the barriers? This chapter proposes two themes as key to understanding their success.

On the one hand, all the programs address a set of common tasks. Successful sites have:

- Developed a coherent mission to explain why serving families and children is the welfare department's job;
- Devoted considerable attention to effective collaboration with children's services agencies, including the development of a common mission and a means of conflict resolution;
- Reached out to bring targeted families into services;
- Chosen and supported staff who were capable of responsive service delivery in an atmosphere of accountability; and
- Identified organizational and funding arrangements that mediated the tensions between responsiveness and accountability.

On the other hand, the successful sites carried out those tasks in quite different ways, depending on their local conditions. Local solutions depended on the political setting, the agency's internal organizational capacity, the capacity of existing child and family service providers in the community, and the particular needs of the children and families an agency chose to serve.

This chapter takes up each of the tasks in turn, illustrating the importance of the task and analyzing the alternative approaches to solving it. Chapter 6 draws out key recommendations from these multiple approaches.

MISSION

Chapter 1 asked why the well-being of poor children might be the welfare department's job. Perhaps children who are not doing well prevent their parents from concentrating on education or employment. Perhaps it is the welfare department's job at least to avoid harming children in its pursuit of self-sufficiency for their mothers. Perhaps there are broader reasons for involvement: Helping children grow up healthier or better educated might reduce future welfare caseloads. Or perhaps the reason is broader still: helping children grow up into self-sufficient and healthy adults is every agency's job, with the welfare department having some special opportunities to contribute to it.

This section looks more closely at the ways in which the study sites answered the pair of questions: What, exactly, is the job to be done here for children and families on welfare, and why is it the welfare department's job? In other words, it looks at the definition of mission that is accepted at the welfare department in each site in regard to children and families. The section argues that developing a conception of mission is frequently critical to successful efforts at change in large public agencies, and that, according to the site evidence, changing welfare agencies to serve children and families is no exception. The section then goes on to describe the range of different missions that have been articulated at the sites and to analyze the local circumstances that support them.

Mission and Change in Public Agencies

Several recent writings on management have suggested that a persuasive and clear mission definition plays a key role in supporting major changes in agency operations across a wide variety of organizations. The reason is that such a conception of mission can keep external supporters on board and motivate staff internally during periods of change.[1] For example, in his study of the ET CHOICES innovation, Robert Behn found that managers in the Massachusetts Department of Public Welfare (DPW) paid great attention to developing and articulating a clear conception of mission. In order to transform the jobs of welfare department staff, DPW managers articulated a new mission of lifting families out of poverty to replace the old mission of issuing accurate checks for welfare benefits. Both within and outside the agency, they took care to draw on this mission to explain and set a context for the many changes that they made in agency policies, job responsibilities, training, and personnel evaluation procedures.[2]

A welfare agency seeking to move into child and family services might well need a new, clearly defined, and persuasive mission even more than other public agencies that are engaged in reform efforts. The reason, as the analysis in Chapter 3 suggests, is that the current mission of many welfare agencies, as defined by their political mandates and the beliefs of their staffs, is quite inconsistent with the needs of many families and children. If the agency is not simply to ignore the tension between the demands of steady, accurate, low-cost processing and the needs of families for responsive services, it needs to secure a new mandate founded on a somewhat different definition of its fundamental mission.

Several of the case examples illustrate the difficulties that a welfare agency's mandate, as currently defined, can create for delivering high-quality services to families and children. In the San Francisco collaboration between TAPP, a nonprofit agency serving pregnant and parenting teens, and GAIN, the welfare-to-work program operated by the city Department of Social Services, the TAPP staff constantly felt frustrated by rules that they thought restricted their clients' access to resources and ignored their individuality. For example, they criticized a rule that forbids the payment of child care while a GAIN client completed a four-year college program and they objected to the requirement that teens attend an adult job-search program that the TAPP counselors thought was unsuited to the special needs of teens. DSS staff, on the other hand, saw some of these rules as being directly required by the GAIN legislation and others as needed to ensure equity and distribute scarce resources fairly.

In another example, staff at the TASA Next Step site in Chemung County, New York, saw state regulations as being sometimes so specific and routinized as to threaten the effectiveness of care for some clients. For example, they found that the state forms for assessment did not fit some clients, and the state time frames for assessment and service planning could jeopardize service to more difficult clients if taken literally.

Not surprisingly, however, the most powerful examples of the tension between agency mandate and family needs come from eligibility workers, who are most driven by the mandate. At several sites, eligibility workers explained why they could not imagine having broader responsibility for families at the same time as their present obligations. Even in the Massachusetts ET CHOICES adult case management program, in which the eligibility worker's job is substantially broader than in other agencies, some staff still described a tension between the financial eligibility mission and a broader mission that could truly help families. According to an intake worker: "I think I went in with not a very realistic perspective of what the job entailed. . . . I didn't realize it was as controlled by bureaucracy, rules and regulations as it is. I thought I would be coming in and really being . . . more of a social worker. . . . Sometimes I think of myself as a bank teller, processing forms to determine financial eligibility."

When a welfare agency is constrained to a mission so narrow that workers see themselves as bank tellers, it is unlikely to have the space to serve children and families well. It is not surprising, therefore, that the sites generally tried to change the metaphor.

Mission and Change at the Sites

The evidence from the sites confirms the role of a new, broader, and persuasive mission in supporting service to children and families. Almost all the sites have developed such a conception in order to explain why serving children and families is the welfare department's business. However, the two sites that are no longer serving children in conjunction with the welfare system, PACE and TAPP/GAIN, do not seem to have developed such a definition.[3] While there may be other reasons for the difference in success, or at least in its longevity, the difference in mission appears to be at least part of the explanation.

In one of these two sites, the department mission (at least as interpreted at the local level) was clearly *not* compatible with serving families and children. Specifically, the collaboration between PACE and the Department of Social Insurance (DSI) in Kentucky did not last, in part because at the local level DSI was primarily driven by the mission of providing accurate benefit checks. A local DSI director, for example, argued that in the short run, the burden of finding out about the PACE program would have to fall on the client because workers had to focus on eligibility. Apparently as a result of conflicting demands on the eligibility workers— who were required to focus largely on benefits but, in addition, were asked to refer clients to PACE—both the PACE/DSI collaborative projects had difficulty filling the 10 PACE slots that were assigned to welfare recipients. (New legislation passed in 1990 has put PACE programs into Family Resource Centers which are run by the Department of Social Services, Kentucky's family and children's services agency, where the collaboration may well work more smoothly.)

The other site that is no longer operating (the TAPP/GAIN collaboration in San Francisco) is harder to analyze because the program was primarily run through a community agency and the case study interviews were concentrated there; consequently, the evidence about the conception of mission at the welfare department (the Department of Social Services) is limited. A likely interpretation of the available evidence is that the new DSS management supported the collaboration precisely *because* they wanted to move the agency toward a broader mission that would accommodate services to families and children. However, they had not at the time of the site visit succeeded in persuading line staff to adopt this broader sense of mission. One administrator saw the limited staff perspective as a reason that the TAPP collaboration was not accepted and ultimately dissolved in 1990.

In the other five sites, both interviews and other evidence suggested that many welfare agency staff held clear conceptions of the agency's role in services to families and children. For example, in at least four sites, welfare administrators were convinced that "reaching out to families" through intensive social work was a key goal for the agency and that the historical move to separate financial eligibility from social work had been a mistake. In these sites, welfare administrators saw a link between the historical goal of family social work and the new goal of economic self-sufficiency because they saw intensive work with the family as the only way of motivating families to change. The next section offers a more detailed account of the different conceptions of mission that underlay the different programs.

The final piece of evidence suggesting the importance of a clear mission definition at the study sites is the role that such definitions played in solving particular political and operational problems. For example, the director of Chemung County's TASA Next Step program responded successfully to the troublesome state regulations on assessment at least in part by drawing on the conception of mission that she shares with state DSS officials: the conception of intensive services to the most hard-to-reach, long-term welfare recipients. She reported that her approach has been to articulate her concerns and tell state officials that she will do what she feels is necessary to maintain program quality, implying that if necessary, she might disregard rules that would damage service in a particular case. State officials have accepted this response so far, and one likely reason is that the director's clear conception of the program's mission (combined with her personal reputation) has convinced them that they can trust her to carry out the spirit, if not always the letter, of the rules.

What Is the Mission of the Welfare Agency in Serving Children and Families?

In the five sites in which welfare agency staff articulated fairly clear conceptions of the agency's role in services to families and children, those mission conceptions fell into two groups. The more limited conception of the two (though it is still much broader than most states are likely to implement under FSA) sees family services as a support for the mother's primary goal of self-sufficiency. One agency fits clearly into this category: the Massachusetts Department of Public Welfare as observed through the ET CHOICES/Voucher Child Care and the ET adult case management site visits.

In the Massachusetts sites, the welfare department plays a role for families and children in order to avoid harming children through their mothers' education and employment activities and in order to help mothers gain peace of mind about their children's care. In the research site, the Lawrence Child Care Circuit, the latter role has been expanded to include helping mothers resolve any conflicts they may experience between their roles as provider and parent. Thus, the welfare department's mission in regard to children and families is to enable mothers to make a transition to self-sufficiency while not endangering their children or their family life.

The case examples offer some reason to believe that this definition of mission is as far as a welfare agency with a narrowly defined set of organizational responsibilities (determining eligibility only, rather than child protective services and other social services) can move toward family and children's services. The two welfare agencies in the case examples that have organizational responsibilities defined this narrowly also have relatively narrow missions: Kentucky's Department of Social Insurance, which focused, at the time of the site visit, on the accurate determination of benefits, and the Massachusetts Department of Public Welfare, which focused on self-sufficiency. On the other hand, the agencies with broader missions (described next) also have broader organizational responsibilities, including child protective services and other social services. All but one of these agencies has the title Department of Social Services; the exception is the Department of Human Services in Oklahoma, which has an even broader range of functions, such as rehabilitative services for the disabled.

In the second group of programs, covering the four remaining sites, administrators saw a broader and more long-term mission, which generally included several of the following features:

- *Prevention:* It is the welfare agency's job to reach families before they experience crisis in order to prevent foster care; to reach young women before or soon after they become pregnant in order to prevent ill health, family difficulties, and long-term dependence on welfare; and to reach children in welfare families while they are young in order to give them the educational background and motivation that they will need to support themselves as adults. In the long run (but not the short run), prevention should mean lower caseloads for cash assistance and child protective services.

- *Social Work, Motivation, and Self-Esteem:* It is the welfare agency's job to reach out to families and individuals on welfare and offer the kind of counseling and personal connection that will enable them to achieve economic self-sufficiency and a healthy family life. For many families, administrators argue, this kind of social work is a prerequisite to self-sufficiency because family members need to develop motivation and self-confidence before they can take jobs. Almost all the administrators linked this element of the mission to the welfare department's past, before eligibility and services were separated: "This program is really nothing that we didn't used to do" (Detroit).

- *Supporting Families:* The mission of the welfare agency includes supporting the development of healthy families that can take care of their members. For example, the formal mission statement of Michigan's DSS includes "support [of] family life" as a focus of the department's programs.

- *Collaboration:* The mission of the welfare department includes reaching out into the community, to other public and private agencies, in order to "sell" AFDC families (that is, persuade other agencies not to give up on them) and in order to put resources together to solve problems, prevent crises, and change family lives. In San Diego, "community relations" is an explicit part of the DSS director's "Vision for Social Services into the 1990's," and he thinks the prevention aim cannot possibly be achieved without it.

- *Long-Run Cost Savings, without Short-Run Cuts:* In the long run, it is the welfare agency's job to stop acting as a "growth industry" and to prevent rising caseloads. To achieve this, though, it is important to argue against the shortsighted view that merely "closing and reopening a case" (through punitive programs, for example) will save money.

These underlying themes developed into different specific missions at the different sites, according to the nature of local problems and opportunities and a variety of historical accidents. For example, in both Michigan and Chemung County, New York, DSS managers expressed a commitment to the principle of social work as it used to be done, and both groups were looking for an opportunity to reach out to AFDC families using that principle. In Michigan, the opportunity came with an apparent threat: DSS staff feared that the legislature would pass legislation similar to Wisconsin's "Learnfare" which would penalize AFDC families for a child's failure to attend school. They offered to try out an alternative approach instead: to put DSS workers into the schools to work with children and families in order "to show that if we reach out to families, we can get the dropout rate to decrease." As a result of the program's success, staff in Detroit's DSS now aim to hold down Detroit's dropout rate and to develop a wide range of collaborations with the schools to aid at-risk children.

In Chemung County, on the other hand, the opportunity to return to social work for AFDC families came in the context of services to teen parents and their children. When New York State passed the Teenage Services Act (TASA) and was looking for pilot sites, a local DSS administrator reported that she saw the initiative as a way to move back toward social work and away from the separation of services from financial assistance. Since she knew that DSS could not provide social work for the whole caseload, she thought services to teens was a good place to start. Because the county already had a rich network of health and developmental services for young mothers and their children, she felt that she could give these young families a good start in life physically, emotionally, and educationally without funding new services, just by providing case management to link them to existing services.

In Oklahoma, the specific mission that governs IFS seems to have evolved from the same basic principles as in the other sites. Yet as in each site, common principles evolved into a specific mission through the influence of unique local opportunities. One underlying principle in Oklahoma was a commitment to supporting families: The IFS director reported that the State of Oklahoma wanted to develop a program to support families at the time when the federal government advertised for grant proposals to provide integrated services. The state seized on the federal grant as a first step. Another principle was collaboration, which is reflected in the organization of virtually all Oklahoma's human services programs under one large umbrella agency. For example, the federal report on the early stages of the grant noted that Oklahoma had three of the required elements of integration across program areas in place even before the grant period began.

As in Detroit and Chemung County, however, the mission that has evolved along with IFS's development and success is even more ambitious than the original principles. The IFS mission now goes beyond providing family support and preventive services for individual families, and even beyond encouraging collaboration among DHS workers, to knitting together entire community service systems. When asked how this broad mission can sustain political and financial support, the IFS director reported that the testimony of families and service deliverers about what the system has done for them is politically persuasive.

In San Diego, the DSS director has chosen to use explicit discussion of the agency's mission (or, in his words, "vision") as a key part of his management strategy. In his conversation, formal speeches, and memos, he argues for the vision sketched in Chapter 1: a vision of collaboration on behalf of families by a whole range of human services and education agencies that operate from different levels of government. In his view, long-run financial realities prove that there is no other way to go because the same group of poor, multineed families shows up as a problem in all the systems (as dropouts, criminal offenders, welfare recipients, and so forth) and the band-aid services that each system can provide without more far-reaching collaboration will never be enough. Thus, to make a difference, and to do so with scarce resources, requires over the long run that agencies get together and revamp their service systems collectively to meet the needs of families. Several San Diego DSS administrators emphasized these points when talking about their programs: They reported, for example, that DSS tries to be a "catalyst" in the community and to meet community needs. The administrators also spoke of the kind of social work that will be necessary to make a real difference with families, sometimes, as in the other sites, referring back to the agency's history and sometimes suggesting that the new social work will be better than the old because it encourages more client independence.

When asked how he can sustain this mission conception in the face of more immediate pressure to control welfare costs and keep error rates low, the DSS director offered several answers. First, San Diego DSS has already made considerable progress on error rates and costs through automation and fraud control. Second, the agency runs well internally, so he can concentrate his attention externally. Third, however, to enable other welfare agencies to make the same shift, the federal government will have to change its incentives. For example, he argued that the Family Support Act will never be implemented as planned unless the federal government stops emphasizing error rate sanctions at the same time, since managers have to pay attention to what can hurt them.

What Local Conditions Support Broad Missions?

The broad conceptions offered by these agencies of the role of the welfare agency are substantively appealing from the perspective of child and family needs, but how can these agencies possibly sustain such broad conceptions in the face of all the pressures for narrow accountability? The answer, based on the evidence of these sites, is not the universal appeal of any single mission definition but rather the way in which these agency managers have developed *different* definitions, each of which is uniquely suited to local circumstances and opportunities.

More specifically, the sites suggest that five kinds of local conditions sustained the broad mission conceptions. First, the welfare eligibility agency may be in a better position to expand services to families and children when eligibility is only one of its functions, as in most Departments of Social Services or Human Services. Not surprisingly, when an agency's mandate goes beyond eligibility to include various social services, family-oriented services fit more logically. For example, a family-oriented service as broad as Oklahoma's Integrated Family Services might be difficult to house in an agency with a narrower mandate than that of the Department of Human Services. A closely related point is that the history of linkage between social services and welfare eligibility—a history that staff might see as particularly relevant in agencies that still house the two functions under the same organizational roof, even though different workers carry them out—is clearly on the minds of welfare administrators who are thinking about their purposes and the justification for those purposes.

Second, the local importance of a population with cross-cutting needs (dropouts or teen parents, for example) can be a source of support for a broad mission definition by the welfare agency. Targeting a broad mission on a specific group of local importance provides a rationale for the broader mission and also limits costs. Both Detroit and Chemung County followed this strategy in selecting particular groups of welfare families as the focus for their broad interest in reaching out to provide family-oriented services. And in Oklahoma, which has quite a broad target group at the state level ("families in crisis"), individual communities are encouraged to identify more particular groups that are local priorities, such as youth in trouble with the law in one county. In fact, one reason for the broad state-level definition is precisely to allow different communities to choose target groups that meet locally defined needs.

Third, collaboration may itself be a source of political support for a broader mission when other agencies support the welfare agency's broader ambitions through an account of the benefits they and their clients have received. In Oklahoma, such support reportedly helps to explain the state's financial commitment to the program in times of tight budgets. In San Diego, the DSS director reported that he works explicitly with the superintendent of the Unified School District to testify before each other's governing bodies on issues that affect their common clients (for example, school health clinics).

Fourth, these programs have sustained political and organizational support for their broad missions through a match between the precise form of the mission and locally defined problems and needs. For example, the broad focus of Detroit's DSS on school dropouts has gained support over time because it came out of a clear and politically salient local concern.

Finally, it is possible, but not certain, from these examples that the emphasis on self-sufficiency and education in the Family Support Act could be a new source of political support for welfare agencies choosing to carry out a broader, family-oriented mission. In San Diego and in Chemung County, state legislation emphasizing long-term self-sufficiency through education provided local administrators who were already committed to a set of family-oriented principles with another opportunity to carry them out. On the other hand, program administrators warned that self-sufficiency that is conceived in a short-term way, without a belief in its links to motivation, self-esteem, and family functioning, might conflict with broader conceptions of mission rather than supporting them.

The site examples, then, suggest that several different conceptions of the welfare department's mission might provide a justification for its role toward children and families as well as a framework for organizing services and orienting staff. No single mission will be sustainable everywhere. Instead, the examples suggest that the organizational structure of the welfare agency, its capacity and history, and both enduring and temporary features of its political environment shape its possible future directions. At the same time, the sheer variety of missions adopted by the sites suggests that most welfare agencies ought to be able to move toward some measure of responsibility for the children and families on their caseloads.

COLLABORATION

The second common challenge faced by all the study sites was building links with other agencies to serve children and families. This finding was not expected: At the beginning of the study, we anticipated identifying programs that provided services to children directly. However, as Chapter 3 pointed out, many families and children on welfare need multiple services, which welfare agencies are generally ill-equipped to provide. Therefore, the site programs had to find ways in which to collaborate with a wide range of public and nonprofit agencies.

This section examines the challenge that collaboration poses for welfare agencies and analyzes the range of solutions offered by the sites. Like the last section, it begins by looking at research about other large organizations and then moves to evidence from the study sites. It argues that collaboration is a major managerial challenge for many organizations with complex tasks, that it is a key challenge for welfare agencies entering into family and children's services, and that effective site strategies for collaboration share common themes. Finally, it argues that despite these commonalities, successful collaboration strategies, like successful missions, need to be adapted to local settings.

Collaboration in complex public agencies is bound to be both difficult and important. On the one hand, several writers have noted that collaboration is difficult when different organizations (or parts of organizations) develop different views of the world and how they fit into it— different conceptions of mission, as described in the last section.[4] On the other hand, in organizations that are responding to a complex and changeable environment, these differentiated missions are inevitable and, indeed, necessary: The different organizations are responding to different technologies, circumstances, staff characteristics, and problems. For example, it is probably a good thing that surgeons focus clearly on their differentiated mission of performing effective surgery and that hospitals are organized to support them in doing so—yet it is precisely this differentiation that may make it hard for hospitals to collaborate with social services agencies to provide preventive care for children and families.

What, then, can a manager do when it is important for organizations that are legitimately very differentiated to work together in order to accomplish a crucial purpose? A famous study of private-sector corporations argued that this is precisely the situation in certain industries that are characterized by rapidly changing technologies, markets, and production and a need for constant and innovative response. In these industries, success requires high levels of both differentiation (that is, specialized expertise in very different fields—for example, in basic research and customer relations) *and* integration (that is, collaboration to further the common mission of the firm). The study argued that although there is a trade-off between differentiation and integration, excellent companies do better on both dimensions than weaker companies, relying on a variety of managerial techniques to improve communication and conflict resolution.[5] In other words, successful companies take on collaboration as a critical managerial task.

Welfare agencies embarking on services to children and families may well be in the same position as companies in these difficult industries: Their success at serving children and families may, in fact, depend on excellence at both differentiation and integration. That is, more than most children, very fragile children may need skilled teachers, counselors, and sometimes even surgeons—yet at the same time, more than other children, as Chapter 3 suggested, they need to be helped as whole children and to be seen in the light of other aspects of their lives. To return to an example provided in Chapter 3, responding successfully to the needs of a teen mother with a chronically ill baby may require both the highly differentiated skills of the surgeon and the ability to integrate many different services in response to the family's needs, whether through case management or another approach.

The second theoretical reason for expecting collaboration to present a major managerial challenge to public agencies also seems to apply with particular force to welfare departments. Public agencies are accountable to political overseers and, ultimately, to the public, which has a conception, implicit or explicit, of what those agencies are supposed to be doing.[6] In many cases, these public conceptions are defined in terms of the differentiated missions rather than the integrated ones. Therefore, shifting toward collaboration may look to the public and the agency's political overseers like shifting toward activities that are on the fringe of the agency's mission as opposed to the core. This is the issue that was highlighted by the San Diego DSS director, cited earlier, who explained that he was free to move outward from the traditional accountability of the welfare department—in terms of costs and error rates—only because his agency had already established a record of excellence on cost control, fraud control, and automation.

Collaboration at the Sites

Despite its difficulties, all seven sites chose collaboration as their solution to the multiple needs of families and children on welfare. No site chose the alternative solution, developing capacity to meet all or most needs through the welfare department alone. In fact, as argued in Chapter 3, the collaborations were generally even more complex and ambitious than their program plans anticipated: Sites that were envisioned as two-party collaborations (partnerships between the welfare department and one other agency) tended in practice to require the collaboration of more parties to meet multiple family needs.

Achieving this collaboration at the sites was a difficult managerial challenge for all the reasons that the literature about public organizations would predict. As Chapter 3 documented, the categorical organization of services to families and children; the divergent education, training, and loyalties of service providers; and the involvement of multiple levels of government all erect barriers of mission as well as funding. Further, welfare agencies may be particularly isolated because of the stigma of welfare and the poor reputation of the welfare bureaucracy.

Nonetheless, all seven of the site programs developed collaborations between the welfare agency and other child-serving agencies, of which five collaborations continued in operation as of late 1990, about a year after the site visits. The next section identifies common themes among the successes.

Common Themes of Successful Collaboration

Successful site collaborations shared five common themes:

- *Redefined and overlapping missions:* Collaborating organizations have succeeded in developing overlapping conceptions of mission and have managed to enlarge their missions beyond the conventional limits associated with their agency.
- *Conflict resolution:* In effective collaborations, people do not expect that conflict between the organizations will disappear or attribute such conflict solely to uncooperative personalities, power struggles, or turf battles. Instead, they develop ongoing mechanisms for conflict resolution.

- *Commitment of managerial time:* Managers devote considerable time and attention to collaboration, looking out from their organizations rather than simply up or down within them.
- *Role of personal relationships:* Managers and service deliverers cultivate personal relationships as a basis for collaboration.
- *Exchange relationships:* Collaborating agencies have some basis for exchange—something they can do for each other.

Redefined Missions and Conflict Resolution. If differentiated missions and associated conflicts between agencies explain part of the difficulty of collaboration, then it makes sense that effective collaborations turn for solutions to the first two approaches suggested above: integrating the different missions insofar as possible and developing mechanisms for resolving the remaining conflicts. For example, we might expect that agencies that are engaged in successful collaboration would identify shared values and visions, acknowledge the worth of both points of view when conflicts occur, develop processes for conflict resolution, and perhaps develop specific integrating mechanisms, such as units or people whose job is to link existing organizational units.[7] We would expect that successful collaborators would not suppress conflicts or view them solely as personal or bureaucratic power struggles.

The evidence from the sites about successful approaches to collaboration is consistent with this overall framework. For example, the collaboration between the Massachusetts Department of Public Welfare and the Lawrence Child Care Circuit illustrates considerable agreement on a broad mission conception, along with conflict resolution procedures for disagreements about particular tough issues. In the interviews, welfare eligibility workers, ET (employment and training) workers at the welfare agency, and parent counselors at the Child Care Circuit all described their jobs in terms of a common mission: encouraging self-sufficiency for mothers on welfare through the provision of services including good child care. Department of Public Welfare staff described the role of good child care in a successful employment and training program, and the parent counselors at the Child Care Circuit, when asked about success stories in their experience, all selected examples in which child care had contributed to economic self-sufficiency.

Despite having an overlapping conception of their broad mission, however, workers in the two agencies may disagree considerably about their priorities for a particular family, requiring approaches to conflict resolution. For example, parent counselors reported that they might disagree with the welfare department's ET specialists about the timing of a mother's entry into training: Should she start right away, or should she wait until the next program cycle in order to first become more comfortable with her child care arrangements? They reported a clear sense of how they would resolve that conflict: They would encourage the client to delay entry (which she is able to do under a voluntary program), speak to the ET worker if necessary, and perhaps try to "educate" workers at the DPW office as a whole about the nature of adjustment to child care. The example suggests that the overlap of mission between the two organizations, the willingness to acknowledge and resolve particular disagreements, and an informal personal relationship between the workers involved all make collaboration possible.

A second example, drawn from Oklahoma's IFS, illustrates that the process of developing a common mission and the process of resolving particular conflicts can sometimes happen together, in this case through a team approach to a family's problems. A child protective services (CPS) worker described her own change of attitude during the team staffing process when she realized that a mother whom she had seen as incompetent could, in fact, be a good parent with the right support. The team process helped produce a common sense of mission (serving the family) by resolving an apparent conflict between the CPS worker's view of her job as protecting the child and other professionals' jobs of serving the mother.

On the other hand, site evidence suggests that where a common mission has not developed *or* where there is no clear process for conflict resolution, collaboration does not succeed. In the case of Kentucky's PACE, the program's internal workings offer a successful example of the development of a common mission: Adult education teachers and early childhood teachers have integrated their approaches toward a joint task of working with the family. Externally, however, PACE teachers and staff at the Department of Social Insurance had, at the time of the site visit, very different conceptions of their purpose for families and no clear means for resolving their differences. The two agencies began their collaboration because it appeared to meet both their needs: PACE had difficulty recruiting families, and the welfare department was interested in education programs for mothers, particularly given their convenient pairing with child care. However, the collaboration did not survive early difficulties, most likely because the local welfare office saw its primary mission as following the rules on benefit checks and processing clients who were mandated to register for training programs. Because the families with young children who were appropriate for the family literacy program were not mandated registrants, welfare workers found it difficult to refer enough families to fill the program, and local office administrators found it equally difficult to move beyond their mission and improvise an agreement to solve the problem. Intervention from the welfare agency's central office filled the program in its first year, but the welfare agency chose not to participate again in the second year.

In the TAPP/DSS relationship in San Francisco, there appeared to be more progress toward an overlapping mission, at least at the top levels of the agencies, but there was no clear process for resolving the conflicts that inevitably remained. Instead, at the time of the site visit, conflicts appeared to drag on, without personal meetings or negotiation, and rather to be elevated through exchanges of high-level memos and occasional testimony at public or legislative hearings. For example, one continuing and unresolved conflict was about whether, upon high school graduation, teens should move into a Job Club specially designed for them (as proposed by TAPP) or into a regular adult Job Club (as proposed by DSS). By contrast, when a similar conflict came up in San Diego, it was resolved quite easily and informally. While the GAIN legislation requires Job Clubs as a next step after a teen's high school graduation, many staff members did not believe that a job (rather than vocational training) was best for a 17-year-old mother with a child to support and few skills. Therefore, the informal resolution was that teen specialists (the caseworkers in the GAIN Teen Parent project) would refer a teen to Job Club but would also agree beforehand with the Job Club leader that the teen should use the time to learn about the working world, with the expectation that she would go on to vocational training afterwards.[8]

Commitment of Managerial Time. The program managers of successful site collaborations devoted enormous amounts of time and attention to collaboration—to facing outward from their organizations rather than merely looking up or down within them. For example, the founder and director of the San Diego Teen Parent Project reported that her proudest achievement from the program's first year was developing a strong reputation in the community. She continues to reserve considerable time to make presentations, develop relationships, and meet with administrators and staff in a variety of agencies *outside* the welfare department, including regular monthly meetings with the two agencies with which she collaborates most closely. In the summer of 1990, the Teen Parent Project sponsored a week of workshops and activities for the teens. While the major purpose was to keep the teens engaged over the summer months so that they would be more likely to return to school, a second purpose was to offer an opportunity for even more collaboration with diverse elements of the community: a local utility, which presented a career day; a local television station, which broadcast a news report; and more predictable involvement from the school system and community agencies. The director's advice to other jurisdictions is to make sure to establish linkages to other organizations before attending to any other aspect of a project.

Similarly, the director of the Next Step teen parent program described her long-standing and constructive relationships with a wide variety of community service providers as "key, key, key" in getting services to clients, and said "We make it our business to know how to get in the back door." The Detroit DSS director and founder of the Detroit dropout prevention program reported repeated trips to school committee meetings and public events where she could get to know school personnel and talk about her idea of a joint project. At the service delivery level, as well, caseworkers in many of the programs reported a great deal of time spent in contact with other providers, ranging from formalized roles as on-site liaisons to other agencies (the TAPP/GAIN collaboration) and conveners of "team staffings" (Oklahoma IFS) to less structured roles in other case management programs.

Role of Personal Relationships. The data from the site visits are consistent with an observation widely reported in the literature on collaboration and case management: "Institutions don't collaborate, people do."[9] That is, collaboration in the sites is associated with a network of personal relationships, built over time, between the major participants. In Elmira, New York (TASA Next Step), the relationships have been built over decades; in San Diego and San Francisco, over the last 5 to 10 years; and in other programs, more recently. Where staff are setting out to build such relationships, as in Detroit and the Oklahoma IFS sites, they select strategies with a personal element: for example, face-to-face meetings instead of communications by phone or memo and colocation or outstationing of workers wherever possible so that staff get to know each other. Among the examples of successful techniques using this approach:

- In Elmira, New York, the director of TASA Next Step attributed the strong relationship between her agency and the DSS eligibility workers partly to the outstationing of a Next Step case manager at DSS part-time.

- In San Diego, the heads of the GAIN Teen Parent Program, the major health center for pregnant teens, and the major community case management program meet in person once a month for a formal meeting and see each other informally much more often.

- In Oklahoma, one local IFS case manager said that at first he doubted the value of the face-to-face meetings of service deliverers that the state requires him to convene because he already talked to them frequently on the phone. He now thinks the meetings are important, however, because "face-to-face is different."

- In San Francisco, the formal interagency agreements developed by TAPP often specify a colocation or outstationing arrangement.

On the other hand, in two instances in which collaboration did not last in the site projects, personal links seem to have been missing:

- In San Francisco, the relationship between TAPP and GAIN did not involve frequent personal contacts at the case manager level; at the time of the site visits, problems were being addressed through memos between the program supervisors.

- In the PACE welfare collaboration in Kentucky, there was personal contact and collaboration at the state level but considerably less at the site level. At the time of the site visit the PACE teachers reported having visited DSI once, but most communication seemed to occur over the phone and to focus narrowly on particular problems.

Exchange Relationships. The collaborations typically involved skill at noticing what one agency (the welfare department in cases where it was the initiator) could do for another. For example, in Oklahoma, when an IFS unit was first set up in a community to work with multineed families who might be falling through gaps in the system, the IFS case managers did not simply arrive and announce that they were there to coordinate other service deliverers. Instead, they spent several months learning how to offer concrete assistance that would build their credibility, for example, by developing an Automated Resource Directory and identifying training and service gaps that they might be able to fill. In Detroit, the dropout prevention program demonstrated in its first two years that it could meet some specific needs of the schools—such as assistance in keeping children in school, a capacity for home visits and connection to families, and an ability to link schools, teachers and families to the DSS bureaucracy— and the schools responded with a commitment of some resources for the planned expansion.

To provide more guidance to welfare agencies entering into collaborations with frequent partners such as the schools, the study looked for common themes in the exchanges between welfare agencies, on the one hand, and schools, early childhood programs, and visiting nurse or other health programs, on the other. While the evidence of such common themes was not strong, the search did turn up starting points that might prove useful for other agencies.

- *Welfare and Schools.* One resource that welfare agencies may be able to offer schools, based on the evidence of the Detroit and San Diego sites, consists of case managers who can visit homes and help keep children in school.Child care and transportation funding for teenage parents are also valuable, particularly in conjunction with case management offered either by the school or the welfare agency. In addition, as noted in regard to the Detroit example, schools may appreciate having a connection with the welfare agency that enables them to understand the child protective services system and gain access to it more easily.

One exchange that seemed natural under the Family Support Act was not, in fact, operating in any of the sites: the use of the welfare agency's child-care funding stream to support on-site, school-based infant care for teen parents. However, the school system and DSS in San Diego reported discussing the concept.

• *Welfare and Early Childhood Programs.* A natural resource for the welfare department to offer to early childhood programs is financing through child care funding available under the FSA's Job Opportunities and Basic Skills (JOBS) program, which deals with education, training, and employment for welfare families. Financing for transportation to child care is also helpful. In addition, the PACE program offers a reminder that the welfare department may also have another resource: people to refer. When excellent early childhood programs have trouble recruiting from the welfare population, there ought to be a good match of needs.

Besides PACE, the sites turned up only one example of a close relationship between the welfare agency and a particular early childhood program. In TASA Next Step, case managers were generally able to enroll the teens' children in the local Head Start program as they reached preschool age, since the same umbrella, community-based organization operated Head Start and Next Step. Other locations had more limited relationships for a variety of reasons, including an emphasis on parental choice of child care and an unwillingness to use programs subsidized from other sources (such as Head Start and California's state preschool program) for welfare recipients who have access to a different stream of child care funding.

• *Welfare and Health Care.* Several of the programs had very close relationships with visiting nurse services and with health clinics specializing in teenage parents and high-risk infants, among others. In the site examples, the welfare department was not contributing financial resources to these relationships. However, clinic staff appeared to appreciate their relationship with a welfare-funded case manager who could bring to bear other community resources besides the medical care available at the clinic. Thus, the major resources that the welfare agency may be able to bring to this partnership are its strengths in case management, counseling, and referral to other services.

The Local Nature of Collaboration

Despite the common themes, effective site collaborations, like effective site missions, were adapted in fundamental ways to idiosyncratic local settings. In all the sites the specific form of collaboration on family and children's services was defined at the local level and its success or failure was determined there—even when the welfare agency was administered statewide, as in Oklahoma, Massachusetts, Michigan, and Kentucky. While states can lead in collaboration on family and children's services, the actual development of the collaboration appears likely to require considerable local autonomy and flexibility for at least four different reasons.

The first and most obvious reason is that schools, early childhood programs, and many other family and children's services are locally organized. For example, Elmira's TASA Next Step program is able to take advantage of a rich local array of maternal and child health services. In San Diego and Detroit, county-level welfare administrators are able to work directly with local school superintendents who cover roughly similar geographical areas. In the ET CHOICES/Voucher Child Care program, the partnership between the welfare department and the day care network is organized at a local rather than statewide level, presumably because the day care market and the networks among providers are so localized that a uniform statewide Voucher Management Agency could not do the job effectively.

Second, the personal relationships described above as being key to collaboration are almost inevitably specific to a particular local setting. They grow out of a history of common experiences and trust among service deliverers who have worked together; consequently, relationships at the state level or in one county do not automatically transfer to another county.

Third, exchanges between the welfare department and its partner agencies will work differently in different communities. The exchange of resources that will work for one school district or family services agency will not work for another because the agencies' needs, the key problems they focus on, and their resources all differ. One school district may be eager to serve teen parents and want to work with the welfare department on case management services and child care for them, while another may be reluctant to address teen pregnancy and prefer to work on reaching families whose children are in middle school. The structure of Oklahoma's IFS program explicitly recognizes this multiplicity of needs in the agencies with which the welfare department needs to cooperate by giving the local IFS teams great flexibility to identify needs and develop particular roles to meet them. For example, at one rural site, the IFS program's priority is farm families in crisis, while at a planned urban site, the IFS team is expected to start by helping a local community group carry out health- and housing-related projects. The state IFS director viewed both projects as consistent with the IFS focus on community capacity to serve troubled families with multiple needs.

Fourth and finally, if strong collaborations require effective and quick conflict resolution, they may well require local programs with the ability to improvise solutions themselves rather than kick the conflicts up to the next bureaucratic layer.[10] Managers in the study programs believed that local staff will act creatively and effectively to resolve conflicts and solve problems *only* if they have considerable autonomy in program development. This model of local ownership and problem solving seems to have guided program development in the Oklahoma, Detroit, and Massachusetts programs. According to Donna Stahl, the founder of Oklahoma's IFS, the key element of program success for IFS has been "attitude, attitude, attitude": a belief that local people can make things happen and "maximum freedom" for them to do so.

If, on the other hand, heads of local programs believe that they have been told by a central office to just follow the rules, they are likely to approach a sticky problem with another agency by trying to apply those rules strictly—which will lead to deadlock if the other agency reacts in the same way—rather than by trying to find a solution that is better for both agencies as well as for the clients. Thus, in Kentucky, the local Department of Social Insurance office interpreted its job as following the rules on benefit checks and referral of WIN-mandatory clients. When collaboration with PACE proved more difficult than anticipated (there were not enough referrals to fill the program), local staff were unable to violate these instructions and improvise an agreement to solve the problem, requiring intervention by the central office.

Overall, then, the cases studied suggest that collaboration is a critical management challenge for welfare agencies attempting to pay attention to the needs of children and that successful collaborations share important common themes. At the same time, however, specific approaches to collaboration will vary with local needs and opportunities, requiring considerable autonomy for local offices in developing effective service networks.

OUTREACH AND INTAKE

Whatever the mission of the welfare agency and the specific nature of the program to serve families and children, a first step to providing services is getting the appropriate families "in the door." Chapter 3 suggested that this task ought to be easy for the welfare department, which is a natural intake point for poor families. However, the site experiences suggest that far from being easy, outreach and intake represent a third important managerial challenge. At least two of the sites had initial problems with intake because they did not anticipate the challenge, and one had not resolved the problem at the time of our visit. The other sites had succeeded at reaching the families they wanted to reach, but only by investing considerable effort.

Two features of the welfare agency's circumstances, as described in Chapter 3, explain why intake is a major challenge rather than an obvious and easy part of serving families and children on welfare. The first barrier has to do with the eligibility worker's job, and the second, with the emotions and experiences—isolation, mistrust, anger, and depression—

that may characterize some of the families that a program may be designed to serve.

The Eligibility Worker's Job and Outreach/Intake

For the many needy families who pass through the welfare department to obtain benefits, the eligibility worker is the key point of contact. It is natural to think of taking advantage of that contact to provide a referral stream for special services. However, in settings where eligibility workers are overwhelmed by other tasks, measured on other criteria, and lacking in knowledge or enthusiasm about the special services to which they are asked to refer, they will not provide an effective link. In the PACE program, the experimental program dedicated to AFDC recipients did not fill its quota of 10 recipients until the agency commissioner intervened personally, primarily because the workers were overwhelmed with other duties and the targeted group for PACE was not relevant to any of those tasks. In the San Francisco TAPP/GAIN collaboration, TAPP staff reported that they initially expected either DSS eligibility workers or DSS GAIN workers to refer clients, but when the arrangement did not work out, they developed other referral routes.

Successful programs took one of two approaches to the potential roadblock presented by eligibility workers: Either they dedicated considerable time and personal attention to ensuring a smooth flow through the eligibility system or they developed alternative referral sources in order to bypass it. The three programs that took the first approach—TASA Next Step, the ET CHOICES/Voucher Child Care program, and Oklahoma IFS—used a range of specific techniques to make the process work:

- In TASA Next Step, a Next Step case manager is on-site part-time at the DSS office. If a teen walks in while he or she is there, the worker may enroll her directly; if, as is much more frequent, the case manager does not meet a teen directly, the eligibility worker makes a written referral to Next Step and a Next Step case manager follows up. Next Step does not have the eligibility worker introduce the program to the teen in order not to risk a client refusal on the basis of a less complete or persuasive presentation than the case manager could give. Interestingly, the TASA director feels that it is important to maintain some hours on-site at DSS even though the colocation turns out not to be particularly effective at its original purpose, which was enrolling teens as they walk in the door. Instead, she feels that the primary purpose of colocation is to cement relations with the DSS eligibility staff.
- In Oklahoma, IFS case managers reported that they go personally to the AFDC workers to ask about families who might benefit from IFS

services. They also get cases from other referral sources, and in those instances, they will include the AFDC worker in the "team staffing," or case conference, that they call on the case.

- In the ET CHOICES/Voucher Child Care program, the referral to child care is made in the context of a multi-year approach to changing the role and sense of mission of the agency's eligibility workers. Eligibility workers are evaluated on referrals to the ET CHOICES program (which provides employment-related case management to adults and then refers parents on one more step to voucher child care) as well as on the traditional criteria of accuracy and speed, and a whole range of department actions in the years since ET CHOICES began in 1983 have been devoted to changing workers' conception of the job and of themselves.

Two programs chose from the beginning to use other referral sources instead of the eligibility workers. In the GAIN Teen Parent Program, staff have developed referral contacts from community service providers who see teens. They have also relied directly on the AFDC computer files, bypassing the eligibility workers, to provide a mailing list for recruitment letters to all teenagers heading AFDC cases. In addition they hope to develop a pilot project that involves a closer relationship with eligibility workers in one of the quieter offices outside the city limits. In Detroit, the children to be served by the DSS dropout prevention workers are identified by the schools based on a record of poor attendance.

Family Emotions and Experiences

The second reason why outreach requires effort is the set of experiences and attitudes described in Chapter 3 and characteristic of at least some of the families that may need services for children. Families that are in the most need may be socially isolated, mistrustful of professionals (especially professionals who ask about their children), angry, depressed, and wary of more bad experiences with public services.

Some programs, particularly those that explicitly intend to serve the hardest-to-reach portion of the AFDC population, solve this problem through intensive, time-consuming, personal outreach. This approach is characteristic of TASA Next Step, which sends staff members on repeated home visits, sometimes in the face of implied rejection, until the teen accepts case management. As a result, TASA Next Step reported enrolling 85–95 percent of all teen parents on AFDC, even though the program is voluntary. Case managers reported that they cultivate a nonthreatening and supportive approach that responds to the teen's needs as she herself sees them. The community case managers in the SANDAPP program (part of the San Diego partnership serving teens), the San Francisco TAPP case managers, and the teachers in the rural PACE site all reported similar approaches involving a great deal of home visiting and personal responsiveness.

Other programs, while also marketing their services and trying to respond to families' perceived needs, solve the problem by allowing families that see themselves as a good match to the program to enter and allowing others to screen themselves out. For example, a teenager who really cannot manage her life sufficiently to go to school is not a good candidate for San Diego GAIN case management, although she may be appropriate for the SAN-DAPP community case managers. At Oklahoma IFS, the entry of a family into case management is voluntary for both the family and the case manager: the case manager has the discretion to choose families that he or she expects will benefit from the service. In the IFS case, the family is also quite likely to be in crisis, which may provide a motivation for entering services that is not as likely to be present in the other programs.

Theoretically, a third option for overcoming this barrier to intake and outreach would be mandating family participation. This option was extremely rare among the site programs: A few teens in the Next Step program were mandated by Child Protective Services to take part in the Family Life Education groups, and children in the Detroit program, while not mandated to be in the program, are mandated by school attendance laws to be in school. Program staff who worked with mandated participants reported that their task was to make their clients feel as though they were present voluntarily. While the evidence is limited, mandates alone do not seem to solve either of the outreach and intake barriers: Drawing appropriate families into services and motivating family involvement continue to be central challenges, no matter what the legal status of a family's participation.

SELECTION AND SUPPORT OF STAFF

Chapter 3 argued that many families on welfare require services that are delivered in the context of a trusting, personal relationship and by a worker who is comfortable moving across traditional service boundaries. Delivering this kind of high-quality, highly discretionary, responsive service is not easy, particularly in a welfare agency that is set up for a very different kind of service delivery. An inadequately supported or unqualified worker can easily cause considerable damage: for example, by interfering in a family's life in a way that ultimately harms a child, by treating families inequitably, or by spending discretionary resources in a way that causes public or political concern.

As a result, all the programs we observed shared a common emphasis on the importance of recruitment and hiring as managerial tasks. In virtually all the programs, managers saw the selection of the right people for the job as an important part of their own managerial responsibilities. In the smaller programs, such as the GAIN Teen Parent Program and TASA Next Step, program directors described their criteria for the right kind of service provider and their personal involvement in interviewing and screening. In Oklahoma's IFS, despite the high degree of local flexibility in decision making, interviewing and selecting candidates for new IFS teams is the combined job of the state IFS director, field staff, and the local supervisor. They find this task so crucial that they have learned to start again if the first pool of applicants does not yield someone who meets their criteria, rather than selecting someone second best.

Thus, meeting the managerial challenge of selecting (and supporting) high-quality staff helps mediate the tension between discretionary, responsive services and the need of the welfare agency to be accountable for its performance. If staff have been recruited to share the mission of the program and to bring to the job the basic capacities it requires, and if they are then supported with supervision, training, appropriate caseload sizes, consultant expertise, and appropriate authority, they can make flexible, discretionary decisions that are nonetheless consistent with standards of quality and with the agency's purpose. This section discusses two kinds of approaches to this challenge: approaches to staff qualifications and recruitment and approaches to staff support.

Staff Qualifications and Recruitment

All the sites devoted a great deal of managerial attention to staff hiring, but they did not all hire the same kinds of people. In fact, the sites illustrated three somewhat different conceptions of the best kind of person to serve welfare families. A fourth possible conception, that welfare eligibility workers should be able to do the job themselves, was not explored at the sites.

Existing Welfare Staff. Programs in the first group recruited program staff from inside the welfare or human services department. They looked for volunteers who were excited about the new initiative, willing to work hard, entrepreneurial, service-oriented, and perhaps (in two of three cases) already knowledgeable about some aspect of child or adolescent services. Examples include the GAIN Teen Parent Program, the Detroit dropout prevention program, and the Oklahoma Integrated Family Services program.

The approach had several advantages in these sites. In two of the three sites, it enabled administrators to get started quickly on a promising new program and to avoid requesting new money or authorization. In all three, it gave talented and eager staff an outlet for their energies, and it yielded staff who knew the public human services system well enough to intervene in it effectively on behalf of clients. In Oklahoma, where the community organizing role was crucial, it also yielded staff who began the job with credibility in their communities.

On the other hand, the disadvantage of this approach may be that staff in eligibility and child protective services positions do not typically start out with the experience, knowledge, or attitudes that will enable them to build strong relationships with clients, although careful selection and training may be successful in overcoming this limitation.[11] In all the programs, we thought that supervisors had clearly selected people with a warm and caring attitude toward clients. However, in San Diego and Detroit, site visitors, along with some workers and administrators at the sites, thought that workers would benefit from additional training and experience in counseling and interacting with clients. For example, one worker said that she felt she was relying entirely on her own childhood in building connections to young clients.

Diverse Community Service Professionals. The second approach to staffing service delivery, which is exemplified by two community-based agencies (TASA Next Step and SANDAPP in San Diego), is to recruit staff from a wide variety of backgrounds who meet a set of standards for personal qualities and skills. In both these programs, supervisors had strong views about the kind of person they wanted as a case manager: mature, open, qualified through diverse life experience, knowledgeable about adolescent development, experienced in working with teenagers, and enthusiastic about being with them. Because supervisors in these programs did not associate these qualities with a specific professional degree, they hired case managers with a mix of educational backgrounds, ranging from no college degree to master's degrees, and they particularly emphasized a candidate's relevant work and volunteer experience.

To offset one possible disadvantage of this approach—that staff might not have the skills to meet new situations—both programs provided very involved and supportive supervision, ongoing training, and considerable work with peers. Case managers felt that they were trusted to plan their time on their own, but they also felt free to consult with the supervisor whenever they wanted to, were grateful for frequent, regularly scheduled case conferences, and had the sense that their supervisor knew their cases as well as they did. Training was frequent and intended to keep case managers up-to-date on a range of issues as well as to get them in the habit of learning and asking questions. In addition, both programs took advantage of the variety of staff backgrounds through very frequent formal and informal peer conferences, which provided multiple perspectives on difficult cases. The intensive supervision and extensive peer support available in these programs seemed to pay off in considerable staff sophistication about both the client relationship and the service delivery system.

Credentialed Professionals. A third approach to selecting service deliverers, which was represented among the sites by the San Francisco TAPP program, emphasizes the professional qualifications of case managers. In TAPP, the qualification is a master's degree in social work or counseling; in other programs, it might be an R.N. degree, for example. This approach is consistent with Lisbeth and Daniel Schorr's conclusion from their review of the evaluation literature that professional skill is critical in working with difficult populations.[12] On the other hand, programs that choose to hire only staff with professional credentials may face some difficulty in connecting across functional boundaries to other service systems with different professional traditions. In addition, of course, professionally credentialed staff are more expensive. In the case of TAPP, staff salaries that are fairly low for the required professional level have led to a very young staff, often just out of social work school, in contrast to the considerably older, but on average less credentialed, staff at SANDAPP and TASA Next Step.

Eligibility Workers Plus. A possible fourth approach would be to change the description and capabilities of welfare eligibility workers so that all of them are capable of responding to child and family needs—in contrast to the first three approaches with their focus on developing a special unit of service deliverers who can respond to those needs. While no site tried a full version of this approach, ET CHOICES Adult Case Management (the supplemental site) broadened the jobs of all eligibility workers substantially. However, it did not try to enable workers to respond to the full range of family needs; instead, it modified eligibility workers' jobs to make them case managers for the much narrower set of services required to enable adult recipients to become self-sufficient.

Nonetheless, even this somewhat less ambitious change involved a major commitment to training, salary upgrading, and revised performance standards over a period of about five years.[13] In the first phase of this change, ET workers who were separate from the eligibility workers were hired to be case managers. In the second phase, the eligibility workers took on case management responsibilities, and the ET workers became specialists supporting the case managers by providing intensive advice to interested clients, keeping up to date on vendors and community services and consulting to the case managers as needed.

In addition to the long time required for implementation, the ET CHOICES model uses several techniques to reconcile the multiple demands on case managers with the job of the eligibility worker. Under ET CHOICES (at least as initially conceived), a team of specialists, including the ET worker, is available to support the eligibility worker/case manager. In addition, the case manager's assessment and follow-up are structured through a set of forms that make up the Family Independence Plan. Thus, the case manager has a broader and more discretionary job than that of the other eligibility workers we visited, but a much less discretionary job than the intensive case managers in other sites who deal with child and family services.

In fact, the evidence presented in Chapter 3 about the nature of child and family needs suggests that it would not be possible for case managers charged with serving families and children to rely very heavily on a structured form like the Family Independence Plan: The task is inherently more discretionary and individualized. Therefore, ET CHOICES does not offer direct evidence about whether eligibility workers or workers in another one of the large service bureaucracies (child protective services, for example) could take on the greater demands of building a relationship and negotiating services in that more private and complex world.

Support of Staff Once They Are Selected

The site programs supported the quality of decisions by frontline staff in several ways. Most impressive was the commitment described earlier to supervision, peer consultation and review, and training, particularly in the intensive case management programs. Besides training and supervision, however, another way of supporting staff to make high-quality decisions is granting them time through low caseloads. More time can lead to higher-quality services by allowing more opportunity to build a relationship with a family that may lead to change and by permitting more persistent negotiations with other service delivery agencies. On the other hand, in agencies that are accountable for the use of scarce resources, allowing more time per case is a difficult policy to defend.

We would have expected, based on the account of family needs in Chapter 3, that caseloads ought to vary depending on the needs of the families to be served: Those families who only need referral to services will take little time, while those whose multiple needs, pessimism, isolation, or other incapacities prevent them from finding their own way through the system will take much more. In addition, direct service caseloads will probably vary depending on the extent to which the case manager is also expected to work on system change or community organizing, as in the IFS system. Finally, caseloads may vary depending on the other case management available to clients: Under team arrangements, one client could have several case managers with different substantive backgrounds or specialties but only the lead case manager would need to put in the time to get to know the client extremely well.

Despite these trade-offs, however, caseloads in the sites were typically low, with five programs offering intensive services to hard-to-serve families at caseloads between 20 and 50 families per worker. IFS was at the low end, because case managers there have responsibility for community organizing as well as direct service. Others in this group are TAPP,

TASA Next Step, the Detroit dropout prevention program, and the SANDAPP case managers in San Diego (who reported that caseloads are supposed to stay around 35 but have crept up to near 50 for some case managers).

On the other hand, the GAIN teen parent specialists and the ET CHOICES adult case managers had caseloads in the 100–150 range at the time of the site visits. The GAIN specialists carried about 100 cases, but many of those were adult cases; the number of teens ranged from a handful for the newest teen specialists to about 60 for the longest-standing. Somehow, the teen specialists found time to make home visits and lead evening support groups even with these caseloads, presumably by balancing off the more limited time commitment required by the adult cases. Some of their teen cases also had a SANDAPP case manager; in those cases, the GAIN worker could play a more limited supporting role. The ET CHOICES case managers carried about 100 cases in the consolidated office (where they did intake as well as ongoing eligibility reviews) and 130–140 in the nonconsolidated office at the time of the interviews. However, the ET CHOICES case managers were playing a more limited role than the other service deliverers, as they were case managers for adult services that are related directly to self-sufficiency.

At the high end, the caseload of parent counselors in the ET CHOICES/Voucher Child Care site was about 200 welfare families plus additional nonwelfare families. Counselors did report developing strong relationships with some families, but they did not do a great deal of brokering across agencies. Brokering for services related to self-sufficiency is, of course, the job of the ET specialist and the case manager at the welfare department, so the team arrangement limits the demands on parent counselors.

DEVELOPING ORGANIZATIONAL AND FUNDING ARRANGEMENTS

Finally, the sites faced the task of identifying financial and organizational arrangements that could mediate conflicts between the responsive services required by families and the narrower accountability required by the welfare agency's mandate. Several of the strategies identified earlier, such as articulating a powerful mission and hiring high-quality staff, clearly reduced the scope of these conflicts. Nonetheless, agencies needed to figure out how to finance services and how to locate service delivery within or outside the organization in order to respond to these multiple demands.

Funding Streams

Because funding streams come with strings attached in the form of legislation and regulations, the choice of funding stream may affect the nature of services and case management. The sites we visited tapped a variety of funding sources (not including the Family Support Act, which was not yet in effect at the time of our visits). In California, Massachusetts, and the pilot sites in Kentucky, services were funded through the state welfare-to-work programs that preceded the Family Support Act. Two programs, however, had more flexible and wide-ranging funding sources: The TASA Next Step case managers were funded through Medicaid funds that are available for case management and Oklahoma's Integrated Family Services is currently supported by state funds with a federal match where appropriate, after three years of start-up support through a federal demonstration grant.

Administrators of these programs may or may not seek funding through the FSA. The administrator for one program reported that the FSA funding had been discussed in her state but she preferred state funding because federal reimbursement comes with "parameters," while "the beauty of what we do is no parameters."

Organizational Structure

Welfare agencies might choose to mediate the tensions between the flexibility of responsive service delivery and the tight accountability demanded of the welfare eligibility function through three different organizational arrangements. First, they might choose to place the two functions, family services and eligibility determination, as far apart as possible by contracting out family service delivery to a nonprofit, community-based agency that is in a position to escape some of the pressures of bureaucratic accountability. Second, they might choose to locate the two functions a little closer, both within the welfare agency but in separate units. Third, they might choose to locate the two functions in the same unit, changing the eligibility worker's job to include family services.

The sites offered successful examples of the first two models but no complete example of the third. Again, however, ET CHOICES offers hints of what might be required to make the third model work.

Case Management through a Community Agency. Several sites chose this approach in order to put distance between the eligibility function and family-oriented case management or to take advantage of community expertise in serving hard-to-reach families. For example, the TAPP/GAIN collaboration involved a contract between the Department of Social Services, the school system, and a community-based nonprofit organization; the TASA Next Step program involved a more complicated arrangement in which a community-based non-profit provided case management with Medicaid funding and oversight by the county DSS office; and in San Diego, the SANDAPP community case management program worked collegially with the GAIN Teen Parent Project to provide a more intensive service to the most needy teenagers in the community, using GAIN funding to support child care where appropriate.

The big advantages of this approach ought to be responsiveness, flexibility, and community experience at the point of service delivery. A potential disadvantage, however, is the possibility of ongoing conflict between the welfare agency and the community service deliverer, as seems to have occurred in the TAPP/GAIN collaboration. In the TASA Next Step and San Diego GAIN/SANDAPP programs, however, conflicts arose but were resolved through negotiation based on long-time personal relationships and a generally shared sense of mission.

Case Management through a Special Unit. A second approach locates the responsive case management service inside the welfare agency but not within the welfare eligibility unit. For example, case managers might work in a unit that specializes in employment and training (San Diego GAIN Teen Parent program), a family services unit (the Detroit dropout prevention program) or a freestanding separate unit (Oklahoma IFS). Depending on the accountability demands of the funding stream, this approach may allow almost as much flexibility in service delivery as the community agency approach (Oklahoma IFS), or it may require some compromise and informal negotiation, as when GAIN Teen Parent staff reported that they had to be "creative" in order to bring program rules into line with the needs of their clientele.

Possible advantages of this approach include the ability of workers located within the human services department to intervene in the agency's core functions (eligibility and child protective services) on behalf of clients, the clout such workers may have in the community service delivery network, and quick program start-up, compared to the other two approaches. On the other hand, managers may find it impossible under this approach to sustain caseloads as low or a service as intensive or flexible as in community-based case management systems, though this has not been the case in Oklahoma. In addition, the approach may leave untouched the client's experience with the basic eligibility function, a disadvantage compared with the third approach.

Case Management through the Eligibility Worker. There is no complete example of this approach for family-oriented case management. However, the ET CHOICES supplemental site illustrates a version of this model for a simpler form of case management: case management of adults toward self-sufficiency. Under ET CHOICES case management, individual eligibility workers are responsible for case management of services directed toward self-sufficiency, a job that requires each worker, supervisor, and local office director to manage the tension between accountability and flexible service within his or her own job. ET CHOICES appears to support workers in ways that make this balancing act possible: relatively low caseloads (compared to those of other eligibility workers but not intensive case managers), assistance from specialist workers, and limitations on the scope of case management through the Family Independence Plan.

The choice to move the eligibility worker's job in the direction of case management could have several advantages for families. It might improve the client's eligibility experience, offer the opportunity to make small improvements in children's services for *all* families (for example, referrals for pediatric care), and enable eligibility workers to work effectively as part of a team with family-oriented service deliverers. That is, eligibility workers who see their job as case management, even in a limited form, might be more inclined to see clients as individuals and collaborate with others who can provide more specialized services.

On the other hand, the possible disadvantages of such a move include a very long time horizon—changing the operation of the whole welfare eligibility service system is a long-term task—and the risk of error rate increases that would be unacceptable to political overseers (although in Massachusetts, the error rate went down at the same time that case management was being implemented). In addition, lower eligibility worker caseloads are costly and may, as the Massachusetts case illustrates, be difficult to sustain in fiscal hard times.

In any case, the changes in the eligibility workers' job represented by ET CHOICES case management are far from the full scope of intensive, family-oriented case management as illustrated by the other sites. The balancing act required of the ET CHOICES eligibility worker is much easier than the one that an eligibility worker would have to carry off in order to case-manage the more intimate, unpredictable, and complex service needs of families and children. Thus, the experience of the ET CHOICES site does suggest that the eligibility worker's job can be changed substantially by a large enough managerial investment—but it does *not* permit the conclusion that the job can be turned into case management of comprehensive family services.

CONCLUSIONS

This chapter has argued that the successful sites overcame the considerable barriers identified in Chapter 3 by addressing a common set of tasks that grow out of the common characteristics of welfare agencies and poor families. Yet each successful agency developed its own approach to those tasks in order to respond to the unique local setting, politics, and history; the array of local services; the agency's own staff and resource possibilities and limitations; and the specific local needs of families and children.

The next chapter takes on the task of crystallizing recommendations from these multiple approaches. Not surprisingly, it argues that agencies will be able to do the most for children and families on welfare not by adopting particular program models but rather by identifying approaches to serving children that fit their unique circumstances—and then drawing on the opportunities provided by the Family Support Act for funding and authorization to carry them out.

6

Recommendations for Action

The Introduction to this volume asked whether this country's large public welfare agencies can play a richer role for young children in poverty, a role better attuned to what we know about children's needs, family functioning, and child development. Based on the evidence from the seven study sites, the answer is yes: The welfare department can, in fact, serve as a catalyst for action on behalf of young children and families. Welfare department staff can help families identify child-related needs, refer or link families to other services, and counsel families directly; welfare agencies can fund other, more expert or more community-based providers to offer early education, health care, or case management services to welfare families; and welfare administrators can lobby, organize, and influence other service providers on behalf of welfare families.

But in order to do any of these things well, in a way that helps, rather than harms, the children and their families, the welfare agency needs to attend to a delicate balance: the balance between its own mission and capacity and the needs of the children and families it hopes to serve. The previous chapters have explored the many and subtle techniques used by skillful and committed administrators to improve the apparently odd match between child development and the large and impersonal welfare system in order to move their agencies gently toward two-generational programs that identify and take seriously the needs of both children and adults.

This chapter provides recommendations for attaining that delicate balance for the use of advocates, policymakers, administrators, and others committed to the needs of poor children and families. The recommendations are presented in three sections. The first section explores the guiding principles that should frame this balance and guide the expansion of welfare agencies into services to children and families. The section begins by offering two possible scenarios for change and then draws from them a set of overall recommendations. The second section develops these broad principles into a set of much more specific recommendations for action with particular relevance to the implementation of the Family Support Act: recommendations for case management, assessment, child care, adult programs, and the targeting of services. Finally, the third section suggests some implications of these recommendations for the other large public service systems that see young children and their families.

GUIDING PRINCIPLES AND RECOMMENDATIONS

What makes the development of recommendations difficult in this case is the central theme and finding of the study: There is no single right way to go about serving children through the welfare department. In fact, the study sites suggest that the right approach for one setting is probably the wrong approach for another: wrong for the political setting, wrong for workers, and wrong for families.

More specifically, the study sites suggest that a welfare agency's approach to serving children and families needs to be adapted in three important ways to the agency's circumstances and purposes: The approach must fit the mission that the agency can sustain on behalf of children and families, the opportunities it has to collaborate with other service deliverers to meet family needs, and the capacity of its staff to serve families rather than simply to process them. Each of these requirements for a successful approach is supported by particular evidence from the study sites. The approach must fit the mission, based on the evidence that a lasting program requires a mission that can link the welfare department's traditional tasks with the needs of children and families, and that the right definition of that mission needs to be adapted to local history, politics, and needs. The approach must fit the local opportunities for collaboration, based on the evidence that welfare agencies generally must turn to collaboration to serve children and families rather than expanding their own in-house service delivery. Finally, the approach must fit staff and organizational capacity, based on the evidence that successful intake, effective delivery of high-quality services, and successful organization and financing of services all require establishing a careful balance between the needs of families and the demands of the eligibility function.

What might be the most useful principles for serving children and families through the welfare department, given this finding about each site's individual nature? This section begins to answer that question in a somewhat unconventional way by developing two concrete scenarios adapted to two quite different settings. Both scenarios are based loosely on the experiences of the research sites but do not exactly resemble any one site. In order to be useful to welfare agencies implementing the FSA, both scenarios describe the way in which welfare agencies choose to design the JOBS component of the FSA, which deals with education, training, and employment for welfare families. The scenarios are intended to illustrate two distinctive approaches to building a role for the welfare department in the broader network of family and children's services and to provide a context for the principles described in the second part of this section.

Two Scenarios

Scenario No. 1: The Department of Income Maintenance. In the Department of Income Maintenance of State A, top administrators are clear that their central focus in implementing JOBS is to encourage financial self-sufficiency. At the same time, however, they want to support parents on AFDC in their family life for two reasons: They believe that anxiety about the well-being of children makes it much harder for a parent to succeed in training or on the job, and they want the welfare department to avoid having harmful effects on the lives of young children.

Therefore, they have chosen to target for family-related services those JOBS participants who have young children (under school age). A first step in serving these families is communicating to eligibility and JOBS workers the agency's commitment to both economic self-sufficiency *and* a family life. All the agency's written materials on JOBS emphasize that a mother's concerns for her young children are legitimate and must be respected and that the agency has a variety of ways in which to help her meet those concerns at the same time that she pursues training and employment. The eligibility worker's initial interview now includes questions about whether the family has a pediatrician for the children and whether the mother has any other questions or concerns she would like to raise; the JOBS worker's initial employability assessment includes specific questions about the children's health and how they are doing in school, and it also includes an opportunity for the mother to raise any concerns that she may have.

For mothers with children younger than school age, the agency has taken two additional steps. First, at both the state and local welfare office levels, administrators have sought out providers who might be able to develop programs that pair education, training, or employment activities for the mother with high-quality, developmentally oriented care for young children. Among the programs in development or operation around the state are a family literacy program modeled on PACE, a collaboration between a Head Start program and an English as a Second Language program run by the same community agency, and a school-based program for parenting teens that includes on-site infant care along with hands-on parenting classes in the infant care center for the teens.

Second, the agency has enriched its child care resource and referral component, which in this state is carried out by community agencies under contract, for mothers with young children. The agency has chosen to fund lower caseloads, about 50 to 1, for parent counselors who work with these mothers.

To serve families with young children, parent counselors are expected to get to know the mother and the children, develop an ongoing relationship, and assist mothers both with their own transition to work *and* with any other services to which they might need access. In carrying out this mandate, counselors find themselves doing everything from advocating for a mother with her eligibility worker and looking for drug rehabilitation services to making a joint home visit with a nurse from the developmental disability agency in order to assess a child. The welfare agency has discussed contracting separately with local agencies that have expertise in serving teen parents to do case management for the youngest mothers at a more intensive level, perhaps with caseloads of 30 to 1, but so far it has not carried out this plan.

Scenario No. 2: The Department of Human Resources. In the Department of Human Resources in State B, an organization with a history of working across boundaries within human services, administrators see the JOBS program as a means to further their aim of working with other human services agencies to change family lives across two generations. They believe strongly that only by delivering wide-ranging preventive services to poor children and families can government ever hope to contribute to self-sufficiency in a meaningful way. Agency managers believe that such an approach provides long-run cost savings in income maintenance and foster care, among other areas, and they believe that better family functioning and self-sufficiency are intimately related.

With this perspective, the agency wants to take advantage of JOBS to expand the role of the welfare system in preventive, family-oriented services for particular populations that seem likely to benefit the most. The initial list of target populations identified by planners in the agency includes pregnant and parenting teens and families who identify themselves (or are identified by other service deliverers) as having multiple needs that are not being met well elsewhere. Central office planners also want to allow local offices to identify other specific target populations based on local needs and community priorities (for example, families with children who are often absent from school), but they have not yet worked out how to do this.

So far, the new program is in effect in two local welfare offices that were particularly eager to start and are well connected to the community services network. Referrals of families to the program in these offices come from eligibility workers, child protective services workers, schoolteachers, school nurses, and public health nurses, among others. As the program has grown, there are more self-referrals—families who come in having heard about the services a friend received.

The program, which is tailored to AFDC families with multiple needs and difficulties in getting access to services, offers each of the targeted families intensive case management and referral to a variety of services. Intensive case management means that the case manager sees the family at home as well as in the office, works to develop a personal relationship with all family members, and advocates for services for the family. Case managers aim to carry a case long enough to enable the adults in the family to stabilize crises in their lives and learn how to get what they need from the system so that they can bring up healthy and competent children and provide for the family economically.

The case managers who provide these services are a special group within the broader group of JOBS case managers. These special case managers, who are known as family specialists, have caseloads of 30, compared to 80 for the other JOBS case managers, who deal with a narrower range of services and a clientele judged by administrators to be easier to work with. In addition to carrying the 30 cases, each family specialist is also expected either to lead a parent support group or to act as liaison to another service agency.

While some observers have asked whether a single case manager can have the dual responsibility of moving a family toward self-sufficiency through JOBS and responding to a much broader range of family needs, agency administrators are convinced that the two kinds of services go together and that families cannot progress in one of the two spheres without progressing in the other. They also believe that the Family Support Act's emphasis on education makes the tension between self-sufficiency and family support goals much less than it would be with a narrower emphasis on employment because they believe that education is an important goal for virtually every family whereas, in the short-run at least, employment may not be. However, the dual responsibility does mean that a family with multiple problems in which the mother does not, after a reasonable amount of time, become motivated to enter a training or education program would not be appropriate for continued services. Most likely, the family specialist would close the case (probably excusing the family from JOBS on a temporary basis on the basis of emotional problems or family crisis) and refer the family to a community-based agency where they could get longer-term services.

Families served by the family specialists are routinely linked up with visiting nurse services and with the pediatric clinics at the city hospital (which include a clinic for high-risk infants), in addition to regular Medicaid coverage. The case managers have training in observing child development and child-parent interactions, and they are encouraged to take their questions or concerns to the visiting nurses or to the local agency for developmental disabilities for consultation and to set up a joint home visit.

Families also have access to a local Head Start program, and teens have access for their infants and toddlers to a high-quality program which is on-site at an alternative high school. However, many families are not served by these programs because of capacity limits or specific family needs. The family specialist ensures that these families work with the community agency that provides child care resource and referral assistance, in order to identify child care in the community that is as well-suited as possible to both the child's and the mother's needs.

Like the welfare agency in State A, the Human Resources Department has also tried to communicate the philosophy and specific content of the new program to eligibility workers. The family specialists are located in the same offices and can, therefore, talk with eligibility workers about which of their cases might benefit from services, include eligibility workers in case conferences where appropriate, and let them know what happens to the families as services move along. In addition, the knowledge that the family specialists have accumulated about a wide range of community resources turns out to be useful to eligibility workers who want to refer families to a service that might help them, and the family specialists are encouraged to offer individual advice or conduct more formal training sessions as a means of strengthening the relationship. As a result, at least at the two pilot offices, eligibility workers are knowledgeable and enthusiastic about the Family Specialist program, actively refer pregnant and parenting teens and other appropriate families, and mention the option of family services case management to families who express concerns in the eligibility interview.

Principles

To serve poor children effectively, a welfare agency's approach to children and families needs to meet the three criteria noted above:

- It needs to be consistent with a sustainable mission for the agency;
- It needs to take advantage of opportunities for collaboration at the state and local levels; and
- It needs to balance the needs of families with the capacity and limits of staff and bureaucratic structures at the welfare agency.

The scenarios suggest several implications of these broad criteria.

Sustainable Mission. The scenarios illustrate the two kinds of mission conceptions found in the study sites. The more limited conception (though it is still very ambitious compared to a typical welfare agency today) is illustrated by the Income Maintenance Department of State A. This conception of mission identifies the welfare agency's job for poor children and families as one of enabling mothers to maintain a healthy family life while pursuing self-sufficiency. For welfare agencies without a broader mandate for children's services, this conception is probably the best fit for their legal and historical role—and, as suggested by the first scenario, it can lead to substantial changes in the welfare-to-work process once it is taken seriously. At the very least, a welfare agency that takes this mission seriously will examine its welfare-to-work system to identify effects on children and on family life. At best, as suggested in this scenario, the agency will also look for opportunities to assist mothers in meeting their children's needs in conjunction with their own search for self-sufficiency.

The second conception of mission took many forms in the study sites; one form is illustrated in the second scenario by the Department of Human Resources in State B. In this conception, the welfare agency has a much broader responsibility toward poor families and children than simply to avoid harming family life in the pursuit of parental self-sufficiency. This responsibility may include avoiding foster care, assisting with early education and health care to prevent later "rotten outcomes," improving the self-esteem and motivation of parents and children, and intervening more broadly with both parents and children to strengthen family functioning, promote long-run self-sufficiency, and prevent two-generational poverty. In the research sites, welfare agencies that expressed some version of this broader mission typically:

- Had responsibilities beyond income maintenance (for example, child welfare services); and
- Focused on a particular element of the broad mission, usually a particular target group (such as teen mothers) and a particular set of outcomes for them (for example, self-esteem and education).

Consistent with this evidence, the Department of Human Resources in the scenario is a department with wide-ranging responsibilities, and it has chosen to focus on two groups of AFDC families to begin with: teens (as in several of the research sites) and multineed families (as in Oklahoma IFS).

In both scenarios, agency administrators choose to communicate the mission widely, and in both, they try to select specific next steps that are consistent with their overall purpose. In addition, both make the choice to respond to cost constraints by targeting more intensive services to selected families rather than by diluting services for all families. All these steps are suggested by practices of the study sites that seem likely to contribute to success.

More generally, the scenarios highlight the following principles about how welfare agencies should develop and implement a mission that involves services to children and families. In designing a new role for a welfare agency, advocates, policymakers, and administrators should:

- Begin with a clear conception of the agency's mission and core functions and consider the link between that mission and services to families and children.
- Determine at least whether the agency should be paying attention to the effects of its existing activities on family life, and then consider a broader mission that involves strengthening family life and providing preventive services to children and families.
- Articulate broad purposes as well as identifying specific next steps.
- Avoid adding on particular services without articulating why they are important and relevant to the agency's job.
- Consider identifying a particular group of families for whom the broader mission is especially appropriate.
- Consider targeting limited resources to intensive services for these particular families, rather than spreading resources equally across all families.

Opportunities for Collaboration. As the research sites showed, welfare departments cannot provide directly most of the services that children need to grow up into healthy, educated, and productive adults. Therefore, meeting the needs of children and families on welfare necessarily involves collaboration.

The scenarios illustrate several dimensions of such collaboration. First, in both the scenarios, the collaboration occurs at both the state and local levels. Although Scenario A is more standardized across the state, both state and local offices search for providers that might be able to provide two-generational programs. In Scenario B, the target groups and the nature of services are intended to be tailored to community needs, and the program is piloted in two local offices that have particularly strong ties to the community network of services.

Second, the scenarios illustrate what the welfare department might be able to offer other agencies to encourage them to collaborate. Funding— for child care and for two-generational programs, in particular—is an important element in both scenarios. The welfare department's ability to advocate for the families it serves is less explicit but may be important in (for example) gaining services for welfare families from a separate agency that has expertise in responding to developmental disabilities.

Third, the scenarios suggest that the collaboration with other agencies is based, at least in part, on personal relationships (the case manager and nurse home visitor who consult about a family) rather than solely on formal agreements. Other key elements of effective collaboration identified through the research sites, such as the development of a common mission and a process for conflict resolution, are not explicit in these brief discussions of the scenarios, but they will need to be there for the programs to survive.

Finally, the scenarios reflect two different approaches to the use of welfare agency resources for new programs: resources for new programs that will serve only welfare recipients (such as two-generational programs) and resources to finance referral to existing programs (as in child care resource and referral services). The research sites did not offer persuasive evidence that one of these approaches is generally better than the other; the scenarios suggest that the choice will often depend on what resources are already available in a community and what new programs need to be developed.

The scenarios highlight the following principles for implementing services to children and families that can meet needs through collaboration. Advocates, policymakers, and administrators should:

- Consider at the state level what agencies might be valuable to work with, what resources each might want from the welfare department, what resources each might offer and what common problems or clients might be of joint interest.

- Authorize and encourage local welfare directors, in selected locations or statewide, to investigate services in their own communities.

- Seek out local school systems, early education providers, teen services programs, community health centers, visiting nurse programs, and developmental disability services as likely collaborators.

- Recognize the role of common purposes, conflict resolution arrangements, and personal relationships in effective collaboration.

- Consider collaborative arrangements with providers both to develop new programs and to improve access for welfare families to existing programs.

Balance Between Family Needs and Welfare Department Capacity. Chapters 3 and 5 developed the theme that the needs of many children and families on welfare demand personalized, wide-ranging services delivered in the context of a trusting personal relationship. However, the welfare agency's mandate, history with its clients, and staff capacity may be ill-suited to delivering such services. As a result, a welfare agency hoping to serve children and families effectively confronts three challenges which are identified in those chapters: reaching out to targeted families in order to bring them in the door and then engage them in services, selecting and supporting staff who can delivery quality services to them, and developing organizational and financial arrangements consistent with such services.

The agency's ability, or inability, to meet these challenges successfully has consequences far beyond an internal, bureaucratic judgment about program success or failure. In particular, welfare families and their advocates worry about the possibility that welfare agencies could harm families in the effort to do good through intrusion by ill-trained workers into difficult family situations or through the use of information gained in a "helper" role to reduce benefits in the eligibility role.

The research sites suggest that these worries are legitimate. In particular, there are serious tensions between the role, knowledge, and attitudes of the typical eligibility worker and the kinds of services that families require. At the same time, however, the study sites offered many examples of the techniques that successful programs use to reduce these tensions and take advantage of the capacity of the welfare agency to help families without inadvertently harming them. The two scenarios illustrate a number of their approaches to this delicate balance.

First, both scenarios reflect the judgment that there is a great deal to be gained by serving families more effectively. While there are dangers, they need to be weighed against the dangers and ineffectiveness of the previous system, which imposed requirements on parents without considering their family obligations and failed to take advantage of any of the opportunities that the welfare process provides to attend to the needs of children.

Second, in both scenarios, a key first step is to open up the welfare department's processes to the concerns and requests of the parents. Before proposing elaborate assessments for children and families, both agencies choose instead to make it possible for parents to identify what they think they need.

Third, in both scenarios, eligibility workers are involved but are not the primary service deliverers. The tensions between helping and investigative roles are at their most intense for workers who determine eligibility, and both agencies have therefore chosen not to ask those workers to deliver family services. On the other hand, because eligibility workers see so many families and because their attitude and approach shape families' experience of the whole system, neither state is prepared to leave eligibility workers out of the program completely. In both cases, their role is to help identify families who would benefit from the new services and to allow families to identify child-related needs. In addition, both states understand a key lesson from the research sites: This new role, small as it may seem, can only be created through considerable management attention, given the multiple other demands on eligibility workers.

Fourth, the Income Maintenance Department (State A) has chosen to contract out primary case management responsibility to community child care resource and referral agencies in order to distance family services from the mandating power of the welfare department. The Department of Human Resources (State B) is better-equipped to provide family services and has left the basic case management function in-house, but the in-house case managers work together with outside nonprofit agencies and sometimes refer cases to them.

Finally, in both scenarios the agencies are providing services that are largely voluntary, although families have mandatory responsibilities in relation to the JOBS program as a whole. In State A, a mother's participation in an employability activity is mandatory (in the absence of an exemption), but she has opportunities to select among activities and, therefore, will not be mandated to participate in a particular two-generational program. In addition, at the same time that child care resource and referral counselors are helping mothers find child care that can make an employment or training placement possible, they also advise the parent that she is not required to begin an employment or training opportunity until she finds satisfactory care. In State B, parents are also mandated to participate in an employability activity but they are not required to work with a special family services case manager. Those who do must continue making progress toward participating in an activity, since the family services case manager cannot be reimbursed as a JOBS case manager if she is serving families who are not involved in JOBS. Families who do not make progress may be sanctioned, although in practice, family services case managers generally identify an underlying reason for the lack of progress (such as violence in the home) and issue an exemption. These compromises are not tidy ones, but they represent the best efforts of the states to combine a mandatory employment system with the privacy and discretion required to meet child and family needs.

Once again, therefore, the recommendations highlighted by the scenarios do not fit neatly into specific packages or program models. Rather, they offer alternative responses to the trade-offs and tensions between the welfare department's capacity and the needs of families and children. Therefore, we recommend that advocates, welfare administrators, and policymakers:

- Develop approaches that take seriously the needs of families for trustworthy, responsive, and wide-ranging services and avoid approaches that rely heavily on mandates and sanctions or that are unsuccessful at engaging and involving families.
- Develop approaches that take into account the pressures on welfare agencies and staff that may prevent them from offering trustworthy,

responsive, and wide-ranging services. For example, when asking workers to perform differently, make certain they are offered support—such as training, supervision, and revised job evaluations—for new ways of doing business.

- Consider opening up the process to the concerns of parents about their children.
- In undertaking more systematic assessments of child and family needs, recognize the difficulties of trust between the eligibility worker and the client. Consider whether assessments can be conducted in the course of child care counseling, enrollment in Head Start or other early childhood programs, or interaction with the training provider rather than during eligibility determination.
- Identify ways to include the special knowledge of eligibility workers in the new program and to improve the eligibility process for all families without asking eligibility workers to assume primary responsibility as family service deliverers.
- Consider contracting out portions of the family services where other agencies would be more accessible to welfare recipients or more trusted by them.
- Identify ways to keep services for children and families voluntary within the context of mandated employability services.

SPECIFIC RECOMMENDATIONS: IMPLEMENTING THE FAMILY SUPPORT ACT

As the Introduction suggested, the passage of the Family Support Act in 1988 provided both opportunities and risks for poor families and children. Applying the principles sketched above to the implementation of FSA suggests a number of ways of taking advantage of the opportunities and minimizing the risks. The specific recommendations fall into five categories, corresponding to provisions of FSA that offer states important choices in implementation:

- Using the Family Support Act's case management option to serve families and to cement links with other service providers;
- Offering opportunities for the assessment of child and family needs;
- Implementing the child care provisions of the FSA through enriched child care referral and partnerships with particular, high-quality programs;
- Developing partnerships with high-quality two-generational programs that could pair JOBS services for a parent with services for her child; and

- Selecting target groups for employment and training services under the FSA with some attention to the needs of families for broader, child-oriented services.

Case Management

The Family Support Act allows states the option to deliver services to JOBS participants and their families through case management. If states select this option, they must specify how the case management services will be delivered, by whom, and how families will be assigned to case managers (if not all families statewide will be assigned to case managers).[1] Case managers' salaries are reimbursed by the federal government, as are other direct costs of providing JOBS services, at the higher figure of 60 percent or the state's Medicaid match rate.[2]

Recommendation. States *should* take advantage of the case management option, though perhaps not for all JOBS families. States should consider specifically how they want to use case management to serve families, build partnerships with outside agencies, and improve the service system as a whole. They should also consider the possibility of contracting out to community agencies some case management services, which is allowable under FSA.[3] States may also want to compare the requirements of several different funding streams for case management in order to see which best meets particular policy aims. For example, some study sites used Medicaid case management funding for teens or state funding for multiproblem families.

- *Case Management to Serve Families.* A state that hopes to use case management to solve a range of difficult child and family problems should note the serious attention to skills—through the selection of qualified staff, supervision, training, and peer review—that accompanies intensive, family-oriented case management in the study sites. While a welfare agency may well want to start its case management program with enthusiastic volunteers who now hold other jobs within the system, it should nonetheless plan to recruit and screen carefully, even at the beginning, and should plan on considerable training and supervision as the program matures.

States may also want to consider smaller changes in services to a broader range of families. The other extreme from intensive case management for a few families is a strategy of changing the eligibility worker's job for all families. An eligibility operation that moves toward the level of client responsiveness provided by the ET CHOICES site could provide effective intake and referral to a family-oriented program, share information (as appropriate, given confidentiality guidelines) with other service deliverers, provide basic services to the whole caseload (such as referral to a pediatrician), and provide a more dignified experience for the client.

However, there are clear risks in taking this route: Changing a whole service system is slow, expensive in terms of lower caseloads, and unpredictable in its effect on other important agency goals such as low error rates.

• *Case Management to Build Partnerships.* An unexpected insight from the study sites is that the welfare department's capacity to fund or provide case management offers opportunities to cement partnerships with schools and health providers. Both kinds of provider may appreciate the help of a case manager who knows a family well. Among other roles, the case manager can help family members take advantage of services, troubleshoot when something goes wrong (as when a teen misses school or a young mother fails to bring her child to a health care appointment), and translate the needs and expectations of each party (provider and family) to the other.

• *Case Management to Improve the Service System.* Because case managers learn a great deal about how the system as a whole works for families, they can be invaluable to upper-level managers who want to improve the system but do not know exactly how. Thus, state strategies for using case management may want to build in feedback from case managers to service systems, either directly or by way of upper-level managers. Among the study sites, Oklahoma IFS empowered case managers to make system changes themselves through their role in convening community service providers, while San Diego relied on case managers to provide information about collaboration successes and needs to high-level managers.

Assessment

The Family Support Act requires that states assess an individual's employability, taking into account the individual's needs for supportive services (including child care), skills and experience, and family circumstances.[4] The state is allowed, but not required, to consider the needs of the individual's child or children in the assessment, and the state is allowed to add to the assessment other factors it determines to be relevant.[5] There has been considerable discussion of whether states should take advantage of the option to assess children, through developmental tests, for example.

Recommendation. The assessments carried out for state JOBS programs ought to have several goals: to take advantage of the unique capacity of the welfare department to identify and meet child and family needs; to focus on needs that the program, as defined in a given jurisdiction, can effectively address; and, at the same time, to avoid inaccuracy or damage that might arise from involvement by an untrained worker or through the confusion of assistance with enforcement of eligibility rules. The study sites suggest several characteristics of an assessment process that meets these goals:

- An effective assessment often builds on the needs identified by families themselves, needs that the typical welfare or employability assessment may leave out.

- An accurate assessment develops over time and through trust. Case managers do not expect to understand complex aspects of the family situation on the first or second meeting.

- Case managers attempt to improve parents' ability to assess children's development, and not only to make their own assessments.

- Case managers who attempt to assess child development have specific training and often have access to experts (such as nurse home visitors and developmental disability specialists) who can offer additional advice.

These findings offer guidance on some ways that a JOBS program might gain the advantages of paying attention to children without implementing a potentially inaccurate or damaging process. First, early in the program's contact with families, it should be possible to collect some basic information that would flag serious problems being experienced by the children, particularly problems already identified by the parent and problems that affect either participation in JOBS or the selection of child care. Early on, it might also be possible to identify families that would benefit by more intensive assessment and services directed at child and family needs. Examples of information that could be collected early in the process include whether the child has a health care provider, whether the mother has concerns about a child's health or development, whether the family has acceptable shelter for the children, whether the mother is worried about the child's school progress, and whether, due to fears about a violent or crime-ridden neighborhood, the mother wants her JOBS program to allow her to be home when the children return from school. Opening up early interviews, whether with the eligibility worker or the JOBS worker, to the mother's concerns about her children is a small change that could have a considerable effect on the experience of families with the welfare system.

To address concerns that this information will be misused or interpreted inaccurately, agencies need to think through the role of such information in the eligibility process and the training and support offered to the workers collecting it. For example, the school progress of a 16-year-old has an effect on a mother's eligibility and therefore needs to be collected explicitly as a part of an eligibility determination, and not simply incorporated into an assessment to help the mother and child. To take another example, a well-trained eligibility worker in a system that supports (through reasonable caseloads and supervision) a basic relationship with a family *and* allows the family to refuse services may be able to judge accurately that her client would benefit from more specialized services. A more rushed and untrained eligibility worker should not make that judgment, and no eligibility worker should be able to require families to enter services. The general rule should be that the training and support offered to workers, the extent of contact and relationship between parents and the program, and the ability of parents to make voluntary choices about how they handle information that is developed should govern the degree to which the worker probes for information.

As suggested by both the scenarios, welfare agencies ought to look for ways in which to build more extensive assessments into later steps of the process, at least for some families, but should not necessarily conduct the assessments themselves. Among those workers whose training, support, and functions might enable them to assess family needs are counselors at child care resource and referral agencies, family service workers at Head Start programs, case managers at comprehensive teen services programs, and, in some agencies, JOBS program case managers.

Child Care

The Family Support Act requires states to "guarantee child care necessary to accept or retain employment, to participate in JOBS, and to participate in other approved education or training."[6] State expenditures are reimbursed at the state's Medicaid match rate (from 50 percent for wealthier states to about 80 percent for the poorest states), and reimbursement is open-ended (unlike reimbursement for JOBS expenditures, which is capped). However, expenditures on the development of child care supply (such as provider training or recruitment, technical assistance to providers, and so forth) are not reimbursable.[7]

Recommendation. States should concurrently pursue two routes to better child care: enriched child care referral, whereby knowledgeable parent counselors help parents find child care that suits them and their child, and partnerships with particular high-quality programs, such as Head Start, family literacy programs like PACE, and other programs that may be locally available. There is some tension between the two tracks because many child care providers, whose cooperation is necessary to the first track, are uncomfortable with the second. Nonetheless, given the solid research evidence about the importance of *quality* in child care, particularly for disadvantaged children, an approach based solely on referral has clear limits if there is not a large pool of high-quality care.

In addition, states might consider the child care resource and referral agency or the child care provider as a possible source of multiple services to the family. Staff at these agencies are likely to hear about children's needs and family problems, and they could be supported to play a case management role, if appropriate in a particular community's service structure.

Finally, child care funding, even more than case management funding, offers welfare agencies the opportunity to build partnerships with other providers. In the study sites, the welfare department's access to child care funding gave it a new role in the community service delivery system and a new value to other providers (such as teen services agencies or the school system), which could be traded for services by those other providers to welfare recipients.

We hoped to find more direct kinds of partnerships as well, whereby welfare agencies offered child care resources to other providers who developed child care programs tailored to the needs of welfare families. For example, welfare funding might make it possible to extend a Head Start program from a half to a full day or to provide infant care on-site in a school building in conjunction with a special program for pregnant and parenting teens. Except for the experiment with welfare funding for the PACE program, no such partnerships were operating at the sites, probably because of a mix of logistical difficulties and tensions concerning mission. We would encourage more experiments, with the understanding that developing these programs will not be easy.

Two-Generational JOBS Programs

The Family Support Act requires each state to provide four mandatory components in its JOBS program: education, job skills training, job readiness activities, and job placement and development. The state must also provide two of four optional activities (job search, on-the-job training, work supplementation, and work experience) and may provide other activities.[8] The legislation gives states broad discretion in matching programs to recipients *except* for recipients without a high school diploma, who are to be assigned to basic education, with limited exceptions (and somewhat different rules for those under and over age 20).

Recommendation. The sites offer two examples of programs that seem suited to meeting this requirement for parental education *and* meeting the needs of children in welfare families: family literacy programs, such as PACE, and school-based programs for young mothers that offer on-site, high-quality child care. In the study sites, both types of programs offer education leading to a high school diploma or GED for the parent, high-quality, developmentally oriented care for the child, and opportunities for parent-child interaction and parent education. However, states need to understand that creating partnerships around these programs will not be easy because of the different missions and mandates of early childhood programs, adult education programs, and welfare agencies. In addition, excellent programs of this type are not cheap, in part because high-quality child care is expensive. PACE costs about $5,000 per family, for example, in addition to the cost of child care for other siblings who are not included in the program.

Selection of Target Groups

The Family Support Act requires that states spend the majority of their JOBS resources on four target groups or face a fiscal penalty. The target groups are long-term recipients (on aid for at least 36 of the preceding 60 months); young parents (under age 24) who have not completed high school and are not enrolled; young parents (under 24) who have had little or no work experience in the preceding year; and members of a family in which the youngest child is within two years of being ineligible for AFDC because of age.[9] One question for a state attempting to consider the whole family is how well these target groups correspond to the families that are most in need of child and family services.

Recommendation. The overall goal for policymakers and administrators should be to identify target groups that are consistent with a conception of the welfare agency's mission—what it is trying to do for families. Agencies that are more like the Income Maintenance Department of Scenario A should have no difficulty aligning the families they want to serve intensively with their JOBS target groups since their purpose is to address the needs of families within JOBS who need help achieving self-sufficiency without sacrificing family life. The most obvious target groups for these services are families with young children (which is probably consistent with the emphasis in the legislation on young parents), as well as families whose children have special needs and perhaps other families who find the transition to work particularly stressful.

However, for agencies more like the Department of Human Resources in Scenario B, that want to use the FSA as a funding stream to support a broader mission for children and families, the JOBS target groups may not be consistent with the state's own priorities. Teen parents, a group selected as a priority for services by a number of the research sites, offer a good match: they fit into the priority groups for JOBS services and are on many local lists of families that are in particular need of child-oriented services. Multiproblem families, a group selected as a priority in Scenario B and in the Oklahoma study site, might overlap considerably with the long-term recipients category under JOBS, but there is no solid basis for predictions about how substantial the overlap might be. Other local priority groups, such as families with middle-school children at risk of dropping out (as selected in the Detroit study site) might not overlap particularly closely with any of the categories. In order to serve groups like this, which represent an appealing target for services to families and children in a particular community, states will have to target case management services in ways not entirely driven by the 55 percent funding rule. They may also choose to mix JOBS funding with other sources of case management or service funding.

Whatever the target groups chosen by a state, one of the clearest lessons from the sites is that agencies need to pay careful attention to the strategy for bringing targeted families into services and engaging them once they are enrolled. Neither mandating family participation nor mandating referral by eligibility workers is likely, in itself, to be sufficient to recruit and engage families given the many conflicting demands on both families and workers. Instead, managers will need to spend considerable time developing approaches to outreach and cultivating referral networks, whether through the eligibility system or outside.

Finally, whatever the target group, enrollment into any special family services offered as an adjunct to JOBS (intensive case management, family literacy, special services to teen parents, and so forth) should be voluntary. The reasons are the risk of intrusiveness in delivering these services and, what is probably more important, the crucial role of a trusting personal relationship between client and service deliverer in making the services effective and worthwhile. In any case, whether the program is officially voluntary or mandatory, the importance of the relationship means that the program will need skillful staff who act *as if* the program is voluntary—that is, who devote considerable time to marketing and motivation—no matter what the official status of family participation.

PRINCIPLES FOR FAMILY-ORIENTED, TWO-GENERATIONAL SERVICES

Children who are growing up in poverty or other kinds of need are likely to come into contact with other large public agencies besides the welfare system: the public schools, community health clinics or city hospitals, and, perhaps, sadly, the state's child protective services agency. What are the implications of the findings presented here for the other large public agencies that see poor children and families? To put the question slightly differently, what principles would we apply to each system if we wanted to create a coherent network of services to children?[10] While this study was not designed to investigate other service systems in any detail, the research sites do suggest several intriguing speculations.

First, other agencies besides the welfare department can and should consider what it means to be two-generational. As the research sites and the evidence of other researchers suggest, family needs are often intertwined, whereas the services offered by many of the large systems are limited to a single family member.

A number of program examples from the site visits and other sources illustrate what it means for service providers other than the welfare department to be two-generational in their focus:

- The PACE program in Kentucky, with its combination of adult literacy and preschool education, operates within the public schools. In addition to offering two-generational services to families that are directly enrolled in PACE, the program director sees PACE as a vehicle for changing the thinking of the public schools toward a greater inclusion of parents and other family members.

- Child protective services workers in several of the research sites found that working with intensive case managers helped them appreciate the demands on parents that made it difficult for the latter, in turn, to respond to the needs of the child. This insight lies behind a variety of family support and family preservation programs now being deployed as part of the child welfare services continuum in a number of states. The aim of these programs is to offer services to both parent and child to improve family functioning and enable the child to stay in the home.

- Visiting nurse programs enable health care providers to see parents and children together and serve the whole family. Maternal and child health clinics with other colocated services also offer the opportunity to meet the needs of several family members.

- In several locations in New England, Head Start programs are planning or already operating programs jointly with education and training programs for mothers on welfare. These programs include cooperative projects with vocational high schools and with a community training agency.[11]

Second, however, no agency attempting to move in a two-generational direction should expect the change to be easy. Many of the obstacles experienced by welfare agencies apply just as forcefully to the other large service systems for poor children and families. For example, difficulties of mission plague both schools and child welfare agencies that consider reaching out to parents, just as they hamper welfare agencies that consider reaching out to children. In the school setting, teachers, administrators, and elected overseers may worry that a mission of academic excellence will be compromised by too much attention to the multiple needs that children and their families bring into the classroom. For child welfare agencies, the conflict is even more stark: In an agency whose mission is to protect children, many of whom are in urgent danger, how can it be legitimate to pay comparable attention to their parents? Similarly, each system suffers isolation from other service deliverers and lack of expertise in the multiple problems of families. Each experiences its own set of demands on workers and on the organization as a whole, demands that must be balanced against the needs of families in any successful solution.[12]

Third, the ways in which welfare agencies have overcome these barriers may well offer insights to other agencies. For example, welfare agencies at the successful sites have overcome the limitations of their initial mandate by developing a clear and sustainable mission that makes clear why services to children and families are part of the welfare agency's job. In order to expand services, schools, health clinics, and child protective services agencies may similarly need to articulate connections between an initial, narrower mission and the broader, family-centered mission that they would like to achieve. Thus, schools may conclude that they cannot teach children without a collaborative relationship with parents, that they cannot teach children without addressing the problems that keep them from being ready to learn, or that they cannot teach teen mothers effectively without addressing their roles as parents as well as students. Child protective services agencies may conclude that functions such as enhancing family stability and averting foster care are more effective over the long run than providing after-the-fact treatment.

To take another example, the successful welfare agencies used a variety of techniques to balance the operational demands of the eligibility function against the needs of families for trustworthy and responsive services. By paying attention to outreach, hiring, staff support, organizational structure, and funding streams, the agencies succeeded at engaging families and providing them with high-quality services while still meeting other demands on the system. The other large public agencies experience similar demands that obstruct responsive services in similar ways. While these other agencies (except for child protective services) may have less potential to do harm to families if they misjudge services than do welfare agencies, all of them run the risk of processing rather than serving families and of draining rather than supporting workers.[13]

Quite possibly, the menu of techniques used by the welfare agencies in the study sites can also help mediate these tensions for other agencies. For example, the welfare sites sometimes chose either to contract out services or to supplement in-house services through collaborative relationships with community-based agencies. The same approach might be helpful for child protective services agencies; in fact, such relationships developed informally at several research sites when hard-pressed child protective workers informally asked community-based case managers to keep an eye on a family. To take another example, successful welfare agencies often chose to involve eligibility workers, who do the agency's demanding core function, in the family services program but not to give them direct responsibility for providing family services. Similarly, schools might make considerable efforts to involve teachers in a family services program but not ask them to make home visits or take the lead role in making services referrals to outside agencies.[14]

More important than each of these specific suggestions, however, is the vision suggested by the sites taken as a whole: a vision of large public agencies that have moved toward knitting together their different efforts on behalf of children and families. That larger task, while certainly difficult, is too important to abandon. From their different perspectives, both

Sandra—the teenager from Chapter 3 who fought her way back into school and into a teen parent program in the welfare office—and Richard Jacobsen—director of the San Diego County Department of Social Services at the time of the site visit—argue that agencies cannot afford to keep up their isolation and single-minded focus on one client and one service. The incongruity between that narrow focus and the needs of children is too great, and the consequences of failing to pay attention to children in need are too frightening.

CONCLUSION

For the young woman sketched in Chapter 1, who went into an eligibility interview with a range of worries about her children and was unlikely to receive help with any of them, either of the two scenarios offered above would represent a substantial improvement. Under either scenario, the welfare agency will stop wasting the opportunity it has as an organization to notice the well-being of young children and intervene on their behalf, and it will start taking advantage of the knowledge and energy of its staff and the resources it has at its disposal to affect community delivery of services to poor families and children.

At the same time, reaching the point at which a welfare agency can respond to family needs as responsively and flexibly as in the scenarios will not be easy. The study sites suggest that welfare agencies can, in fact, serve poor children and families far more richly than most do now, but they also underline the challenges to be met on the way. Agencies cannot take for granted the challenges of defining a sustainable mission, collaborating with other organizations, reaching out to suitable families, delivering responsive and high-quality services, or balancing responsiveness with the need for political and bureaucratic accountability.

Thus, the conclusions of this research are both optimistic and guarded. On the one hand, the evidence from the research sites suggests that welfare agencies can play a role in improving the lives of poor children and families. Over the long run, they can even serve as catalysts and coordinators in the reform of the service system for those families. After all, the welfare agency is in a position to speak for families that other service deliverers may prefer to forget, such as children who are difficult in school, mothers with few skills to take into an occupational training program, and teenagers who irritate doctors by missing appointments or bringing a crying baby into the waiting room. On the other hand, convincing as is the research on children's needs and the power of intervention, changes in the mission and services of welfare agencies will take a considerable investment of time, managerial resources, money, and political commitment. This study is meant to provide both a prod and a framework for that investment.

Appendix A: The Case Studies

This Appendix tells the stories of the study sites and how they have gone about linking children and families in the welfare system to much-needed services. In order to convey the full flavor of these experiments in service delivery, the first four stories are told at considerable length, while the remaining stories are more briefly summarized. In general, the longer cases are based on the most extensive interview evidence and raise a particularly wide array of themes.

The cases reflect the situation at the time of the site visits in the summer and fall of 1989. All the sites have experienced some change and development since that time, and in Massachusetts and California in particular, tight budgets have substantially affected the shape of the program. Selected important changes since the site visits are noted in the text, but there has been no effort to bring the cases completely up-to-date.

OKLAHOMA: INTEGRATED FAMILY SERVICES

Case Management and Community Capacity Building

Introduction. More than any other of the sites, Oklahoma's Integrated Family Services (IFS) system is deliberately designed to change the way in which service delivery institutions work at the same time that it delivers services to individual families. Operated by the Oklahoma Department of Human Services in 9 counties across the state, IFS provides intense, short-run (three- to six-month) case management to families in crisis, many of whom are AFDC recipients. Through "team staffings" with other service deliverers, IFS case managers link families up to a wide range of needed services in the community. At the same time, the case managers and the program have a crucial second function: to build community capacity for family-oriented services through such activities as convening a regular working group of service deliverers, developing a community resource directory, conducting workshops or training sessions for staff, and identifying service gaps and seeking out resources to fill them. In the first few months at each site, IFS case managers concentrate exclusively on the community capacity-building task; after that, each worker both carries a caseload *and* works at the broader community level. The program currently serves 9 of Oklahoma's 77 counties, with plans to expand to 8 to 13 more counties over the next couple of years, as funds allow.

Background. The IFS system (originally called Integrated Services Project) began in May 1985 as one of five demonstration projects in integrated services funded nationwide by the U.S. Department of Health and Human Services (HHS). The purpose of the demonstration was to find a way in which to integrate social services for especially needy AFDC families, such as long-term recipients and teens, in order to decrease their dependence on public services over the long run. The demonstration period was marked by some negotiation between the federal government and the state about appropriate purposes and target groups, with the federal government emphasizing AFDC families and Oklahoma emphasizing a broader group of families in crisis. In the spring of 1989, when the state took the program over as a permanent component of its service system, it received its current name to mark the commitment to family-oriented services.

IFS is housed in the Division of Field Operations of the Oklahoma Department of Human Services (DHS). Field Operations has traditionally crossed programmatic boundaries within DHS, while other divisions carry out the specific tasks of AFDC eligibility, JOBS implementation, child protective services, and so forth. Thus, the IFS staff are within the same umbrella agency as a wide range of human services programs but not under any one program.

Goals. For the individual families they serve, IFS case managers express goals related both to self-sufficiency and to family functioning, which they see as closely related. One worker emphasized the need for case management for all family members regardless of individual service needs, "since each one impacts the self-sufficiency and healthy functioning of the other." Another said, "It's important to focus on the mother's needs in order to help the child. What the child really [may] need is a mother who can cope." One important goal is reminiscent of that in several other sites: IFS case managers aim to create a relationship of "real trust" that empowers the families to solve problems themselves. According to one case manager, "The most important thing we give to them is ourselves."

In addition, the IFS case managers have particular goals that are related to the short-term nature of their intervention and their place in the service system. In some cases, their key goal is to stabilize a family and pull it through a crisis. In other cases, their goal is to galvanize other service deliverers that are working with the same family but are at cross-purposes, so that the team of professionals can create an effective service plan. According to one IFS case manager describing a successful intervention: "We literally made a pie, and everybody [the various service deliverers] got a piece of a pie, and I mean a cut up piece of paper. It was something she [the client] understood and it was something they understood. And the plan that they were involved in was their piece."

The truly unique aspect of IFS, however, is the combination of these individual case management goals with goals for the service delivery system as a whole. According to the manual for IFS case managers, it is their "obligation" to identify and try to fill community service gaps. It is also their job to pull community service deliverers together and to build effective links between the community and DHS. The same case manager quoted above offered this element of the job as the key lesson she would offer to other states: "I think that [what is important is] the whole [notion] of making a community own the problems of this family through the welfare department. This family belongs to all of us. . . . We can get together and help the family better than any one agency can help the family."

Finally, at the state level, a key goal has been to promote local ownership, flexibility, and innovation. The sites represented in our interviews reported somewhat different priorities for families to be served and quite different initiatives for new services. Donna Stahl, the program's founder and director, cited a rural county that developed a creative new program to work with farm families that had been devastated by the threat of losing their farms, while an urban county that is slated to receive an IFS unit in the next expansion is eager to work on case management related to the health needs of AFDC families.

Services to Children. Because the philosophy of IFS is family-oriented, children are part of the program at every turn. The cases cited as examples reflect the complexity of the IFS case manager's role: Children are served through the counseling and coordinating role of the case manager as well as through specific brokered services. For example:

- A seven-year-old boy came to the attention of a school principal because of both physical and emotional health problems. The boy had long been prone to seizures and self-destructive behavior and was just starting to threaten other children. When the principal called IFS, he found that IFS was already working with the family because the mother was on AFDC and herself had multiple problems. The IFS worker called a meeting of all the agencies who had contact with the family to talk about the child's needs. As a result, the boy was admitted and sent to a diagnostic center for several months of testing and treatment; the mother received needed services such as mental health treatment and literacy training; and the Child Protective Services worker reported that, as a result of the IFS intervention, she now saw the family in a different light and realized that the mother had the potential to be an adequate parent.

• A 16-year-old boy, who was living with his aunt because his mother had been murdered, was developing behavioral problems, including alcohol abuse. The IFS case manager called together a team staffing (including the AFDC worker), with the result that the boy was admitted to a temporary youth shelter for three weeks and now sees a psychologist weekly. Relations between aunt and nephew reportedly improved.

• The most frequent service that IFS case managers in Washington County report referring families to is WIC, and the second most frequent is children's health services.

Children loom equally large in the community capacity-building task of the IFS case managers. The spin-off programs created by IFS in various counties include MATCH, a program of volunteer parent aides for teen mothers; a community-based tutoring center for youth; and a school referral system whereby IFS case managers intervene with students before truancy occurs. In addition, IFS played a supportive role in the development of Families First, a program of intensive in-home mental health services to prevent placement of a child.

Case Management. Case management at IFS shares many features with case management at other study sites: an emphasis on personal relationships, small caseloads (about 20), and a holistic approach to services. More unusual features of the case management approach include:

1. While other programs may reach out to the whole family from a primary client (such as the teen mother), IFS is explicitly *family-oriented*.

2. Besides functioning as counselors, brokers, and advocates, IFS case managers are *conveners*, bringing together multiple service deliverers who may be involved with a family and assisting them to develop a common vision of the family's needs. According to Stahl, it "isn't productive" to aim for a single case management system for these families; rather, the aim is to enable existing systems, with their special populations and special expertise, to work together for the whole family.

3. One reason for the IFS case managers' credibility in this role is their position *inside the state DHS system*. This position reportedly gives them clout with service delivery agencies and, sometimes, with clients. For

example, a service deliverer in the schools said that she took the IFS case manager with her to see a mother who was not sending her child to school, and the mother responded well for the first time because "just his presence [alone] has power."

4. Participation in IFS is *voluntary* both for the client and for the agency: That is, IFS is allowed to select those clients it wants to serve and believes it can help and families are free to accept or decline involvement at any time in the process.

5. From what we could tell, IFS provides an interesting *mixed strategy for targeting* families with limited resources: There is considerable local discretion, but at least some sites appear to mix intensive case management to very needy families with simpler referral services for less needy families, while at the same time working to improve the community network of services for all families. Among the reported characteristics of the IFS caseload statewide are a history of alcohol or substance abuse, domestic violence or a history of physical abuse, depression, a "lack of role modeling" for adults now trying to be parents, and, in the case of the "new poor," recent financial catastrophe.

6. The strategy for recruiting families relies on a *personal referral network* (for example, conferences between the IFS case manager and the AFDC worker about what families might benefit from IFS) but not necessarily on personal contacts with the families themselves.

Community Capacity Building. The IFS approach to community capacity building involves several features:

1. IFS case managers make a substantial *up-front time commitment* to gaining knowledge about community services and credibility with service deliverers. Early in the development of an IFS site, case managers are expected to set up an Automated Resource Directory, a process that increases both their knowledge and their credibility.

2. Both IFS case managers and service deliverers in their communities emphasize the extent of *face-to-face personal contact* involved in the approach. An IFS case manager said he initially wondered why the state required him to set up a Community Council (a regular gathering of local service deliverers) when he talked on the phone to other service deliverers every day. Now he's glad, however, because "face-to-face is different."

3. IFS case managers work hard to learn *what they can do for other service deliverers*: for example, provide the automated resource directory, offer posters, or supply information. Two workers made an analogy between building links with service deliverers and building links with families on their caseloads: "We did the same thing then with the resource people that we now do with families. We assess their strengths, their needs; we share."

4. The IFS approach means that "everybody gets to keep their own system": IFS *supports rather than substitutes for* the case managers who

serve specific, categorical populations. Occasionally, however, the result of this philosophy is that a service deliverer in another system may wonder, as did one child protective worker, "What do they [IFS case managers] do?"

The effects of IFS on community service delivery were reported by individuals whom we interviewed, both outside and inside IFS, to be quite impressive. The reported results included a new level of information on the part of service deliverers about each others' services and about individual families; improved relationships and reduced "red tape" among service deliverers; some change in attitudes toward families; and a wide variety of spin-off programs initiated in response to IFS's mandate to identify and respond to gaps in community services. In addition to the three spin-off programs described above as services to children, other initiatives about which we heard included several cross-agency training programs for staff, a new model of preemployment training for children, and a program staffed by volunteers to help families with budgeting. In the case of the Families First program, IFS not only identified the need but also helped provide the political clout to gain resources from the state legislature by documenting that 200 families could use the service.

Challenges

1. A key challenge for the future relates to *program scale*: Can IFS obtain funding to move from a small number of sites to statewide services over the next few years, and will it be able to maintain the same level of county and caseworker flexibility as it does so?

2. For other jurisdictions considering the adoption of IFS, another challenge may be *gaining political support for a freestanding program* of family services that is not linked to the existing categorical programs. While services like those of IFS could perhaps be funded by the Family Support Act's case management provision or some medical provisions, Oklahoma has chosen not to seek such categorical funds in order to retain flexibility in program operation.

SAN DIEGO, CALIFORNIA: THE GAIN TEEN PARENT PROJECT

Collaboration from the Bottom Up and from the Top Down

Introduction. The most distinctive feature of the GAIN Teen Parent Project is the mix of service delivery–level collaboration by case managers and administrative collaboration by higher-level officials. Operated by the county of San Diego Department of Social Services (DSS), the project assigns selected caseworkers from GAIN (Greater Avenues for Independence), California's welfare-to-work program, to work with pregnant and parenting AFDC teenagers.

Like the case managers in the other teen programs (TAPP and TASA Next Step), the GAIN teen specialists try to develop personal relationships with the teens that will enable them to address underlying issues of self-esteem at the same time that they assist teens to attain specific goals such as school completion and self-sufficiency. Unlike case managers in the other teen programs, however, the GAIN teen specialists are part of a large public agency with a legislative mandate that is specific about the steps a young woman should take to attain education, employment, and economic self-sufficiency. One teen specialist, when asked if this situation required bending the rules, responded, "Not really bending them but being creative." At the same time, the GAIN teen specialists bring with them the advantages, as well as the disadvantages, of association with a large public agency: In particular, they have the resources to pay for child care and transportation, which fill the major gaps seen by the community-based case managers who work with the same teen parent population.

At the service delivery level, we were struck on our site visit by the way in which the GAIN Teen Parent Project fits in as one component of a community network of services to AFDC teenagers and their children. GAIN teen specialists may fund child care for girls whose primary case manager is at a community agency: most likely, the San Diego Adolescent Pregnancy and Parenting Program (SANDAPP). Or, they may take on primary case management responsibility for a girl whom SANDAPP is unable to serve due to an overload of cases: According to an agreement worked out at a meeting of the program directors, SANDAPP keeps the younger and more at-risk teens but may refer older teens to GAIN. Similarly, teens receiving health-oriented case management through a special program at the University of California at San Diego (UCSD) Medical Center Teen OB clinic may be referred to GAIN for child care or other employability-related services. The Teen OB clinic, in turn, has provided in-service training in adolescent development to GAIN staff. According to the director of the Teen OB program, the relationship among the directors of the three programs (GAIN Teen Parent Project, SANDAPP, and Teen OB), having been bolstered by regular meetings, is "much stronger than simply referrals [and] . . . much more personal."

At the administrative level, the program fits the long-standing interest of the DSS director at the time of the site visit, Richard W. Jacobsen, in collaboration among agencies. Jacobsen has worked with top administrators of the county, the city, the San Diego Unified School District (the largest of some 40 school districts in San Diego County), and the San Diego Community College District on a collaboration project called New Beginnings. While the Teen Parent Project did not grow directly out of New Beginnings, the interest in collaboration of top DSS and school officials clearly contributed to its development. According to Marilyn

Stewart, the chief of GAIN Operations and also the founder and manager of the Teen Parent Project, the director's "advance work" with the school system led to collaboration with SANDAPP (which is technically housed in the school system), and thus to the Teen Parent Project, when the SANDAPP coordinator came to her and "started talking teens."

Background. San Diego County adjoins Mexico and has experienced considerable recent immigration from Asia and the Pacific Islands. According to service deliverers interviewed during the site visit, the poor teenagers served through the programs come from many different backgrounds: Besides both black and white teens born in the United States, many of the girls are recent immigrants from Mexico, Central America, Southeast Asia, Samoa, and the Philippines.

The county of San Diego Department of Social Services administers the GAIN program along with welfare (AFDC and other public assistance programs), child protective services, adult protective services, and community action partnerships. The GAIN program, which was enacted in 1985 and implemented in San Diego in October 1987, is California's program to provide job search, education, and training services to welfare recipients. GAIN is a mandatory program for many recipients, but at the time of our visit (before the shift to the new eligibility rules of the JOBS program), the teenagers served by the teen specialists were voluntary enrollees because their children were younger than age six.

Goals. In the first year of the Teen Parent Project, a key goal for Stewart was to build credibility and referral links with the other agencies that form the community network. Her advice to other jurisdictions is to make sure that linkages to other agencies are taken care of first in carrying out a new program.

Even after that first step, effective collaboration continues to be a key goal for her and for the project. For example, she reported that since the site visit, she has found a new way to link services to the schools through work with the Student Attendance Review Board, which deals with youth who have serious attendance problems. In another current project, she is meeting with both the schools and the Private Industry Council with the aim of setting up an alternative school with on-site child care. In addition, she reported that a key Teen Parent Project achievement over the summer was the first Teen Parent Summerfest, which was an opportunity to keep the teens engaged and also broadened the base of community support for the project beyond the schools and service delivery agencies to include private employers and the local radio and television stations. When asked why she is so committed to bringing in other organizations, she said she was "throwing a net around" the teens: "We can't be with them all the time, the schools can't—we need a tight team."

At the service delivery level, key goals for the teen specialists are to identify eligible teens and bring them into the program, to enable teens to complete high school, and to build supportive personal relationships with them. At the same time, the mandate for case managers under GAIN is to provide employment-related counseling, not personal counseling, and the GAIN legislation provides a step-by-step process for reaching employment goals that seems at variance with the more individualized process that would grow out of a case management relationship. At both the administrative and the case manager levels, staff seem to feel that these two approaches can often be reconciled through a variety of informal arrangements. For example, one teen specialist reported that when one of her teens graduates from high school, she agrees informally with the leader of the Job Club (the next step required of that teen by the GAIN legislation) that the teen will benefit from Job Club as a learning experience before going on to further training but would not benefit from taking a job immediately. ("These are special clients—please teach them all you can about looking for a job.") Further, while children are not officially part of the GAIN mission, the teen specialist with the most experience in the program defined success in terms of the future of a little boy whose mother is on her caseload: Success for her would be if child grows up to be happy, healthy, and "able to break the cycle."

However, several less experienced teen specialists did express some uncertainty about their purposes. One told of trying repeatedly and unsuccessfully to make contact with a teen and wondered how to define the limits of her job: "It's as if I had four or five cases. [I'm] wondering—is this the amount of work for every [teen] case? How can we handle it? I don't see how I could feel good about doing this job if I had a lot of these cases, because I would feel I needed to keep calling, keep seeing them."

Services to Children and Families. GAIN funds child care for the children of the teens while they are in school (or, in a few cases, in other GAIN components such as employment and training programs). In addition, the Teen Parent Project offers a number of other services for the children of the teens, either directly or through well-developed referral links. Directly, the teen specialists offer a support group for the GAIN teens, which had just started at the time of our site visit. At the enthusiastically received first meeting, the teens expressed considerable interest in sessions on parenting and child development. (Since the site visit, additional support groups have been added addressing issues such as parenting, health care, substance abuse, goal setting, and relationships within the family.)

As in IFS, another important service to children comes from the informal relationship between the teen and her case manager. In particular, the SANDAPP case managers have training in observing children with an eye to child development and parent-child interactions. They reported noticing problems with child development and referring the child to a health care provider; they also reported very frequent interactions with the teens and their mothers around child development and parenting. According to one case manager, "Our job is to help mother understand child development: no, your baby will not walk at four months, and no, you cannot give her table food for her to put in her mouth, even if your mother says that."

At the other two programs, the program directors reported an interest in training case managers and other providers to more fully observe child development and parent-child interactions. According to the director of Teen OB: "If the baby is in trouble medically, we notice . . . [but] we don't know if he's developing emotionally and socially[,] . . . if he's being stimulated[, or] . . . if they're reading to him."

Case Management and the Case Managers. At the San Diego site, we were able to interview two different sets of case managers, the GAIN teen specialists and the SANDAPP community-based case managers. With different histories, organizational roles, legislative mandates, and staff characteristics, the two programs practiced somewhat different styles of case management although with some similar themes.

The Teen Parent Project was still evolving at the time we visited, with several teen specialists having been added to the program very recently. Among the important characteristics of case management by the teen specialists:

1. The teen specialists are generally *experienced in the DSS system* (often having worked as eligibility workers or child protective services workers before they became GAIN workers), and they are all *committed volunteers* to the Teen Parent Project. Some also have volunteer experience or an academic background in working with children or adolescents. Because Stewart had no extra positions available to hire teen specialists, she asked for volunteers from among her current GAIN social workers and tried to identify those who had the experience and talent to become teen specialists. She was not able to give them a salary increase and was, in her words, "only able to promise them more work."

2. *Caseloads for the teen specialists are high* (at the time of the site visit, close to the San Diego GAIN average of 100), and all carry mixed caseloads of teens and adults (ranging from 60 teens to 2 or 3). By redirecting the assignment of new cases, Stewart eventually hoped to reduce caseload size to about 80 and create specialized, all-teen caseloads. (In the short run, however, this hope may not be achievable. Since our visit, budget constraints, combined with civil service rules, have forced the reassignment of some teen specialists out of the GAIN program.)

3. Despite these difficulties, *teen specialists reported loving the job* for the personal contact and sense of achievement: "I love working with the girls. I was a happy teenager, and I . . . would like to see all the young girls that I work with lead happy and fruitful lives." "I absolutely love it. It's

been my life goal to get this job. It's everything I ever thought it would be.''

4. Despite the constraints posed by their caseloads, workers aim for a *trusting personal relationship* with the teens that includes, but goes beyond, employment and educational issues. One teen specialist reported that her first conversation with a teen generally covers the expected school graduation date and child care, but that issues about boyfriends often come up too, and she makes many referrals for counseling on relationship issues.

5. At the same time, other agencies see *the special contribution of GAIN in help with child care and vocational decisions,* with personal support more often coming from other sources. Most of the examples clients gave us of assistance from GAIN case managers related in some way to these core areas (for example, advice to go to summer school full time rather than try to combine school and work), though one young woman was very enthusiastic about the Teen Support Group and its focus on self-esteem.

6. Despite the demands of a high caseload, case managers reported *visiting the teens at home and being flexible* enough to run errands with them and make time available to lead the teen support group.

The SANDAPP case managers, while they are organizationally located in the San Diego Unified School System (reporting to the head of the school nurses), have a community-based mission and approach. Among the key characteristics of case management as they conceive it:

1. The *community-based* mission of the SANDAPP case managers is reflected in their racial and ethnic diversity, in professional backgrounds that include community advocacy as well as health and social services experience, and in an image of themselves as "going into the battlefield," where even "the police won't go without back-up."

2. *Caseloads are lower than for the GAIN teen specialists* but higher than in some other intensive case management programs: Workers are supposed to carry about 35 cases, but some have more than 50.

3. Their relationship with the teens is *intense, personal, and at times almost parental*. Case managers report that teens "take us as family" and "call us before they call their parents."

4. At the same time, case managers are *alert to the danger of losing perspective*, of trying inappropriately to substitute for family, or of becoming a "crutch" rather than a support for independence. When one case manager "got out of rhythm" and fell into the role of father, he relied on the program coordinator to pull him back.

5. To support the personal relationship, case managers are extremely *flexible* and open to seeing the teens at all times and places: at school, at the office, at their homes, in a Burger King restaurant, or in the park. They take the teens to museums, restaurants, the beach, both in formally organized group trips and informally one-on-one.

6. The counseling relationship between case manager and teen often requires *defusing deep anger or coping with severe depression* on the teen's part. The teens have often experienced violence and sexual abuse. As a result, a trusting relationship may develop slowly and key information may come out only over a period of many months.

7. The case management is *family-oriented*: Case managers develop strong personal relationships, not only with the teen, but with her child, siblings, parents, and in some cases, her partner. Says one case manager, "I end up case managing the family." The mother of a teen on her caseload had just asked her to case manage the teen's emotionally disturbed younger sibling, saying, "I see what you do for my daughter—can you do something for him?"

8. Case management is intended to be *short- to medium-term*, with a goal of self-sufficiency—defined not in terms of financial self-sufficiency but in terms of being able to work the system independently. Case managers will close a case when the teen is in school, keeping health appointments for herself and her child, tied in with GAIN or other child care arrangements, and in general, relatively stable.

9. The case managers say they rely tremendously on *skilled supervision, teamwork, and regular training* to gain the knowledge and the emotional support that they need to work with this population. The diverse backgrounds of the case managers mean that they bring different perspectives to regular case conferences and frequent informal discussions; they see the team as a "family" and emphasize their own mix of "maturity" (all are over 40) and "childlike" qualities. The program coordinator, a Ph.D.-level nurse, meets with the case managers regularly for individual case conferences, and her staff describe her as "loving, terrific." They add that she has a "photographic memory" and warn, "if you get dull, she'll sharpen you."

Collaboration. Administrators at San Diego DSS suggest that several principles make the Teen Parent Project and other collaborations with community service providers work effectively.

1. Behind collaboration at the service delivery level is a *commitment from the top.* The DSS director reported that he has found that when the principals have a strong relationship, problems lower down in the organization can be "kicked upstairs" if necessary—and most likely this will not need to be done. Similarly, a human services administrator outside DSS sees her strong relationship with Stewart as crucial to solving any problems that might come up in serving teens at the case manager level, where from time to time, "it's easy to become possessive of clients."

2. DSS administrators *see community linkages as a high priority, that is worth considerable time and attention.* Stewart identified the Teen Parent Project's reputation in the community as the proudest achievement of the Project's first year, and she continues to allocate time to work with outside providers and community agencies.

3. DSS staff have made a conscious effort *to identify and try to meet the needs of other community partners*, in particular the schools. At the political level, the DSS director testified before the school board in favor of a school health clinic proposal that the superintendent believed was important. It had been defeated once before but passed this time. At the program level, DSS administrators hope that not only the teen parent specialists but also new GAIN education specialists will help the schools keep students attending, which will improve the average daily attendance tallies that drive school funding. According to one DSS administrator, one reason for DSS's determination to serve voluntary GAIN participants is its interest in supplementing the schools' efforts by funding child care for teens with very young children when the school-based child care slots are full.

Challenges. In the first year of the Teen Parent Project, the key challenges were to get the program up and running with no additional funds and to develop credibility with the community agencies that serve teens. Now that these goals have been accomplished, future challenges include:

1. *Staff training and supervision*: The teen specialists reported tremendous commitment to and enthusiasm for their work, but they felt some need for additional skills to be able to do it well. Said one teen specialist, "I'm going basically on my own childhood" in figuring out how to relate to the teens.

2. *Relations with the eligibility function*: At the time of our visit, the Teen Parent Project had quite limited links with the welfare eligibility division of DSS, in part because of the view of DSS administrators that eligibility workers were overburdened. For example, eligibility workers generally did not know about the project and did not refer teens. Instead, AFDC teens reached the teen specialists by referral from other community service providers (such as SANDAPP, school nurses, or the Teen OB clinic) or through a mailing to all teen heads of households on the AFDC caseload. However, program administrators were planning to start a pilot project in one of the smaller offices that would give eligibility workers a lead role in referral.

DETROIT, MICHIGAN: EARHART—FORT WAYNE—JACKSON—CONNER-WARREN DROPOUT PREVENTION PROGRAM

The Welfare Department in the Schools

Introduction. Since June 1988, the Wayne County (Detroit) Department of Social Services (DSS), under Director Lilly Tabor, has operated a dropout prevention program in two middle schools for AFDC children identified by the schools as in danger of dropping out. According to Tabor, the program was prompted by concerns about the Learnfare program proposed (and since implemented) by the neighboring state of Wisconsin, a program that reduces a family's AFDC grant if a child drops out of school. Tabor and Patrick Babcock, the Michigan State DSS director, started to talk about an alternative approach that would work with families before the child dropped out rather than punishing them afterwards. They began to write and talk to school officials about the idea in the summer of 1987 and got an interested response by the beginning of 1988. Planning was complicated by the fact that the schools were anticipating layoffs of teachers and school social workers, but the program nonetheless began about six months later, in June 1988.

A year after the site visit, Tabor reported that the program was "more and more exciting all the time," with expansion to two more schools occurring as scheduled in the fall of 1990. For the planned expansion, the school system committed its own staff for the first time, assigning two school social workers to counsel families and children and a person in the superintendent's office to coordinate the effort.

Under the program, DSS workers are assigned to the schools to work with children who are identified as being at risk of dropping out. The exact content of their work varies from school to school, but in general they provide activities for the children, such as field trips, group and individual counseling sessions, and tutoring; make home visits to talk with the parents; refer both children and families to various services; and work with teachers and counselors at the schools on behalf of the children.

Program reports from the 1988–1989 school year indicate that 34 of 55 children served at the two schools, or nearly two-thirds, improved their attendance. At the Jackson School, 94 percent of the students were promoted and all of those in the eighth grade group graduated. At Earhart, 6 of 23 students were named to the honor roll. (These statistics probably do not include children who did not stay with the program for the whole year.)

Goals. The goal most clearly articulated for the program by its originator, and measured in the administrative reports, is to improve school attendance, performance, and graduation rates. The case managers clearly focus on these themes: For example, one worker capped a success story about a withdrawn child who now has friends and is motivated to succeed by reporting that he missed 55 days of school the previous year and only 13 last year.

At the same time, however, the case managers clearly see themselves as approaching these academic goals by way of emotional support for the children. When asked what is the most important thing they do, workers in a focus group identified "support for the child." They saw this support as a role that was missing from the children's lives, both in their families and in other institutions:

One of the most important things that we do is to give the kids personal attention. Because they don't get it from the school, their parents, their relatives or anybody.

We are like an extended family, because for most of them, for one reason or another, their families are not functioning.

Workers expressed somewhat mixed feelings about their goals in relation to the students' families. Some felt that many parents were not supportive of the children and that they could not influence the parents, so they had to be content with teaching the child to "cope": "One of our main goals is to try to give kids coping skills. It would be a crock to say we are going to make this a coping family." Other workers, however, do see themselves working with parents: "We find that we become parents to their parents. . . . Because their parents don't know what they are supposed to do . . . so we get to the point where we have to counsel them too." In working with parents, the goals include improving parents' ability to deal with school officials (to "stand up for your child"), improving their relations with the child, increasing their sense of responsibility for the child's education (such as persuading a mother not to keep a child home for the mother's convenience), and, in some cases, helping parents meet their own needs through referrals to various programs (such as GED programs).

At the administrative level, Tabor's goals for the program include stimulating broader collaboration with the schools on behalf of "all the kids." For example, she is particularly proud that planning for the expansion to two new middle schools is leading to discussion of the elementary schools that feed into them—a discussion that uncovered the fact that one feeder school has no playground. She reported that DSS may be able to send clients in its employment and training program over to landscape a playground.

Services to Children and Families. The two schools have developed slightly different program models, but both include a range of services for the children and their families. Structured activities offered by one or the other program include an after-school tutoring program at which the dropout prevention workers help students with homework and basic academic skills (Jackson School); frequent field trips, ranging from outings to movies and restaurants to motivational trips to a college (both schools); parenting groups for the students' mothers and fathers (offered as part of the program at Earhart and by referral at Jackson); and group discussions touching on personal and career topics of interest to the students (Earhart). The program is also able to fund a number of school-related expenses: school clothes, bus fare, and, in at least one case, glasses. One of the programs also reported buying all the students alarm clocks and dictionaries.

In addition, the workers use their knowledge of DSS and other programs to provide a wide variety of services through referrals. For example, workers reported trying to arrange guardianship for a 14-year-old whose mother was on drugs, making a Child Protective Services referral for a 12-year-old who was in her eighth month of pregnancy and had received no prenatal care (and taking her in for care), referring parents for GED classes and job training, referring a mother and her two daughters for joint counseling, and referring a younger sibling to a Head Start program. They also report that students often ask for drug rehabilitation help for their mothers.

As in other sites, however, workers see the most important services as growing out of the case management relationship between the dropout prevention worker and the student. Workers provide personal counseling, support, and advice to the students on their caseload, whom they see regularly at school and on home visits.

Case Management and the Case Managers. The case managers are employees of DSS who have volunteered for this assignment. The backgrounds of those to whom we talked included Child Protective Services, Michigan Opportunity and Skills Training (Michigan's employment and training program for welfare recipients), and Assistance Payments (welfare eligibility). Workers reported varied backgrounds, some with and others without training in counseling or human services. Caseloads are kept very low to allow for the intensive involvement with students and families: about 20 students per worker.

The approach to personalized case management has many features in common with other sites. Features that are different include:

1. Workers serve *as advocates for the students in the schools.* They explain to teachers the family circumstances of individual children, and in some cases, they appear to have requested changes in school procedures: For example, they asked teachers in one school to provide regular progress reports to indicate how the children are doing.

2. They work to *empower parents to deal with the schools* on behalf of their children. Said one worker, "These parents are so intimidated by the school system that you actually have to say, 'OK, if you don't believe that your child did wrong, then you speak up for your child, and I'll be here to support you.'"

3. To build trust with parents and to solve the real problems that prevent students from attending school, *workers provide help from time to time in negotiating the welfare portion* of the DSS bureaucracy. For example, they figure out how to get extra benefits for families (for example, money to pay the electric bill) and set up appointments for mothers with their eligibility workers.

4. Tabor deliberately gave workers *considerable latitude to invent their own approach*. She reported some initial nervousness from workers who were

used to referring to a manual, but the workers who were eventually recruited into the program found this creative opportunity to be an advantage. According to one worker, "When there are no guidelines—that's my kind of game. This is the first positive job experience I've had working for this agency."

Collaboration. One of the unusual features of this program is clearly its relationship to the schools: Social workers from the welfare department work in the schools carrying out tasks that might be seen as belonging to school personnel. Several features of this relationship stand out:

1. From the beginning, the DSS approach has been *to identify needs of the schools and try to meet them.* For example, the program has helped the schools get families to enroll children on time, as required for state funding. In another example, program staff reported making a home visit to check on a case where school staff were worried about child neglect but did not feel confident enough to file a report with CPS. And a school counselor reported that DSS helps him because the DSS workers can make home visits, which he does not have time to do, and because they can get money for food and clothing.

2. *Demands on the schools in the early stages were limited* to providing a referral list of students and providing space for the DSS workers. However, by the summer of 1990, two years after the program began, the school system chose to commit staff for coordination, evaluation, and direct-service social work.

3. During our site visit, DSS caseworkers reported some evidence that their approach *was starting to influence school procedures for at-risk youngsters.* Caseworkers reported on a building principal who decided to work together with all the sixth-graders who were at risk of failing because she thought that the group approach and special attention offered by the caseworkers were working well. At a broader policy level, caseworkers reported that one school was changing its policy from suspension to in-school detention as a disciplinary measure; while the caseworkers had not suggested this change to the school, they thought that their experiences with children who were simply lost to the educational system after they left school for a suspension might have influenced the decision.

4. From the perspective of effective service delivery to children and families, the site illustrates several possible *advantages of providing school-based family services through workers employed by DSS*: their potential role as advocates for students within the school system, their knowledge of the DSS system, and the potentially greater financial resources of statewide welfare agencies compared to local school systems.

5. One *possible disadvantage of this arrangement,* compared to offering the services through social workers employed by the schools, is that *only AFDC children are eligible.* However, workers in the Detroit site reported that there was no stigma to the program, that children not on AFDC

wanted to come to the group activities, and that they included such children informally from time to time.

Challenges. Remaining challenges faced by this unusual program at the time we visited included:

1. *Training and capacity of dropout prevention workers:* At the time of the site visit, the director reported an interest in providing workers with more skills to carry out the new job, and in particular, the counseling component. At the expansion sites, this need will be at least partially addressed by the assignment of Master's of Social Work–level school social workers to take on more in-depth counseling needs uncovered by the DSS workers.

2. *Expansion:* At the time of the site visit, the program operated on a very small scale (two middle schools and about 60 children). A year later, it was scheduled to expand to two more schools. The challenge will be to move to a larger scale with the same flexibility in spending and staff recruitment and the same individualized relationships with the schools.

3. *Child versus family focus:* As the program develops, staff may feel a need to address more explicitly their relationship with the students' parents: How far should workers go to address the parents' needs, how should they see their role in relation to the parent, and under what circumstances (if any) should they be prepared to give up on support from the parent and work only with the child?

4. *Retention:* While the evidence we gathered was not completely clear, it does seem that a number of students who enroll at the beginning of the year are lost to the program before the end, either because they simply stop coming or because of administrative actions by the schools, such as transfers of children who are seen as disruptive.

ELMIRA, NEW YORK: THE TASA "NEXT STEP" PROGRAM

Community Case Management in a Rich Service Network

Introduction. Through the Next Step program, the New York State Department of Social Services (DSS), the state agency that oversees both welfare and child protective services, funds a community action agency to provide intensive case management to Medicaid-eligible pregnant and parenting teens of Chemung and Schuyler counties. Next Step began as a pilot site for New York State's Teenage Services Act (TASA) in 1986 and is now part of a statewide network of TASA-funded programs. We chose it as a site because it has a particularly strong reputation among TASA programs for leadership, quality of services, and attention to the teen's family, including her children, in addition to the teen herself.

While Next Step's funding relationship is with the state DSS (through Medicaid case management funds), Next Step also has a very strong relationship with the Chemung County DSS commissioner and deputy commissioner. The county DSS administrators encouraged the initial Next Step application for TASA funds because they saw case management services for young mothers as a return to a better, social work–oriented approach to welfare administration. As a result of the program's relationship with the county as well as its "outreach-intensive" approach to case management, Next Step comes very close to its goal of enrolling *all* teens (under 18) who receive AFDC. Consistent with the social work approach, a key reason to enroll teens at the time they apply for AFDC (or Medicaid) is to offer services that might *prevent* the need for foster care and other CPS involvement.

Next Step case managers offer teens a long-term relationship based on extensive informal contact in the teen's home and a philosophy of "unconditional acceptance," which is intended to build the self-esteem of young women who may be socially isolated and caught in abusive relationships. Next Step also offers its teens an extensive program of Family Life Education groups, which include parenting education, parent-child time, and colocated child care. In addition, Next Step serves the teens' children, both informally, through the teen–case manager relationship, and formally, through explicit referrals to a rich network of local maternal-child health services, Head Start, other child care resources, and other social and mental health services.

Background. Chemung County, in New York's Appalachian region, has traditionally had high rates of teen pregnancy and child abuse and neglect along with a weak local economy. At the time of our site visit, the county's small, blue-collar urban center, Elmira, was home to a state maximum-security prison (now, there are two) and, reportedly, to extensive drug trafficking activities via Route 17. Schuyler County is rural and sparsely populated, with isolation, inadequate housing, and lack of transportation as particular problems.

At the same time, Chemung County is the home of a nationally known network of maternal and child health services, known as Comprehensive Interdisciplinary Developmental Services (CIDS). Under CIDS, a program known at the time of our visit as the Maternal-Infant Support Program (MISP) provides home visits during pregnancy and early infancy to high-risk mothers, and the Infant Registry Program enrolls almost all children born in Chemung County into a program of hospital and home visits to provide developmental assessments and service referral. Since our visit, MISP has returned to its original name, Prenatal and Early Infancy Program (PEIP), in order to signal a return to the low caseloads and intensive services that it offered in its original, demonstration form. In that original form, evaluations found that PEIP improved parental care giving and mothers' employment.[1]

The program coordinator and founder of Next Step, Maryann Bryant, helped to found CIDS in 1972. Working through a nonprofit community-based organization, the Economic Opportunity Program (EOP), she went on to develop group activities for teens under a 1983 WIN contract. Still at EOP, she added the one-on-one case management component that created Next Step in response to the interest of local DSS officials in applying to be a pilot project under the TASA legislation. Local human services administrators reported that Bryant's personal reputation and longstanding involvement in the service system are key to the successful operation of Next Step. One administrator noted that the whole county network of services has benefited from a core group of people who have stayed long enough to learn to work together: Of the five major human services organizations, he reported that four of the leaders have been in their roles about 20 years each.

Goals. Next Step staff universally hold the view that developing self-esteem is the teens' first and most important step toward improving their long-term prospects. The most important thing TASA does for teens, according to a case manager, is to promote self-worth and encourage teens to believe in themselves. Bryant argued that "if you believe that [in your own worth], you'll get your high school diploma." These teens are used to being "spit out" by the system and need long-term and unconditional warmth and acceptance in order to improve their lives. According to Next Step staff, nurturing the teens is also crucial to serving their children, because it gives them a model for parenting.

More concretely, case managers focus on meeting the basic needs of the teens and their families—medical care, food, shelter, and physical safety. They strive to enable the teens to care for their children well enough to avoid CPS referrals and foster care placements, or to bring children back from foster care. In addition, in many cases, but not all, case managers emphasize completing high school: However, because of the painful experiences some of the teens have had with school and because of the reportedly high incidence of mentally retarded and learning disabled teens on the caseload, case managers feel that some young women cannot succeed in the school program and would be hurt by a further experience of failure.

Next Step staff regard "self-sufficiency" as a complex, very long-term, and sometimes unrealistic goal for their clients: "This population has a broken spirit. You can't fix a broken spirit in six months, even a year." "There are things more basic in life than financial self-sufficiency." "I rarely think about . . . self-sufficiency but more in terms of meeting basic needs, quality of life, self-worth, completing high school." One case manager thought that about 60 percent of her caseload could achieve self-sufficiency; for the rest, she wants them "to be the best they can" but believes that "best" will always involve financial support from the system. For example, she had just that day seen a mentally retarded teen with a 21-year-old partner who has not been able to hold a long-term job because of his temper; she believes the couple will always be "system-dwellers." For those teens who can eventually become self-sufficient, Next Step case managers believe a long-term process is crucially important: Bryant argued that parents typically support middle-class youngsters emotionally and financially through at least the early twenties, and these teens deserve the same. The program's eligibility criteria support this goal by enabling the program to keep young women until they turn 21, although they must be under 18 at the time of enrollment (this was raised to under 19 at enrollment for 1990).

Finally, besides their goals for the teens, case managers hold clear and carefully measured goals for themselves, focusing on outreach and on the intensity and quality of service delivery. The regular monitoring reports, besides tracking outcomes such as enrollment in education and employment, pay close attention to enrollment as a percent of eligible referrals (the figure consistently exceeds 85–90 percent even though the program is voluntary), the number of "effective visits" (visits at which the teen is home) as a percent of home visits conducted, and the percent of referrals with positive outcomes, meaning that the teen actually received the service.

Services to Children and Families. For Next Step staff, children are an inseparable part of the caseload. They place a high priority on making sure that teens get prenatal care as well as ongoing maternal and child health care through CIDS, and they work with the MISP (now PEIP) nurse if they have a health or developmental concern. For child care, they work closely with the local child care resource and referral agency, and they refer children directly to Head Start (administered by EOP, the same umbrella agency that houses Next Step) when they are old enough— often this occurs as the young women are turning 21 and becoming ineligible for Next Step. They help teens apply for WIC, housing subsidies, and other survival services, and they may try to create new services for families with particularly complex needs. For example, in a recent case, Next Step staff had to find a place to live for a mentally retarded woman with a two-year-old child who was temporarily housed in a "safe house" for battered women but needed a long-term placement. Since no mental retardation residence would take the woman with her child, they found a woman to take them into her home through a local church.

Case managers also encourage teens to enroll in the group component of Next Step, the Family Life Education (FLE) program, which offers 10-week group sessions with a strong parent education component. In FLE's on-site child care, caretakers keep a log on each child's behavior and appearance: The first sign of success with the teen, according to one of the group leaders, is a child who comes in looking healthier and better groomed. Most of the group sessions include time set aside for parents to be with their children, either to play affectionately or to practice more specific skills. In one session, for example, the group leader encourages parents to "tell them [your children] what you wish your parents had said to you."

Perhaps the most important services for children grow out of the case manager's relationship with the teen. Case managers are able to assess each child's development over time, to answer questions or offer advice, and to model appropriate parenting behavior. Said one case manager, "I pay attention to every child, at least visually."

Case Management and the Case Managers. Key characteristics of Next Step case management include:

1. The *outreach-intensive approach* emphasizes home visits as an approach to recruitment and to developing a relationship after the teen is enrolled. Staff consider such outreach onto the teen's "turf" to be absolutely essential, not only to gain a teen's trust but also to develop a true understanding of her circumstances.

2. Consistent with the goal of increasing self-esteem, a central theme of Next Step case management is a *warm, trusting, almost parental relationship* with the teens.

3. The content of case management is *flexible and personalized.* Case managers emphasize that "this is not a 9-to-5 job." They attend high school graduations, buy alarm clocks, give rides, and respond to emergency calls from teens who may be in jail or in labor.

4. *Low caseloads*, about 30 to 35, make this relationship possible.

5. In her hiring of case managers, Bryant looks for the *right qualities* to make this relationship possible: a mature understanding of self and others, self-confidence and flexibility, relevant experience, and knowledge of adolescent development. Interestingly, all the case managers and family life educators are mothers, and in most cases they have seen their children through adolescence.

6. *Ongoing peer consultation and supervision* take place through regular group meetings and individual case conferences as well as frequent informal conversations to bounce concerns or ideas off each other.

7. A unique characteristic of case management at this site is the *link between individual and group services*. Case managers consult frequently with the family life educators who facilitate the groups, since new information about a teen's situation often comes out there.

8. Both *teamwork and advocacy* characterize case managers' relations with other agencies. Next Step staff are in frequent informal contact with CIDS visiting nurses, CPS workers, welfare eligibility workers, school counselors, and other providers. Bryant identified such constructive relationships as "key, key, key," and said that when it comes to finding services for Next Step clients, "we make it our business to know how to get in through the back door." The case managers sometimes ask for her help on particularly difficult advocacy cases in order to take advantage

of the extensive personal relationships that have grown out of her lifelong involvement in the local service network.

Relationship with the Welfare Department. Next Step is one of very few of the sites to have a successful referral arrangement with the welfare eligibility agency. Whenever a teen comes in to apply for AFDC, the eligibility worker makes an automatic referral, either by introducing the teen on the spot to the Next Step case manager or by writing a referral slip on the teen and placing it in the Next Step mailbox. (The eligibility worker is *not* asked to make a lengthy presentation about Next Step because Next Step does not want teens to refuse on the basis of an account that might be less complete or persuasive than a case manager's personal contact.) On receiving the referral, a Next Step case manager takes over with a letter and home visit to the teen. A case manager is on-site at the welfare office for two hours each day, and although this time does not enable Next Step staff to meet most teens at the point of application, it does improve relations with DSS workers substantially, according to Bryant.

Overall relations between Next Step and both the eligibility and child protective sections of DSS are strong, according to all participants. The deputy commissioner of DSS reported that the Next Step approach fits into her own view that DSS needs to move back toward offering more comprehensive case management services; since it would be impossible to do that for all AFDC recipients, she sees the Next Step approach as making a beginning with teenagers. She is responsible to the state DSS for the oversight of Next Step, which she carries out formally through required reviews of a handful of case files. Most of her contact, however, is informal: She talks with Maryann Bryant as often as once a week and answers questions from the case managers as needed. On the Child Protective Services side, overburdened CPS workers find Next Step case managers helpful: They sometimes ask case managers to keep an eye on families about which they are worried but to which they are unable to pay attention as a result of worse crises among their caseloads.

Next Step case managers, on the other hand, relish their role as "pure support," separate from the child protective services and welfare eligibility systems. One case manager, in her desire to avoid appearing "institutional," never carries a briefcase. Another noted, "I have no attitude. I don't tell the teen what to do." The staff members doubt that welfare eligibility workers could carry out such case management because of their large caseloads, concern with regulations, and financial power over clients.

Challenges. Several challenges face Next Step, both in its own community and in its role as a model site for TASA, which is intended to spur replication in other counties.

1. The school systems in Chemung and Schuyler counties do not yet appear to be fully involved in the human services network for pregnant

and parenting teens, which limits the educational services that case managers can arrange and perhaps the emphasis they can place on education. Possibly, the Family Support Act, with its focus on education, might provide some incentive for the schools to increase their responsiveness to this population.

2. The staff members report uncertainty about whether their approach to the teens is working in at least one area: the prevention of repeat pregnancy. More broadly, before committing to the full Next Step model, other locations might want fuller evidence of the links between a very long-term case management model focusing on self-esteem and actual changes in life outcomes for teens. The existing evaluation evidence on programs for teen mothers is consistent with many elements of the Next Step program model (for example, the personal relationship with the young mothers), but it does not clearly answer the question about the very long-term nature of services.

3. The program relies on a rich local network of services and the personal and professional links between those services which have been established over decades. To move toward this model in other jurisdictions would require sustained attention to creating equivalent networks.

SAN FRANCISCO, CALIFORNIA: THE TAPP/GAIN COLLABORATION

An Experiment in Community Case Management

Introduction. In San Francisco's TAPP/GAIN collaboration, as in the Next Step TASA program, a public welfare agency teamed up with a community-based organization to provide intensive case management to pregnant and parenting teens. In the case of TAPP/GAIN, the community-based organization was the Teen-Age Pregnancy and Parenting (TAPP) Program, a partnership between the nonprofit Family Services Agency (FSA) and the San Francisco Unified School District (SFUSD) that has been providing services to teenagers in San Francisco since 1981. The public welfare agency was the San Francisco Department of Social Services (DSS), which delivers both welfare and child protective services and also administers GAIN (Greater Avenues for Independence), California's education, training, and employment program for welfare recipients. (The partnership between GAIN and TAPP was part of a broader effort to serve AFDC teens, which included other community agencies that had expertise in serving teens who are not parents; however, in keeping with the focus on services to children, I will discuss only the services through TAPP to teen parents and their children.)

In 1988, DSS and TAPP began negotiations about a contract through which TAPP would provide case management services for pregnant and parenting teens who were on AFDC and therefore eligible to enroll voluntarily in GAIN. (More specifically, the contract was to be between DSS and SFUSD, with a subcontract from SFUSD to TAPP.) Besides contracting with TAPP for case management, DSS would be able to pay for child care, transportation, and training programs for the teens through GAIN funds. Joint operations under the new contract began in the spring of 1989, a few months before our August site visit, and ended in the summer of 1990 as a result (according to administrators) of statewide GAIN funding cuts and institutional friction.

TAPP Services and Case Management. In a number of ways, case management in TAPP is similar to case management in TASA Next Step. TAPP administrators and case managers see a strong personal relationship with the teen as key to program effectiveness, and they strive to maintain each worker's caseload at no more than 35 to make that relationship more possible. (In fact, the case managers are officially called "continuous counselors" to highlight their ongoing relationship with the teens while other services come and go.) The case management approach is intended to be completely flexible and holistic, with the counselor remaining free to assess and meet whatever needs the teen may have. The program director recruits carefully to identify case managers with the right skills, though in contrast to TASA Next Step, she recruits only from master's degree-level social workers and counselors, reflecting her view that professional education is key to counseling this population effectively. Finally, besides building relationships with the teens, counselors are expected to search actively for the services to meet teens' needs, negotiate effectively for access to those services, and advocate, sometimes passionately, on behalf of the teens.

An interesting feature of TAPP case management that is different from TASA Next Step is the extensive network of formal interagency agreements and colocation arrangements that supports the continuous counselors in their efforts to identify teens and link them to services. One example among more than 50 interagency agreements is the agreement with San Francisco General Hospital (SFGH), which commits TAPP to provide a liaison worker to attend intake meetings of the Teen OB Clinic and enroll teens and commits SFGH to provide access to medical charts, office space, and medical advice as needed. Other linkages of particular importance to the children of TAPP teens include the outstationing of a TAPP counselor at the hospital's clinic for high-risk infants, an agreement with the city's public health clinics to provide each TAPP teen with the opportunity to receive home visits from a public health nurse during her pregnancy and her child's infancy, and an agreement with the Golden Gate Regional Center, which sends a staffer to TAPP intake meetings to identify any teens whose infants or toddlers are at high risk developmentally for follow-up home visits. One explanation for this formal network might be that creating an effective service delivery network in a community as large as San Francisco may simply take more formal structure than in the smaller community of Elmira—although personal relationships and a long history of working together are cited in San Francisco, as they were in Elmira, as an explanation for the success of the TAPP network.

Alone among our study sites, TAPP has been evaluated for its effect on outcomes. According to an evaluation published in 1989, the TAPP network of services has a significant positive effect on birth weights of infants born to teens in the program: Participation in TAPP was associated with an increase in birth weight of 114 grams.[2]

Collaboration. At the time we visited, early in the development of the TAPP/GAIN collaboration, several issues remained to be worked out. For example:

- *Referral:* Teens to be served by the collaboration reached TAPP from its usual referral sources and were then identified as GAIN-eligible. There were no arrangements for referral to TAPP from eligibility workers or GAIN workers within DSS.

- *Different conceptions of mission:* TAPP workers wanted to serve adolescents separately from adults, to operate flexibly based on their own sense of what would be best for the client, and to obtain as many services as possible for their clients. For example, TAPP wanted to operate Job Clubs separately for teenagers rather than asking the teens to join adult groups already contracted for by GAIN, and to fund child care during enrollment in a four-year college. DSS administrators saw TAPP/GAIN in the context both of program rules that had to be applied consistently to teens and adults and of constrained resources.

- *Mechanism for problem resolution:* Both TAPP and GAIN staff expressed some frustration with current approaches to resolving disagreements, approaches that relied heavily on formal channels and public forums such as legislative hearings.

While we hoped at the time when we visited that these issues would be resolved, and although we saw evidence on both sides of a commitment to resolve them, we were not surprised to hear a year later that the contract had been dissolved in the face of statewide cutbacks in GAIN funding. One DSS administrator reported that she hopes to be able to come back to the teen population, and perhaps to this approach, at some time in the future.

MASSACHUSETTS: ET CHOICES/VOUCHER CHILD CARE PROGRAM

The Welfare Department and Child Care

Introduction. The Employment and Training CHOICES (ET CHOICES)/ Voucher Child Care Program is a partnership between the Massachusetts Department of Public Welfare and local nonprofit agencies, called Voucher Management Agencies (VMAs), that specialize in child care resource and referral for AFDC recipients. The VMAs provide AFDC families that are participating in education, training, or employment with assistance in selecting child care from among the array of resources available in the community. The particular VMA we visited, Child Care Circuit (CCC) in the city of Lawrence, also provides child care resource and referral (CCR&R) functions to the general public and works with child care providers to develop the supply of care and to provide training and support. As in the other Massachusetts site (ET CHOICES adult case management), this description reflects the program as it existed at the time of our site visits in the summer and fall of 1990; budgets, staffing, program priorities, and political leadership have changed substantially since then.

At the time of our site visit, ET CHOICES, the Massachusetts employment and training program for welfare recipients, paid for child care for AFDC recipients and former recipients through a voucher payment system for the duration of education or training and for one year after employment. At the time of our site visit (but no longer), the Extended Voucher program continued funding beyond that year if the family continued to be employed but low-income. The administration of the voucher payment system is complex, and the state contracts out financial administration (billing and record keeping) to the VMAs along with recipient assistance.

While this system is not unique—a number of states provided some amount of financial and referral assistance to welfare recipients seeking child care even before passage of the Family Support Act—we selected Massachusetts (and, within Massachusetts, the Child Care Circuit) because of the program's reputation for paying attention to the needs of the child as well as the employment of the parent in counseling parents about child care settings. Statewide administrators reminded us that not all programs are as effective as CCC at preserving time for counseling in the midst of their narrower referral functions.

Services to Children and Families. According to a child care professional who has long observed ET CHOICES child care in Massachusetts, the child development background of counselors in CCR&R agencies like Child Care Circuit substantially affects the nature of their conversations with parents—whether or not on welfare—about child care needs. Instead of focusing only on the logistics of child care, such as the hours or location, she reported that Child Care Circuit counselors are very skilled at eliciting the parent's sense of each child's needs. A Circuit counselor we spoke with gave an example of how she would gain a sense of the child's needs: "We try to get the parent to think about those things, rather than *us* seeing the child and making the evaluation. 'You know your child best. Do you think she's quiet? Would she do better in a smaller setting? Would she get lost in a larger center?'"

In addition, counselors ask specific questions about a child's special health needs that might be relevant to child care. For example, one counselor had just seen a child with a history of asthma who therefore could not go into a family day care home with pets. Counselors also ask about special circumstances such as a history of behavioral problems, but they find, not surprisingly, that parents often prefer not to tell them.

A second important focus of the Circuit counselors in serving children and families is empowering parents to act on behalf of their children. For parents on AFDC, counselors find that empowerment often means developing a parent's self-confidence, which may be very low: "We're the day care pros and the day care center directors and teachers are day care pros, and they're 'just a mom—what do I know about my kid?' We have to re-affirm that 'You know everything about this child.'" Counselors also help mothers gauge which concerns about their children warrant postponing plans for training or employment, and they work with providers to meet the needs of particular children whom providers find difficult. Because the CCC has financial as well as programmatic responsibility for the voucher program, it is able to exercise a certain amount of discretion in resolving these latter cases: For example, if a child care provider wants to expel a child without the usual two weeks' notice because the child bites other children, the CCC can use its authority over the two weeks' funding to make sure that the provider has tried to talk with the mother and work out a solution.

Among more formal activities, the CCC offers programs for providers, some of which are also open to parents, and has recently added programs specifically for parents. CCC counselors also provide referrals to parenting groups and to a variety of social services agencies, and from time to time, they have made referrals to Child Protective Services.

Consistent with their emphasis on parent empowerment, CCC counselors believe strongly in assisting *parents* to assess child care quality but do not believe in telling parents their *own* views about which child care programs provide quality child care. In the counselors' view, it is wrong to substitute their professional assessments for parents' judgment in selecting among licensed programs, even if parents ask. The counselors are able to identify types of programs with which they feel personally uncomfortable, but they feel an obligation to refer parents who are interested to these programs: for example, programs with no content or programming (the counselors note that a parent may say, ''But if he was home, he'd watch soap operas all day'') and programs with very teacher-directed curricula. According to state officials, this philosophy is not universal among VMAs, which differ in their views of whether to develop quality standards beyond licensing.

At the same time that the Circuit's parent counselors serve children and families through counseling, another group of staff, called provider counselors, work on upgrading child care quality through training, loans of equipment and toys, and informal advice about what parents need and want. For example, we heard about a training session on puppet making in which providers would make puppets from CCC-provided materials which they would then be free to take home—a session that was intended to model for providers a creative and relaxed teaching approach that they could then apply to working with children.

Case Management. The parent counselors have caseloads of about 200 AFDC families, in addition to providing services to additional non-AFDC families. Counselors identified several features of their job that resemble features of the intensive case management programs described elsewhere:

1. They work to develop a relationship based on trust and respect. For example, they develop techniques for doing the required paperwork at the same time that they ask open-ended questions about how child care and work are going. These questions frequently elicit responses about the strains of working, which counselors see as an opportunity to help mothers move toward eventual self-sufficiency.

2. They emphasize empowering clients to assert themselves in the service system, particularly with child care providers, and they advocate for parents with the Department of Public Welfare.

3. They take a long-term view, believing, according to the CCC director, that it usually takes two to three years after employment for a woman to be truly self-sufficient—that is, unwilling to return to AFDC even if something goes wrong. According to the director, the counselors have had the opportunity to develop this long-term view because they have been able to see women funded through the Extended Voucher program for a couple of years after employment—which is no longer possible now that this program has been eliminated due to state budget cuts.

On the other hand, given caseloads of 200, the parent counselors' role clearly differs from that of the intensive case managers as well. For example, the parent counselors' responsibility is more narrowly defined: When family concerns that are unrelated to the tension between parenting and work come up in conversation, counselors primarily provide referral to other social services providers.

Collaboration. In contrast to the PACE/AFDC collaboration, in which workers in the early education and welfare systems appeared to have quite different goals and missions, Department of Public Welfare staff and CCC staff saw their goals for clients in overlapping terms, though they would make different judgments in particular situations. For example, they might both agree that a mother should have good child care available when she enters a training program, but they might differ on whether she should enter the training program the next week or take time for a better transition to child care and enter during the following program cycle.

More specifically, on the welfare side, case managers and ET workers saw child care as an integral part of self-sufficiency, and in some, but not all, cases, they saw quality child care as essential. For example, an ET administrator in Lawrence, explaining why he believed that ET should stay voluntary rather than become mandatory, argued that a mandatory program would not work because "we have a commitment to quality day care" and a mandatory program would make it impossible to keep that commitment.

At the CCC, parent counselors clearly saw self-sufficiency as the eventual purpose of their child care assistance. The CCC director and all three site managers, when asked for examples of successes, told stories of families for which child care had made employment possible: a woman who has made such progress in her job that she has now chosen to go off the voucher system and pay for child care herself; a woman who was tremendously excited when for the first time she bought boots with her own money rather than AFDC money or her boyfriend's money; and a woman who went through four years of school, earned her R.N. degree, and is now "out of the system."

Challenges. For both the Massachusetts sites, the future form of the programs is uncertain given the last two years of budget reductions and the possibility of much greater reductions in the future. As of the summer of 1990, the state still funded child care and resource and referral services through the VMA network for AFDC recipients, but funding for former AFDC recipients through the Extended Voucher program had been eliminated. As of the spring of 1992, after a change in governor and political party, key elements of the program had been renamed but reportedly continued in some form: ET CHOICES became Mass. JOBS, and VMAs became Child Care Resource Agencies (CCRAs).

KENTUCKY: PARENT AND CHILD EDUCATION (PACE)

The Welfare Department and Family Literacy

Introduction. Kentucky's Parent and Child Education (PACE) family literacy program began in 1986 as a two-year pilot in 12 school districts. PACE aims to break the inter-generational cycle of educational failure through a school-based program that allows parents to pursue adult education while their children attend a high-quality preschool in the same building. The day also includes time for parents and children to be together and learn through play, and it includes opportunities for parents to discuss issues such as discipline and child development. Funded by the Kentucky General Assembly through the state's Department of Education, the program is open to parents without a high school diploma or GED and their three- and four-year-old children. PACE has gained national recognition from the Kenan Family Trust, the Barbara Bush Foundation for Family Literacy, the Harvard Family Literacy Project, national media, and numerous states and localities seeking to reproduce the model; it has also received an award from the Ford Foundation–Kennedy School awards program for Innovations in State and Local Government.

Given the educational needs of AFDC mothers and children as well as the emphasis of the Family Support Act on education services, PACE seems like a natural fit for the needs of a welfare agency implementing JOBS. From the other direction, a special referral relationship with the welfare agency seemed like a natural fit for PACE, which has always had some difficulty recruiting its desired number of participants per site. Thus, while PACE has always served some AFDC recipients in its regular programs—we heard numbers ranging from 25 percent statewide to 75 percent in one county—it made sense to both agencies to experiment with additional sites specifically for AFDC recipients. In September 1989, the state began operating two such programs that were funded by a WIN demonstration grant from the federal government. To enroll in these programs, AFDC families were to be referred from the Department for Social Insurance (DSI), which operates AFDC, to the Department for Employment Services (DES), which provides job training, and then to the PACE program. When we visited, the programs were not filled because of difficulties in this referral network; personal intervention from top agency administrators reportedly solved the referral problem later in the year.

As of the fall of 1990, however, these programs will no longer be reserved for AFDC recipients. They will be picked up by regular Department of Education funding (rather than DSI or JOBS funding) and will be available, as is the case at other PACE sites, to all families with low education levels. DSI will still be able to refer AFDC families, and those who participate as part of their JOBS obligation will be eligible for DSI funds for transportation and child care for siblings of the PACE child. At the same time, there will be new links between PACE and other community social services, which might provide another route into PACE for AFDC families: Recent legislation mandates that Family Resource Centers overseen by Kentucky's Cabinet for Human Resources (which includes DSI, DES, and the Department of Social Services) be located at elementary schools in counties in which 20 percent or more of the children are eligible for free lunches. Each Family Resource Center is to have a PACE program.

Services to Families and Children. For three days a week, PACE participants travel on the school bus with their three- and four-year-old children. After eating breakfast together, parents and children go into different classrooms for their separate educational components. Parents practice skills required for the GED exam, while children learn through a developmentally-oriented early childhood curriculum. Specific periods during the day are reserved for parent-child play, which is intended to model for parents how they can teach their children and interact with them in new ways, and for parental discussion of issues such as parenting and self-esteem. In addition, PACE organizers are now beginning to incorporate employment skills into the curriculum.[3]

In addition to the services offered formally through the PACE curriculum, PACE teachers reported working with families in a number of other ways. While PACE is one of the sites without an explicit case management component, both adult and preschool teachers established strong personal relationships with families. Said one PACE teacher, "We feel like social workers," while another noted: "We are working real hard to find the right niche. It's different than being a classroom teacher."

More specifically, teachers make home visits as part of recruitment or when parents are sick, refer families to appropriate community services, encourage them to seek health care, and assist them in concrete ways such as picking up participants for class and even chopping wood for needy families. Child care for siblings of the youngster in PACE is a major family need, and in one of the sites, teachers along with a social worker located at the school (through a special project unrelated to PACE) were trying to help families locate care. In addition, at the WIN-funded site that we visited, teachers and the program director also spent time trying to solve problems for clients at the welfare department, such as problems getting a child care check from DSI.

As teachers try to define the right mix of teaching and meeting other needs, they do sometimes find that "it's frustrating not to have a social worker background." However, they seem to resolve the tension by seeing their role as linking rather than providing services: "more of a go-between than getters," in one teacher's words. Still, the practical examples mentioned above suggest that many of them have taken the linkage role quite far as a result of their commitment to the families.

Collaboration. At the time of our site visit, which was still early in the collaboration at the WIN-funded sites, upper-level enthusiasm for the PACE/AFDC linkage had not yet translated fully into service delivery. The official process for a family to be referred to PACE had three steps. First, a mother would apply for AFDC at the DSI office, where a worker would inform her about PACE as an option if she met the eligibility requirements (no GED and a preschool child). Second, if she was interested, she would go to the DES office to volunteer for WIN and would tell the

DES worker that she was specifically interested in PACE. Third, the DES workers would send her over to PACE.

However, our interviews suggested that this process often broke down at the first step, since the local welfare office was overwhelmed with high caseloads and focused on getting out benefit checks and enrolling mandatory WIN participants. At the time (prior to passage of the Family Support Act), families were not mandated to enroll in WIN employment services unless their youngest child was at least six. Consequently, families with preschool children, the group eligible for PACE, were not mandated to enroll. (When the state applied for WIN demonstration funding for the PACE project, it requested a waiver to mandate participation in WIN for mothers with children age three or over, but the waiver request was denied.) Thus, a welfare worker would have no reason to think about the WIN program in general, or PACE in particular, for a woman with a young child, and only a particularly motivated worker would notice the match and make a referral. According to a local office administrator, explaining PACE's recruitment difficulties: "Right now, probably one thing that's affecting it, is that if an individual has a child six or under, they do not have to participate. When JOBS comes in it will be [age] three or under. . . . That will hit right at the age PACE wants. . . . That should really boost things."

As a result, families with preschool children were unlikely to hear about PACE at the welfare office unless they initiated the conversation or happened to meet an enthusiastic worker. The same local welfare administrator expanded on the obstacles to actively recruiting families at the welfare office:

One of the major problems that we have is that in the short time that we have with a client, one of the major things that we are doing is just getting eligibility information and child support, medical programs. . . . And I think that's probably where we could be losing some people that could be potentially interested in the program, just by the sheer volume of everything else we have to tell them. And that's why I'm counting on the video presentation for the clients to hear this while they are waiting. . . . So that at the very least when they get back there [with the worker] they can say, "Can you tell me about this PACE program?"

Interviewer: So you think that the initiative then, is going to have to come from the client?

At this point, I would say yes. There is just too much that worker has to do to get that point over. . . . I never had heard of the program [PACE] until the ladies came in. But right now I am sold on it. I wish that I could get my enthusiasm over to the workers who deal with the clients every day. Changing the attitudes is going to be a long process.

To speed up recruitment, PACE teachers recruited AFDC families through other channels (Parent-Teacher Association meetings, for example), but they or DES staff then had to take those families back through the DSI and DES process to get to PACE. Reportedly, the recruitment problem was solved later in the year, after being brought to the attention of the DSI commissioner, through an intensive push.

Other similar issues for the collaboration were delays in issuing child care reimbursement checks which appeared to be jeopardizing the participation of some families, and reported confusion by welfare workers about the effect of child care reimbursement on AFDC checks. All these issues suggested that even though a partnership like PACE/JOBS offers both sides substantial advantages—a recruitment and referral source for PACE, and a high-quality program that combines education with child care for the JOBS agency—it also may require considerable time to develop clear communication and a joint approach to program mission and implementation.

SUPPLEMENTAL SITE VISIT: MASSACHUSETTS: ET CHOICES CASE MANAGEMENT

Adult Case Management through the Welfare System

Introduction. In contrast to the other case management sites, the ET CHOICES site offers case management by the eligibility workers themselves rather than a community agency under contract or specialized workers. We visited the case management portion of ET CHOICES even though it did not meet our site selection criteria—it does not include a clear emphasis on children—precisely because of this choice of case manager. The purpose of the visit was to compare the nature of case management conducted by eligibility workers on a very large (statewide) scale with case management conducted by specialized workers in small programs, as in our other sites. Even more than in the other sites, it is important to note that this description is time-limited to the summer and fall of 1989: Changes in budget, staffing, caseloads, and program priorities since that time—as well as a 1990 gubernatorial election that led to a change of both governor and party—are not reflected here.

We visited two offices with somewhat different management structures. In Lawrence, an intake worker is responsible for determining initial eligibility, getting the first check to the client, and developing an initial Family Independence Plan that addresses barriers to self-sufficiency in the areas of employability, health care, housing, and child support. After the family starts receiving AFDC, the case passes to an ongoing eligibility worker, called a case manager, who has responsibility for both eligibility and the Family Independence Plan for the duration of the family's stay on AFDC. In Fall River, which operates under a consolidated case management model, the same case manager handles both intake and ongoing functions. Thus, a mother who applies for AFDC stays with the same worker from her first eligibility interview to the end of her stay on AFDC. In both offices, the ET CHOICES specialist, who is assigned to one or more units of AFDC case managers, will work with the mother to identify suitable training programs and to refer her to the VMA for child care if she expresses an interest.

Case Management and the Case Managers. Eligibility workers' jobs seemed different from the stereotype described in Chapter 3 and somewhat like the case management jobs at the other study sites in a number of ways.

1. At the time of our visit, *caseloads*, while higher than in the intensive case management sites, *were lower* than for eligibility workers in other locations: about 100 for the consolidated case manager and about 120–140 cases for the ongoing case managers. Since our visit, fiscal problems in Massachusetts have pushed these caseloads up to 160 cases as a statewide average.

2. Workers talked about *the importance of getting to know clients*, understanding their situations, and building a good relationship. A worker in the consolidated office reported: "One of the reasons for consolidation is to know your client when they first walk in the door. That way, you can do your best for them." She also reported using specific techniques to build the relationship: For example, she typically spent the first interview trying to understand the "trauma" that brought the family to welfare in the first place.

3. Particularly in the four areas identified by the Family Assistance Plan, workers felt *a sense of responsibility for brokering and service referral* (in contrast to the eligibility worker quoted in Chapter 1, who saw all brokering for health and housing as outside her job). An intake worker reported that to do her job, "You have to have a good idea of the various community services that are available." An ongoing worker (case manager) reported that when he heard about a particularly appealing training program, he called around to clients who he thought would be interested, and four enrolled.

On the other hand, even the modified eligibility worker's job is clearly very different from the intensive case management described for the other programs.

1. The relationship is clearly *more distant and formalized* than in the intensive case management programs, both because of time constraints (even at the lower caseloads, ongoing workers see clients only about every six months for an eligibility review) and because of the difficulty of establishing trust. None of the clients we interviewed reported that they would call or speak with their eligibility worker to help them deal with a problem between the regular eligibility reviews, though all reported good experiences at the reviews. A welfare advocate who sees many

recipients thought that they were more likely to have an honest conversation about their futures with the ET CHOICES specialist or a colocated worker from the state employment agency than with the case manager who has power over their income.

2. The eligibility case manager's area of *responsibility is deliberately narrower* than that of the intensive case managers. The responsibility is primarily defined by the Family Independence Plan, which touches on only a handful of family and child issues: child care related to employment, child support, and a question about the child's health and access to a physician. As one worker reported, "We're called Financial Assistance Workers. We don't really handle problems with the children."

Several elements of the framework for ET CHOICES case management seem to make it possible for workers to balance the case management and eligibility roles.

1. Until the recent budget problems, *caseloads have been relatively low.*

2. *Participation* in the ET CHOICES training and employment activities listed in the Family Independence Plan *is voluntary.* (Official policy is that the program is a mandatory program that takes volunteers first, but there have always been enough volunteers to fill available spots.) As a result, workers must market the program to clients, which contributes to their desire to understand client needs and develop a relationship. The voluntary nature of the program also reduces concerns that workers might use their power over the family budget to try to control client behavior inappropriately—for example, by requiring a client to enter a program for which she is not suited.

3. Another feature of ET CHOICES case management that appears to help workers balance their roles is *the Family Independence Plan document* itself, which focuses the case manager's attention on issues that are central to the department's mission and well suited to the strengths of the eligibility worker. For example, ensuring that a child has a pediatrician is reasonably related to the Medicaid function of the department and not particularly intrusive.

4. Finally, *the availability of experts,* such as the ET CHOICES specialist and corresponding workers who specialize in health care and child support, seems to address one concern raised by observers of case management elsewhere: The eligibility worker cannot learn enough about vendors and community resources to serve clients well. In the offices we visited, case managers talked frequently with ET CHOICES specialists, for example, although since our visit, these relationships may have been threatened by the budget cutbacks, which have reduced the number of specialists substantially.

Most workers to whom we spoke found it possible to balance their various roles, given these supporting structures. However, one worker commented on the ambiguities that remain:

If a woman doesn't feel that she should be the one who's responsible to maintain the family, how do I address that? Am I crossing the boundaries of my job? Am I only here for financial assistance? That's my title—Financial Assistance Social Worker. The emphasis in the Department in Massachusetts is becoming more and more casework, but sometimes it's a real conflict. Where do you overstep the boundaries?

Challenges. As noted in the ET CHOICES/Voucher Child Care site, the future of the two Massachusetts sites is uncertain given the recent and anticipated rounds of budget cuts and changes in program and political priorities. The first change in the adult case management program after our visit was an increase in caseload per worker, a result both of cuts in staff and rising total caseloads due to a weakening economy. Administrators reported that the effect of rising worker caseloads was to force attention back to basic eligibility and away from the Family Independence Plan.

Appendix B: Research Approach and Methods

This appendix describes the approach taken by the study to answer the central question: How can states take advantage of the Family Support Act to identify and meet the needs of children, and not just adults, in welfare families? In order to develop practical insights that could help states implement programs to meet those needs, the study relied for its primary source of evidence on programs already operating across the country. The site selection process aimed to identify programs that were operating successfully and seemed likely to make a difference in families' lives, as judged by the best evidence available. The study did *not* try to evaluate the long-run effectiveness of the services at changing life outcomes. Chapter 2 in the text discusses the nature and dimensions of program success across the study sites.

This appendix describes the process of selecting the research sites, the sample of sites as actually selected, the content of the site visits, and the limits of the site selection process and the site visits.

SITE SELECTION: CONSTRAINTS

The process for selecting sites and the criteria for site selection had to respond to a number of constraints on the study. Probably most important, we did not know at the beginning of the project what kinds of programs linking welfare and the needs of children would be in existence and operating. No inventory existed—no description of the universe from which sites were to be selected—and in fact, one by-product of the site selection process was a reasonable sketch of that universe.

As a result of this constraint, we developed a multistage site selection process. The first stage was to develop both a list of possible sites *and* a list of possible selection criteria, the second stage was to receive outside comment on both, and the third stage was to refine the criteria and select final sites. This process represented one response to the underlying difficulty of specifying criteria before anyone knew just what programs existed.

The second constraint had to do with the small number of sites funded by the project: originally six, they were expanded to seven as it turned out some visits could be combined. One reason for keeping the number of sites small was funding, but there were at least two other reasons. First, in the absence of any kind of inventory, we did not know at the beginning whether we would find even six appropriate programs in operation. We did, in fact, find more than six, but not many more. Second, because the project aims to influence state decisions about Family Support Act implementation, its timeliness is important. Consequently, the research design aimed to produce tentative suggestions from a small number of sites quickly rather than firmer suggestions from more sites over a longer period of time.

The most important result of this constraint was that the selection criteria had to be relatively simple. In particular, a small number of sites did not allow for systematic variation on more than a few dimensions.

SITE SELECTION: CRITERIA AND PROCESS

The criteria on which we eventually settled required that programs have three characteristics:

- A record of successful program operation (preferably, at least a year of operation);
- Provision of services that focus on the needs of children, not only adults; and
- Strong links to the welfare system.

Within the pool of programs meeting these characteristics, we looked for variation on three dimensions:

- Substantive focus of the programs (for example, teen parent programs or early childhood education programs);
- Organizational location (within or outside the welfare department); and
- Case management approaches versus non–case management approaches.

Although we wanted to include some sites that did not use case management, we were particularly interested in identifying a substantial subgroup that did. Our interest in case management was twofold: First, we suspected that case management would be a particularly effective way to link poor children to needed services; and second, the Family Support Act offers reimbursement for case management services in connection with the JOBS program. As it turns out, almost all the sites that met our other criteria also used case management. This result may have had something to do with our interest in finding case management sites, but we conclude, as explained in the text, that it also reflects family needs.

We identified the selection criteria and the sites themselves through four major steps:

1. Through several weeks of document review and telephone conversations with a range of experts, we conducted an initial search for as many programs as we could find at the state, local, or community level that linked the welfare system and the needs of children.

2. After identifying these programs, we gathered preliminary information about them through telephone conversations with program staff, review of program documents, and conversations with a variety of experts, including, but not limited to, the members of our advisory board (Dr. J. Lawrence Aber, Dr. Jerome Kagan, Dr. Sharon Lynn Kagan, Allen Kraus, Gwen Morgan, Dr. Julius Richmond, and Lucy Williams). Based on this preliminary information, we identified 11 programs as serious candidates for a site visit.

3. At the same time, we developed the site selection criteria. The criterion of successful operation came directly from the underlying assumptions of the research, as described in Chapter 1. The decision to look at programs with strong links to the welfare system rather than solely programs operated by the welfare system, and indeed to seek variation in the organizational location of the programs, came from our growing knowledge of what programs were, in fact, operating. Similarly, our review of actual programs led us to identify four substantive categories: teen parent programs, services to multiproblem families, early childhood education, and services to school-age children.

4. Finally, we circulated the 11 candidates for site visits and the site selection criteria to our advisory board and other informal advisors for comments and suggestions. This review led to two changes:

- We expanded the early childhood category to include not only programs that provide special early childhood services but also programs that link children on welfare to community child care. This category reflected the comment from the advisory board that we should not assume that targeted programs for low-income children (for example, Head Start or state equivalents) were the best way to achieve the benefits of a high-quality preschool experience for those children. Rather, we decided to include one program that attempted to link children on welfare to a wide range of day care programs available in the community, including high-quality and high-cost programs previously available only to children from better-off families. The program included for this purpose was the Voucher Child Care component of ET CHOICES in Massachusetts.

- We had explicitly asked in the initial site selection memo whether we should visit a location with a strong reputation for adult case management for welfare recipients in order to understand as a baseline what a system focused on adults does for children and in order to understand more fully the implementation of a highly developed case management system. In response to comments suggesting that this would be desirable, we chose to make a supplemental visit to ET CHOICES offices in Lawrence and Fall River, Massachusetts.

THE SAMPLE AS ACTUALLY SELECTED

In general, the seven sites that were finally selected met our criteria. Of the seven sites, three share a substantive focus on teen parents. Since two of these are operated from outside the welfare department and one from inside, they offer a useful contrast in administrative arrangements. The other four sites represent three different substantive foci: services to school-age children, services to young children (early childhood education), and services to multineed families. These four programs include two that are operated within the welfare department (or rather, the umbrella human services agency that includes welfare eligibility as one of its functions), one that is operated outside the welfare department, and one that has components both in- and outside. The seven sites, as listed in Chapter 1, Table 1, are as follows:

Teen Parent Programs
Chemung and Schuyler Counties, New York: TASA Next Step Program
San Diego, California: GAIN Teen Parent Project
San Francisco, California: TAPP/GAIN Collaboration

Services to School-Age Children
Detroit, Michigan: Earhart—Fort Wayne—Jackson—Conner-Warren Dropout Prevention Program

Services to Young Children
Massachusetts: ET CHOICES/Voucher Child Care Program
Kentucky: Parent and Child Education (PACE)

Services to Multineed Families

Oklahoma: Integrated Family Services System (IFS)

At the time of sample selection, we thought that four programs included case management and three did not—the Kentucky PACE program, the Detroit dropout prevention program, and the Voucher Child Care component of ET CHOICES (which is nested in a larger program that does include case management). The site visits, however, revealed that workers in the Michigan program offered case management services, leaving only two programs not offering case management. Further, as the text reports, even those programs have found that some staff members expand their jobs in the direction of case management in order to respond to the multiple needs of participants.

CONTENT OF THE SITE VISITS

Because, as noted in the Introduction, this study takes the interaction between street-level workers and families as the central element of service delivery, the site visits combined an in-depth look at street-level program operation with a less detailed overview of other key program elements. The visits were also designed to probe for multiple perspectives on issues that were expected to be difficult or characterized by conflict: for example, the roles of various agencies, the relationships among agencies, program goals, possible conflicts among goals, and the nature of client experiences.

In preparation for each site visit, research staff conducted telephone interviews with program administrators, collected program documents, and planned a site visit itinerary in cooperation with program staff. With the exception of the ET CHOICES/Voucher Child Care site visit (which was shorter because it was partly combined with the supplemental visit that focused on ET CHOICES adult case management), each site visit lasted at least two days and included interviews with 15 to 20 people. In every site, those interviewed included line workers for the central program being visited (in most cases, *all* the line workers at the study location), welfare eligibility workers, line workers for other programs that collaborate with the central program (such as child protective services caseworkers, community program case managers, or visiting nurses), program clients, and program administrators. To supplement the interviews, the research staff directly observed program operations where possible.

LIMITS OF SITE SELECTION AND THE SITE VISITS

As a result of the constraints of time, money, and advance knowledge described above, the sample selected has several limits for research purposes. Four limits seem most important:

1. The initial search for programs, while as comprehensive as we could make it in the time available, undoubtedly missed some programs that would fit the criteria. It is particularly likely that the search missed extremely local programs and programs limited only to one substantive area of children's services. In particular, we feel least confident about our success in identifying programs that link child health services to children on welfare.

The process included a number of safeguards against missing important programs, most significantly, review of the site selection memorandum by a wide circle of experts. In addition, the interim report of the study was also widely circulated. In response to these reviews, only a handful of programs were identified that could potentially meet the study criteria. Therefore, while some programs undoubtedly were missed, these omissions are probably not numerous and probably do not distort the overall picture—with the possible exception of programs limited only to child heath, which are not represented at all within the sample.

2. The design of the site visit incorporated many precautions to ensure the accuracy and objectivity of the site descriptions. These precautions included the deliberate selection of interviewees who would express alternative points of view about key program issues, as well as repeated checks for accuracy after the fact through the circulation of case write-ups and each draft of the analysis to the sites for comment.

Nonetheless, there are inevitably limits to the completeness and reliability of the site descriptions. The most important of these limitations is the incomplete representation of the client perspective. While every site visit included interviews with some families receiving services, the site visit schedules aimed to represent as many perspectives as possible within the limited time available, not to include a significant sample of a single group. As a result, the number of client interviews per site ranged from two to five. Therefore, the client interviews were able to suggest interpretations or insights different from those of workers and to provide a reality check on worker views, but they were not numerous enough to provide a generalizable client perspective.

A second limitation of the client interviews was that (with the exception of ET CHOICES) the program administrators selected the clients to be interviewed. Nevertheless, despite this limit, the client interviews always provided unexpected insights about the operation of the program and usefully supplemented the staff perspectives.

3. As discussed much more fully in Chapter 2 of the text, the available evidence about successful program operation is quite limited for many of the programs and was particularly limited at the time of site selection, *before* the site visits. Many of the programs are new and have not been formally evaluated, so that evidence of successful operation comes from professional judgments about the program itself, professional judgments

about the consistency of the program model with available evaluation evidence, and the longevity of the actual operating experience.

The evidence for the other two selection criteria, focus on children and links to the welfare department, was also incomplete at the time of site selection. The fuller evidence developed through the site visits did confirm that the sites offered services that were focused on children. However, the links to the welfare department turned out in some cases to be weaker than anticipated. This observation forms part of the evidence about the nature and difficulties of collaboration discussed in the text.

4. All research based on case study evidence raises the question of the generalizability of the results. Would another set of successfully operating programs have yielded different conclusions about the important challenges, themes, and approaches? We have attempted to respond to this concern by testing out the ideas on a wide circle of experts and practitioners through the interim reports, presentations in various settings, and circulation of this book in draft. Our conclusion is that while another selection of sites might well have yielded a set of themes and approaches that was not identical, we expect that it would have had considerable overlap. The issues we highlight generally seem both familiar and important to other practitioners in the field, and the approaches of the study sites seem impressive and plausible.

Notes

CHAPTER 1

1. The estimate of the number of welfare workers is drawn from Steve Jenkins, Cheryl Dorsey, and Olivia Golden, "Characteristics of Service Deliverers: Who Delivers Services to Poor Children?" (Unpublished paper prepared for the executive session, entitled "Making the System Work for Poor Children," Cambridge, MA: Harvard University, Kennedy School of Government, Wiener Center for Social Policy, updated June 1989), 8, n. 29.

The average monthly number of families on AFDC in fiscal year 1990 was 3.97 million. See U.S. Congress, House, Committee on Ways and Means, *Overview of Entitlement Programs: 1991 Green Book, Background Material and Data on Programs within the Jurisdiction of the Committee on Ways and Means.* 102nd Congr., 1st session (Washington, DC: U.S. Government Printing Office, 1991), 618.

2. Lisbeth Schorr with Daniel Schorr, *Within Our Reach: Breaking the Cycle of Disadvantage* (New York: Doubleday, Anchor Press, 1988), xvii-xix.

3. U.S. Bureau of the Census, Series P-60, no. 175, Current Population Reports, *Poverty in the United States: 1990* (Washington, DC: U.S. Government Printing Office, 1991), 2, 18, and 195.

For a discussion of trends in child poverty and the characteristics of poor children, see Clifford M. Johnson, Leticia Miranda, Arloc Sherman, and James D. Weill, *Child Poverty in America* (Washington, DC: Children's Defense Fund, 1991).

4. See, for example, reviews of the evidence in:

Naomi Carol Goldstein, "Explaining Socioeconomic Differences in Children's Cognitive Test Scores," Discussion paper H-90-1 (Cambridge, MA: Wiener Center for Social Policy, Kennedy School of Government, Harvard University, January 1990).

Naomi Carol Goldstein, "Why Poverty Is Bad for Children," (Unpublished Ph.D. dissertation, (Harvard University, 1991), 21-62.

National Center for Children in Poverty, *Five Million Children: A Statistical Profile of Our Poorest Young Citizens* (New York: Columbia University School of Public Health, 1990), 50–74.

Schorr and Schorr, *Within Our Reach*, 29–32.

Sheila Smith, Susan Blank, and James T. Bond, *One Program, Two Generations: A Report of the Forum on Children and the Family Support Act* (New York: Foundation for Child Development, in partnership with the National Center for Children in Poverty, 1990), 7.

5. Goldstein, "Why Poverty Is Bad," 82–83.

6. David T. Ellwood, *Poor Support: Poverty in the American Family* (New York: Basic Books, 1988), 84–85.

7. Goldstein, "Why Poverty Is Bad," 107.

8. Ibid., 108.

9. For an overview of this literature, see:

Schorr and Schorr, *Within Our Reach*, 64–110, 179–214, 256–83.

Bernice Weissbourd and Carol Emig, "Early Childhood Programs for Children in Poverty: A Good Place To Start," in George Miller, ed., *Giving Children a Chance: The Case for More Effective National Policies* (Washington, DC: Center for National Policy Press, 1989), 1–22.

For reviews of evidence on Head Start and early childhood education programs, see:

W. Steven Barnett and Colette M. Escobar, "The Economics of Early Educational Intervention: A Review," *Review of Educational Research* 57, no. 4 (1987): 393–404.

Donna M. Bryant and Craig T. Ramey, "An Analysis of the Effectiveness of Early Intervention Programs for Environmentally At-Risk Children," in Michael J. Guralnick and Forrest C. Bennett, eds., *The Effectiveness of Early Intervention for At-Risk and Handicapped Children* (San Diego, CA: Academic Press, 1987), 33–75.

Lawrence J. Schweinhart and David P. Weikart, "What Do We Know So Far? A Review of the Head Start Synthesis Project," *Young Children* 4, no. 2 (January 1986): 49–55.

For a review of evidence on home visit programs, see:

David L. Olds and Charles R. Henderson, Jr., "The Prevention of Maltreatment," in Dante Cicchetti and Vicki Carlson, eds., *Child Maltreatment: Theory and Research on the Causes and Consequences of Child Abuse and Neglect* (New York: Cambridge University Press, 1989), 722–63.

10. U.S. Congress, *Overview of Entitlement Programs*, 621.

11. Ibid., 622–23.

12. Nicholas Zill, Kristin Moore, and Thomas Steif, "Progress Report: Analysis of Employment-Related Characteristics of AFDC Mothers in National Survey Data Bases" (Unpublished paper, Child Trends, Inc., 1989), 2, 5.

13. U.S. Congress: *Overview of Entitlement Programs*, 622.

14. See, for example, the review of the literature on child care quality in: Cheryl D. Hayes, John L. Palmer, and Martha J. Zaslow, eds., *Who Cares for America's Children? Child Care Policy for the 1990s* (Washington, DC: National Academy Press, 1990), 65–77, 84–104.

15. On strategic management, see, for example:

Philip B. Heymann, *The Politics of Public Management* (New Haven, CT: Yale University Press, 1987), ch. 2, pp. 12–24.

Jay Lorsch, "Organizational Design: A Situational Perspective," in J. Richard Hackman, Edward E. Lawler, III, and Lyman W. Porter, eds., *Perspectives on Behavior in Organizations* (New York: McGraw-Hill, 1983), 439–41.

Mark Moore, "Creating Public Value: Strategic Management in the Public Sector" (Unpublished paper, Harvard University, Kennedy School of Government, 1992), chapter 3, 72–74.

CHAPTER 2

1. These conclusions draw on site interviews, observation, and review of documents such as management indicator reports and client evaluations, which, taken together, provided considerable evidence about the dimensions of operational effectiveness at each program. However, it is important to remember that the study's purpose was not to evaluate individual programs, and the site visits were not designed to do so.

2. As suggested above, this evidence is easiest to gather and interpret for those study sites that aim to change families more than systems and that are relatively mature in their stage of development. For example, Kentucky PACE, San Francisco TAPP, and TASA Next Step might fit in this category of programs which are most easily assessed through outcome evaluation. Such evaluation is harder to carry out well for programs that aim to change systems as well as serve individual families, and it is probably least appropriate for those programs at an early stage of their development, at the point where the primary purpose is to get a system started so that it can be refined later. Among the programs that are more difficult to assess through outcome evaluation—because of either systemwide aims or an early stage of development, or both—are the San Diego GAIN Teen Parent Program, the Detroit dropout prevention program, the ET CHOICES Voucher Child Care Program, and the Oklahoma Integrated Family Services System.

3. Carol C. Korenbrot, Jonathan Showstack, Amy Loomis, and Clair Brindis, "Birth Weight Outcomes in a Teenage Pregnancy Case Management Project," *Journal of Adolescent Health Care* 10 (1989): 97–104.

4. For the most recent findings from Project Redirection, see Denise F. Polit, Janet C. Quint, and James A. Riccio, *The Challenge of Serving Teenage Mothers: Lessons from Project Redirection* (New York: Manpower Demonstration Research Corporation, 1988).

5. See:

David L. Olds, Charles R. Henderson, Jr., Robert Tatelbaum, and Robert Chamberlin, "Improving the Life-Course Development of Socially Disadvantaged Mothers: A Randomized Trial of Nurse Home Visitation," *American Journal of Public Health* 78, no. 11 (1988): 1436–45.

David L. Olds and Charles R. Henderson, Jr., "The Prevention of Maltreatment," in Dante Cicchetti and Vicki Carlson, eds., *Child Maltreatment: Theory and Research on the Causes and Consequences of Child Abuse and Neglect* (New York: Cambridge University Press, 1989), 722–63.

6. Janet C. Quint and Cynthia A. Guy, *New Chance: Lessons from the Pilot Phase* (New York: Manpower Demonstration Research Corporation, 1989), 6–11.

7. Denise F. Polit and Joseph J. O'Hara, "Support Services," in Phoebe Cottingham and David Ellwood, eds., *Welfare Policy for the 1990s* (Cambridge, MA: Harvard University Press, 1989), 165–98.

8. Ibid., 192.

9. Quint and Guy, *New Chance*, 7.

10. This description of Next Step's program ethos is based on the range of interviews conducted during the visit to the project site. The program director noted that, in her view, self-esteem and education are intimately connected and therefore, both are emphasized.

11. Cheryl D. Hayes, John L. Palmer, and Martha J. Zaslow, eds., *Who Cares for America's Children? Child Care Policy for the 1990's* (Washington, DC: National Academy Press, 1990), 97, 101–3.

12. Naomi Carol Goldstein, "Why Poverty Is Bad for Children" (Unpublished Ph.D. dissertation, Harvard University, January 1991), 153.

13. Lisbeth Schorr with Daniel Schorr, *Within Our Reach: Breaking the Cycle of Disadvantage* (New York: Doubleday, Anchor Press, 1988), 256–60.

14. Polit and O'Hara, "Support Services," 182.

15. Hayes, Palmer, and Zaslow, *Who Cares for America's Children?* 72–77.

CHAPTER 3

1. James A. Riccio with Kay F. Sherwood, *Key Decisions in Implementing JOBS: Lessons from California's GAIN Program* (New York: Manpower Demonstration Research Corporation, June 1990), 46.

2. Ibid., 39.

3. The phrase is from Lisbeth Schorr with Daniel Schorr, *Within Our Reach: Breaking the Cycle of Disadvantage* (New York: Doubleday, Anchor Press, 1988), xvii-xix.

4. See, for example, Tom Kane, "The Caseworker-Client Relationship and Welfare Reform," Working paper no. H-90-9 (Cambridge, MA: Wiener Center for Social Policy, Kennedy School of Government, Harvard University, September 1990).

Riccio and Sherwood, *Key Decisions*.

5. See, for example:

Center for the Study of Social Policy, "A Framework for Child Welfare Reform" (Unpublished paper prepared for the Annie E. Casey Foundation, December 1987), 6–13.

Sheila B. Kamerman and Alfred J. Kahn. *Social Services for Children, Youth, and Families in the United States* (Greenwich, CT: Annie E. Casey Foundation, June 1989).

Schorr and Schorr, *Within Our Reach*, 260 ff.

Rick Weissbourd, "Making the System Work for Poor Children," Working paper ES-91-4 (Cambridge, MA: Wiener Center for Social Policy, Kennedy School of Government, Harvard University, 1991).

Mary Jo Bane, "Paying Attention to Children: Services, Settings, and Systems," Working paper ES-91-3 (Cambridge, MA: Wiener Center for Social Policy, Kennedy School of Government, Harvard University, 1991.)

Sid Gardner, "Failure by Fragmentation," *California Tomorrow*, Fall 1989, 20–21.

6. See Charles Bruner, *Thinking Collaboratively: Ten Questions and Answers to Help Policy-Makers Improve Children's Services* (Washington, DC: Education and Human Services Consortium, 1991).

Charles Bruner, "State-Level Approaches to Foster Local-Level Collaboration: Iowa's Initiatives to Improve Children's Welfare" (Unpublished first draft prepared for the National Conference of State Legislatures, July 1990), 14.

7. For this experience from the teacher's point of view, see Rick Weissbourd, "Public Elementary Schools: A Ladder Out of Poverty?" Discussion paper H-89-3 (Cambridge, MA: Wiener Center for Social Policy, Kennedy School of Government, Harvard University, 1989).

8. See Appendix B for details of the case study design. For a fascinating account of the differences between reports on family problems by case managers and reports from the families themselves, see:
New Beginnings: A Feasibility Study of Integrated Services for Children and Families, Final Report (San Diego, CA: San Diego City Schools, 1990), 22–24.

9. Naomi Carol Goldstein, "Why Poverty Is Bad for Children," (Unpublished Ph.D. dissertation, Harvard University, 1991), 144.

10. Mary Jo Bane and David T. Ellwood, "The Dynamics of Dependence: The Routes to Self-Sufficiency" (Unpublished paper prepared for the U.S. Department of Health and Human Services, Urban Systems Research and Engineering, 1983), 10.

11. Schorr and Schorr, *Within Our Reach*, 258–59.

12. Janet C. Quint and Cynthia A. Guy, *New Chance: Lessons from the Pilot Phase* (New York Manpower Demonstration Research Corporation, 1989), 7.

13. Riccio and Sherwood, *Key Decisions*, 22.

14. Denise F. Polit and Joseph J. O'Hara, "Support Services," in Phoebe Cottingham and David Ellwood, eds., *Welfare Policy for the 1990s* (Cambridge, MA: Harvard University Press, 1989), 192.

15. Ibid., 190.

16. See, for example:
American Public Welfare Association (APWA), "Case Management and Welfare Reform," W-Memo no. W-7 (Washington, DC, July 1987), 3–6.

Fred Doolittle and James Riccio, "Case Management in Welfare Employment Programs" (Unpublished paper prepared for a conference entitled "Evaluation Design for Welfare and Training Programs," sponsored by the Institute for Research on Poverty of the University of Wisconsin-Madison and the Office of the Assistant Secretary for Planning and Evaluation of the U.S. Department of Health and Human Services, April 1990), 7–16.

17. In addition to the works cited separately in notes 18 and 19, see also:
APWA, "Case Management and Welfare Reform," 1.
Kamerman and Kahn, *Social Services for Children, Youth, and Families*.

Toby Herr and Robert Halpern with Aimee Conrad, "Changing What Counts: Rethinking the Journey Out of Welfare," Research and Policy Reports Series (Evanston, IL: Center for Urban Affairs and Policy Research, Northwestern University, 1991).

18. Center for the Study of Social Policy, "A Framework for Child Welfare Reform," 21–22.

19. Julius R. Ballew and George Mink, *Case Management in the Human Services* (Springfield, IL: Charles C. Thomas Publishers, 1986), 3.

20. Ibid., 9–27.

CHAPTER 4

1. In addition to the site visits conducted for this study, the description of the parent education components of PACE also draws on Bonnie Hausman and Kathryn Parsons, "PACE: Breaking the Cycle of Intergenerational Illiteracy," *Equity and Choice* 5, no. 3 (May 1989): 57–58.

2. Judith S. Musick and Robert Halpern, "Giving Children A Chance: What Role Community-Based Parenting Interventions?" in George Miller, eds., *Giving Children a Chance: The Case for More Effective National Policies* (Washington, DC: Center for National Policy Press, 1989), 183–85.

3. For a discussion of the difficulty of parenting, see, Ibid., 177, 183–85.

CHAPTER 5

1. See, for example:

Robert Behn, *The Management of ET CHOICES in Massachusetts* (Durham, NC: Duke University, Institute of Policy Sciences and Public Affairs, 1989), ch. 6, 15–19 and ch. 7, 7–8.

Mark Moore, "Creating Public Value: Strategic Management in the Public Sector" (Unpublished paper, Kennedy School of Government, Harvard University, 1992), ch. 3, 62–72.

Tom Peters and Nancy Austin, *A Passion for Excellence: The Leadership Difference* (New York: Warner Books, 1985; reprinted with new Afterword, 1986), 319–320 and 334–339.

2. Behn, *Management of ET CHOICES*, ch. 4, 13–14; ch. 6, 15–19.

3. Two caveats are important here. First, the evidence for this finding is suggestive rather than conclusive because we interviewed more widely within the special programs than within the welfare agency as a whole and we did very few interviews with elected and appointed figures not in the welfare agency, whose views about its mission are nonetheless very important. However, our sources did include selected interviews with welfare agency administrators and staff, views from special program staff not in the welfare agency, evidence about actual historical events that might demonstrate the mission in action, documents issued by the welfare agency, and comments by agency administrators on drafts of this report.

Second, the two programs identified in the text are the only ones that had stopped serving children in conjunction with the welfare system as of fall 1990, about a year after the site visits. Since then, other programs may have changed substantially or been discontinued.

4. See, for example:

Paul R. Lawrence and Jay W. Lorsch, *Organization and Environment: Managing Differentiation and Integration* (Boston, MA: Harvard University, Graduate School of Business Administration, Division of Research, 1967).

Janet A. Weiss, "Substance vs. Symbol in Administrative Reform: The Case of Human Services Coordination," *Policy Analysis* 7 (Winter 1981): 20–45.

5. Lawrence and Lorsch, *Organization and Environment*, 52–53.

6. See Moore, "Creating Public Value," chs. 1–3.

7. For examples of these techniques in the private sector, see Lawrence and Lorsch, *Organization and Environment*.

8. For examples of other, similar informal approaches to the job search requirement in the GAIN program, see James Riccio with Kay Sherwood, *Key Decisions in Implementing JOBS: Lessons from California's GAIN Program* (New York: Manpower Demonstration Research Corporation, June 1990), 25–29.

9. See Bruner, *Thinking Collaboratively*, 9–10.

10. Ibid., 18.

11. See Riccio and Sherwood, *Key Decisions in Implementing JOBS*, 44–47, for a discussion of the experience of California counties in hiring GAIN case managers from among eligibility workers.

12. Lisbeth Schorr with Daniel Schorr, *Within Our Reach: Breaking the Cycle of Disadvantage* (New York: Anchor Press, 1988), 258, 273–75.

13. For a discussion of training, supervision, and performance standards, see Jolie Bain Pillsbury, "Reform at the State Level," *Public Welfare* 47 (Spring 1989): 11–12.

For a discussion of changes over the first five years of implementation see Behn, *Management of ET CHOICES*, ch. 1, 8; ch. 3, 7–14; ch. 4, 1–25; and ch. 7, 1–8.

CHAPTER 6

1. Mark Greenberg, *The JOBS Program: Answers and Questions* (Washington, DC: Center for Law and Social Policy, July 1990), 45.

2. Ibid., 100.

3. Ibid., 35.

4. This section benefited from particularly detailed and thoughtful comments by Sheila Smith of the Foundation for Child Development.

5. Greenberg, *The JOBS Program: Answers and Questions*, 39.

6. Ibid., 122.

7. Ibid., 141.

8. Ibid., 6.

9. Ibid., 20.

10. For another exploration of this question, see Mary Jo Bane, "Paying Attention to Children: Services, Settings, and Systems," Working paper ES-91-3 (Cambridge, MA: Wiener Center for Social Policy, Kennedy School of Government, Harvard University, 1991).

11. For an analysis of the difficulties faced by one community agency attempting to develop a joint Head Start–employment and training program, see Ruth Baker, "Parents as Providers: Integrating an Adult Education and Training Program with Head Start," Working paper H-91-1 (Cambridge, MA: Wiener Center for Social Policy, Kennedy School of Government, Harvard University, 1990).

12. For explorations of these issues in different family service agencies, see:

Center for the Future of Children, The David and Lucile Packard Foundation, "School-Linked Services." Special issue of *The Future of Children* 2, no. 1 (Spring 1992).

Ruth J. Liberman, "Clearing the Path to Recovery: Health and Social Service Collaboration for Boston's Pregnant Addicts," Working paper H-91-9 (Cambridge, MA: Wiener Center for Social Policy, Kennedy School of Government, Harvard University, 1990).

Rick Weissbourd, "Public Elementary Schools: A Ladder Out of Poverty?" Discussion paper H-89-3 (Cambridge, MA: Wiener Center for Social Policy, Kennedy School of Government, Harvard University, 1989).

13. For an analysis of this problem across a range of human services agencies, see Michael Lipsky, *Street-Level Bureaucracy: Dilemmas of the Individual in Public Services* (New York: Russell Sage Foundation, 1980).

14. For a discussion of the role various school personnel should take in school-based services programs, see Jeanne Jehl and Michael Kirst, "Getting Ready to Provide School Linked Services: What Schools Must Do," in Center for the Future of Children, *The Future of Children* 2, no. 1 (Spring 1992): 95–106.

APPENDIX A

1. See David L. Olds, Charles R. Henderson, Jr., Robert Tatelbaum, and Robert Chamberlin, "Improving the Life-Course Development of Socially Disadvantaged Mothers: A Randomized Trial of Nurse Home Visitation," *American Journal of Public Health* 78 (1988): 1436–45. Also David L. Olds and Charles R. Henderson, Jr., "The Prevention of Maltreatment," in Dante Cicchetti and Vicki Carlson, eds., *Child Maltreatment: Theory and Research on the Causes and Consequences of Child Abuse and Neglect* (New York: Cambridge University Press, 1989), 722–63.

2. Carol C. Korenbrot, Jonathan Showstack, Amy Loomis, and Claire Brindis, "Birth Weight Outcomes in a Teenage Pregnancy Case Management Project," *Journal of Adolescent Health Care* 10 (1989): 97–104.

3. In addition to our site visits, this summary of services draws from Bonnie Hausman and Kathryn Parsons, "PACE: Breaking the Cycle of Intergenerational Illiteracy," *Equity and Choice* 5, no. 3 (May 1989): 57–58.

Selected Bibliography

Aaronson, May. "The Case Manager–Home Visitor." *Child Welfare* 68, no. 3 (May–June 1989): 339–46.

American Public Welfare Association. "Case Management and Welfare Reform." *W-Memo* no. W-7 (July 1987): 1–15.

——— . "JOBS Implementation." *W-Memo* 1, no. 8-9 (November 1989): 2–12.

——— . *Success 1988: Innovation and Excellence in Public Human Services.* Washington, DC: The American Public Welfare Association, 1988.

——— . Center for Law and Social Policy, Center for the Study of Social Policy, Children's Defense Fund, Council of Chief State School Officers, Institute for Educational Leadership, National Alliance of Business, National Association of State Boards of Education, and National Governors' Association. *New Partnerships: Education's Stake in the Family Support Act of 1988.* Washington, DC: W. T. Grant Foundation, undated.

Annie E. Casey Foundation. *An Implementation Guide for the New Futures Initiatives.* Greenwich, CT, undated.

Baker, Ruth. "Parents as Providers: Integrating an Adult Education and Training Program with Head Start." Working paper no. H–91-1. Cambridge, MA: Wiener Center for Social Policy, Kennedy School of Government, Harvard University, 1990.

Ballew, Julius R., and George Mink. *Case Management in the Human Services.* Springfield, IL: Charles C. Thomas Publishers, 1986.

Bane, Mary Jo. "Paying Attention to Children: Services, Settings, and Systems." Working paper no. ES-91-3. Cambridge, MA: Wiener Center for Social Policy, Kennedy School of Government, Harvard University, 1991.

Bane, Mary Jo, and David Ellwood. "The Dynamics of Dependency: The Routes to Self-Sufficiency." Unpublished report to the U.S. Department of Health and Human Services. Cambridge, MA: Urban Systems Research and Engineering, 1983.

Barnett, W. Steven, and Colette M. Escobar. "The Economics of Early Educa-
    tional Intervention: A Review." *Review of Educational Research* 57, no. 4 (1987):
    393–404.
Behn, Robert D. *The Management of ET CHOICES in Massachusetts.* Durham, NC:
    Duke University, Institute of Policy Sciences and Public Affairs, 1989.
Berlin, Gordon. "The New Poverty Among Families: A Service Categorization
    Response." New York: Manpower Demonstration Research Corporation,
    undated.
Brindis, Claire, Richard P. Barth, and Amy B. Loomis. "Continuous Counsel-
    ing: Case Management with Teenage Parents." *Social Casework: The Journal
    of Contemporary Social Work.* March 1987: 164–72.
Brooks, Eve E., and Brigit Hurley. *For Mommy and Me: Toward a Child Develop-
    ment Policy for Welfare Recipients.* Rochester, NY: Statewide Youth Advocacy,
    November 1988.
Bruner, Charles. "Is Change From Above Possible? State-Level Strategies for Sup-
    porting Street-Level Services." Working Paper no. ES-91-6. Cambridge, MA:
    Wiener Center for Social Policy, Kennedy School of Government, Harvard
    University, 1991.
──── . "State-Level Approaches to Foster Local-Level Collaboration: Iowa's In-
    itiatives To Improve Children's Welfare." Unpublished first draft prepared
    for the National Conference of State Legislatures, July 1990.
──── . *Thinking Collaboratively: Ten Questions and Answers To Help Policy Makers
    Improve Children's Services.* Washington, DC: Education and Human Ser-
    vices Consortium, 1991.
Bruner, Charles, and George Oster, eds. *Family Development and Self-Sufficiency
    Demonstration Grant Program. Proceedings of the Program Implementation
    Workshop: A Focus on Iowa's Support Programs.* Des Moines: Child and Family
    Policy Center, 1989.
Bryant, Donna M., and Craig T. Ramey. "An Analysis of the Effectiveness of
    Early Intervention Programs for Environmentally At-Risk Children." In *The
    Effectiveness of Early Intervention for At-Risk and Handicapped Children,* edited
    by Michael J. Guralnick and Forrest C. Bennett. San Diego: Academic Press,
    1987.
Burbridge, Lynn C. "Will Welfare Be Reformed? The Possible Effects of the Family
    Support Act on Children." *Urban League Review* (1989): 29–41.
Burt, Martha, Madeline Kimmich, Jane Goldmuntz, and Freya L. Sonenstein. *Help-
    ing Pregnant Adolescents: Outcomes and Costs of Service Delivery. Final Report
    on the Evaluation of Adolescent Pregnancy Programs.* Washington, DC: Urban
    Institute, 1984.
California Child Care Resource and Referral Network—Partners in Prevention.
    Making a Difference: A Handbook for Child Care Providers. Oakland: California
    Child Care Resource and Referral Network, 1986.
Center for the Future of Children, The David and Lucile Packard Foundation.
    "School-Linked Services." *The Future of Children* 2, no. 1 (Spring 1992).
Center for Human Resources, Heller School, Brandeis University. "About Case
    Management." *Youth Programs* (Fall 1988): 2–7, 15.
──── . *A Guide to Case Management for At-Risk Youth.* Waltham, MA, 1989.

Center for Law and Social Policy. "Child Care and the Family Support Act." Special issue of *Family Matters* 1, no. 3 (Spring 1989).

——. "Teens and the Family Support Act." Special issue of *Family Matters* 2, no. 1 (January 1990).

——. "The Need for Cooperation: Why Should Educators Be Concerned about Developments in the Welfare System?" Special issue of *The Partnership: Welfare, Education, Job Training* 1 (Spring 1988).

Center for the Study of Social Policy. "A Framework for Child Welfare Reform." Unpublished paper, prepared for the Annie E. Casey Foundation. Greenwich, CT, December 1987.

——. "Case Management and System Reform: Issues in Examining the Skills and Training Needed by New Front-Line Workers." Washington, DC, undated.

Child Care Circuit. Lawrence, MA. Miscellaneous program documents and memoranda.

Children's Council of San Francisco. *The Invisible Child: San Francisco's Solution to the Latch Key Problem*. San Francisco: Children's Council of San Francisco, 1988.

Clewell, Beatriz Chu, J. Brooks-Gunn, and April A. Benasich. "Evaluating Child-Related Outcomes of Teenage Parenting Programs." *Family Relations* 38 (April 1989): 201–209.

Cottingham, Phoebe H., and David T. Ellwood, eds. *Welfare Policy for the 1990's*. Cambridge, MA: Harvard University Press, 1989.

Darling, Sharon. "The Kenan Trust Family Literacy Project. Preliminary Final Report." Chapel Hill, NC: William R. Kenan, Jr. Charitable Trust Fund, 1989.

Doolittle, Fred, and James Riccio. "Case Management in Welfare Employment Programs." Unpublished paper prepared for a conference entitled "Evaluation Design for Welfare and Training Programs," sponsored by the Institute for Research on Poverty of the University of Wisconsin-Madison and the Office of the Assistant Secretary for Planning and Evaluation of the U.S. Department of Health and Human Services, April 1990.

Ebb, Nancy. *Steps Every State Should Take To Implement the Child Care Provisions of the Family Support Act: A Preliminary Guide to P.L. 100-485*. Washington, DC: Children's Defense Fund, September 1989.

Ellwood, David T. *Poor Support: Poverty in the American Family*. New York: Basic Books, 1988.

Family Service Agency of San Francisco, San Francisco Unified School District, and the Ella Hill Hutch Teen Father Program. "GAIN Teen-Age Pregnancy and Parenting Program (TAPP): A Family Approach for Intergenerational Self-Sufficiency (GAIN/TAPP)." Proposal to the Department of Social Services, San Francisco, revised March 30, 1988.

Gardner, Sidney L. "Community Accountability for Children: Cross-Cutting Outcome Measures at the Community Level." Working paper no. ES-91-5. Cambridge, MA: Wiener Center for Social Policy, Kennedy School of Government, Harvard University, 1991.

Gardner, Sid. "Failure by Fragmentation." *California Tomorrow* (Fall 1989): 19–24.

Goldstein, Naomi Carol. "Explaining Socioeconomic Differences in Children's Cognitive Test Scores." Discussion paper no. H-90-1. Cambridge, MA: Wiener Center for Social Policy, Kennedy School of Government, Harvard University, January 1990.

———. "Why Poverty Is Bad for Children." Unpublished Ph.D. dissertation. Cambridge, MA: Harvard University, 1991.

Greenberg, Mark. *Family Support Act of 1988: JOBS Program and Related Amendments: Requirements, Issues, and Options.* Washington, DC: Center for Law and Social Policy, November 1988.

———. *The Final JOBS Regulations: HHS Resolution of Key Issues and Some Implications for JOBS Planning.* Washington, DC: Center for Law and Social Policy, October 1989.

———. *The JOBS Program: Answers and Questions.* Washington, DC: Center for Law and Social Policy, July 1990.

———. *JOBS Provisions of the Family Support Act of 1988: Ten Early Choices.* Washington, DC: Center for Law and Social Policy, November 1988.

Greenberg, Mark, and Jodie Levin-Epstein. *The JOBS Program: Good Ideas and Some Concerns in the First Round of State Plans.* Washington, DC: Center for Law and Social Policy, August 1989.

Guba, Egon G., and Yvonna S. Lincoln. *Effective Evaluation.* San Francisco: Jossey-Bass, 1982.

Hausman, Bonnie, and Kathryn Parsons. "PACE: Breaking the Cycle of Intergenerational Illiteracy." *Equity and Choice* 5, no. 3 (May 1989): 57–58.

Hayes, Cheryl D., John L. Palmer, and Martha J. Zaslow, eds. *Who Cares for America's Children? Child Care Policy for the 1990's.* Washington, DC: National Academy Press, 1990.

Herr, Toby, and Robert Halpern with Aimee Conrad. "Changing What Counts: Re-Thinking the Journey Out Of Welfare." Research and Policy Reports Series. Evanston, IL: Center for Urban Affairs and Policy Research, Northwestern University, 1991.

Heyman, Philip B. *The Politics of Public Management.* New Haven, CT: Yale University Press, 1987.

Himmelman, Arthur T. "Communities Working Collaboratively for a Change." Minneapolis: Humphrey Institute of Public Affairs, University of Minnesota, May 1990.

Hodgkinson, Harold L. *The Same Client: The Demographics of Education and Service Delivery Systems.* Washington, DC: Institute for Educational Leadership and Center for Demographic Policy, 1989.

Jehl, Jeanne, and Michael Kirst. "Getting Ready To Provide School-Linked Services: What Schools Must Do." *The Future of Children* 2, no. 1 (Spring 1992): 95–106.

Jenkins, Steve, Cheryl Dorsey, and Olivia Golden. "Characteristics of Service Deliverers: Who Delivers Services to Poor Children?" Unpublished paper prepared for the executive session entitled "Making the System Work for Poor Children." Cambridge, MA: Wiener Center for Social Policy, Kennedy School of Government, Harvard University, updated June 1989.

Johnson, Clifford M., Leticia Miranda, Arloc Sherman, and James D. Weill. *Child Poverty in America.* Washington, DC: Children's Defense Fund, 1991.

Kagan, Sharon L., Ann Marie Rivera, and Faith Lamb Parker. *Collaborations in Action: Reshaping Services for Young Children and Their Families.* New Haven, CT: The Bush Center in Child Development and Social Policy, Yale University, 1990.

Kamerman, Sheila B., and Alfred J. Kahn. *Social Services for Children, Youth and Families in the United States.* Greenwich, CT: Annie E. Casey Foundation, 1989.

Kane, Thomas J. "The Caseworker-Client Relationship and Welfare Reform." Working paper no. H-90-9. Cambridge, MA: Wiener Center for Social Policy, Kennedy School of Government, Harvard University, 1990.

Kenyon, V. Sheffield. "Case Management." Unpublished paper, available from the National Center for Children in Poverty, New York, 1988.

Korenbrot, Carol C., Jonathan Showstack, Amy Loomis, and Claire Brindis. "Birth Weight Outcomes in a Teenage Pregnancy Case Management Project." *Journal of Adolescent Health Care* 10 (1989): 97–104.

Kosterlitz, Julie. "Devil in the Details." *National Journal* (December 2, 1989): 2942–46.

Lawrence, Paul R., and Jay W. Lorsch. *Organization and Environment: Managing Differentiation and Integration.* Cambridge, MA: Harvard University, Graduate School of Business Administration, Division of Research, 1967.

Lemov, Penelope. "Bringing the Children of the Underclass into the Mainstream." *Governing* (June 1989): 34–39.

Levy, Janet E., with Carol Copple. *Joining Forces: A Report from the First Year.* Alexandria, VA: National Association of State Boards of Education, 1989.

Liberman, Ruth J. "Clearing the Path to Recovery: Health and Social Service Collaboration for Boston's Pregnant Addicts." Working paper no. H-91-9. Cambridge, MA: Wiener Center for Social Policy, Kennedy School of Government, Harvard University, August 1991.

Lipsky, Michael. *Street-Level Bureaucracy: Dilemmas of the Individual in Public Services.* New York: Russell Sage Foundation, 1980.

Loomis, Amy, Claire Brindis, and Carol Korenbrot. *A Formula for School Dropout Prevention: Teen-Age Pregnancy and Parenting Program (TAPP).* Presented to the California State Department of Education. San Francisco: Teenage Pregnancy and Parenting Program, June 1987.

Lorsch, Jay. "Organizational Design: A Situational Perspective." In *Perspectives on Behavior in Organizations,* edited by J. Richard Hackman, Edward E. Lawler III, and Lyman W. Porter. New York: McGraw-Hill, 1983.

Martinson, Karin, and James Riccio. *GAIN: Child Care in a Welfare Employment Initiative.* New York: Manpower Demonstration Research Corporation, 1989.

Massachusetts Department of Public Welfare. *The Massachusetts Employment and Training Choices Program: Program Plan and Budget Narrative, FY 89.* Boston, 1988.

——— . *Case Management Guide.* Boston, April, 1987.

Massachusetts Department of Public Welfare and Department of Employment and Training. Miscellaneous program documents and memoranda.

Melaville, Atelia I., with Martin J. Blank. *What It Takes: Structuring Interagency Partnerships To Connect Children and Families with Comprehensive Services.* Washington, DC: Education and Human Services Consortium, 1991.

Michigan Department of Social Services, Michigan Opportunity and Skills Training (MOST). Miscellaneous program documents and memoranda.

Michigan Department of Social Services, Wayne County Office. Miscellaneous program documents and memoranda.

Miller, George, ed. *Giving Children a Chance: The Case for More Effective National Policies.* Washington, DC: Center for National Policy Press, 1989.

Moore, Mark. "Creating Public Value: Strategic Management in the Public Sector." Unpublished paper, Harvard University, Kennedy School of Government, 1992.

Mumma, Edward W. "Reform at the Local Level: Virginia Beach Empowers Both Clients and Workers." *Public Welfare* 47 (Spring 1989): 15–24.

Musick, Judith S., and Robert Halpern. "Giving Children a Chance: What Role Community-Based Parenting Interventions?" In *Giving Children a Chance: The Case for More Effective National Policies,* edited by George Miller. Washington, DC: Center for National Policy Press, 1989.

Nash, Margaret A., and Margaret Dunkle. *The Need for a Warming Trend: A Survey of the School Climate for Pregnant and Parenting Teens.* Washington, DC: Equality Center, 1989.

Nathan, Richard P. "Implementation Research: Studying the Institutional Challenge of the JOBS Program." Paper prepared for conference entitled "Evaluation Design for Welfare and Training Programs," April 19–21, 1990.

———. "The New Bargain Between Welfare and Work." In *Emerging Issues* series. Albany: State University of New York at Albany, undated.

National Center for Children in Poverty. *Five Million Children: A Statistical Profile of Our Poorest Young Citizens.* New York: Columbia School of Public Health, 1990.

National Governors' Association. *Coordinating Prenatal Care.* Washington, DC, 1989.

New Beginnings Team. *New Beginnings: A Feasibility Study of Integrated Services for Children and Families.* San Diego: San Diego City Schools, July 1990.

Next Step TASA Program, Economic Opportunity Program of Chemung and Schuyler Counties, New York. Miscellaneous program documents and memoranda.

Oklahoma Department of Human Services, Field Operations, Integrated Family Services. *MATCH (Mothers Affirming, Teaching, Caring, and Helping) Training Manual: A Program To Provide Positive Parenting Role Models.* May 1989.

———. *Pre-Employment Assessment Training Manual: Job Selection, Job Search, Job Success.* Revised May 1989.

———. Miscellaneous program documents and memoranda.

Olds, David L., and Charles R. Henderson, Jr. "The Prevention of Maltreatment." In *Child Maltreatment: Theory and Research on the Causes and Consequences of Child Abuse and Neglect,* edited by Dante Cicchetti and Vicki Carlson. New York: Cambridge University Press, 1989.

Olds, David L., Charles R. Henderson, Jr., Robert Tatelbaum, and Robert Chamberlin. "Improving the Life-Course Development of Socially Disadvantaged Mothers: A Randomized Trial of Nurse Home Visitation." *American Journal of Public Health* 78, no. 11 (November 1988): 1436–45.

Peters, Tom, and Nancy Austin. *A Passion for Excellence: The Leadership Difference.* New York: Warner Books, 1985; reprinted with new Afterword, 1986.

Petit, Michael. "Issues Surrounding State-Level Collaboration on Services to At-Risk, Preschool Age Children." Presented to the Summer Institute of the Council of Chief State School Officers, Portland, ME, August 3, 1988.

Pillsbury, Jolie Bain. "Reform at the State Level: In Massachusetts, Eligibility Workers Have Become Case Managers." *Public Welfare* 47 (Spring 1989): 8–14.

Polit, Denise F., Janet Kahn, and David Stevens. *Final Impacts from Project Redirection: A Program for Pregnant and Parenting Teens.* New York: Manpower Demonstration Research Corporation, 1985.

Polit, Denise F., and Joseph J. O'Hara. "Support Services." In *Welfare Policy for the 1990's,* edited by Phoebe Cottingham and David Ellwood. Cambridge, MA: Harvard University Press, 1989.

Polit, Denise F., Janet C. Quint, and James A. Riccio. *The Challenge of Serving Teenage Mothers: Lessons from Project Redirection.* New York: Manpower Demonstration Research Corporation, 1988.

Quint, Janet C., and Cynthia A. Guy. *New Chance: Lessons from the Pilot Phase.* New York: Manpower Demonstration Research Corporation, 1989.

Riccio, James, Barbara Goldman, Gayle Hamilton, Karin Martinson, and Alan Orenstein. *GAIN: Early Implementation Experiences and Lessons.* New York: Manpower Demonstration Research Corporation, 1989.

Riccio, James, with Kay E. Sherwood. *Key Decisions in Implementing JOBS: Lessons from California's GAIN Program.* New York: Manpower Demonstration Research Corporation, 1990.

Robinson, Estelle R., and Aleta You Mastny. *Linking Schools and Community Services.* New Brunswick, NJ: Center for Community Education, School of Social Work, Rutgers, State University of New Jersey, 1989.

Roditti, Martha, and Libby Denebeim. *Guide to Services for Children, Youth, and Families in San Francisco.* San Francisco: The Children's Council of San Francisco, sixth edition, 1989.

Romig, Candace L., ed. "Family Policy: Recommendations for State Action." Washington, DC: National Conference of State Legislatures, Children, Families, and Social Services Committee, December 1989.

Rosenthal, Stephen R. *Managing Government Operations.* Chicago: Scott, Foresman, 1982.

San Diego City Schools, San Diego Adolescent Pregnancy and Parenting Program (SANDAPP). Miscellaneous program documents and memoranda.

San Diego County (CA) Department of Social Services, GAIN Program. Miscellaneous program documents and memoranda.

Schorr, Lisbeth B., Deborah Both, and Carol Copple, eds. *Effective Services for Young Children.* Report of a workshop sponsored by the National Forum on the Future of Children and Families, National Research Council, and Institute of Medicine. Washington, DC: National Academy Press, 1991.

Schorr, Lisbeth B., with Daniel Schorr. *Within Our Reach: Breaking the Cycle of Disadvantage.* New York: Doubleday, Anchor Press, 1988.

Schweinhart, Lawrence J., and David P. Weikart. "What Do We Know So Far? A Review of the Head Start Synthesis Project." *Young Children* 41, no. 2 (January 1986): 49–55.

Sherman, Arloc, and Alan W. Houseman. *Welfare Reform and the Education Provisions: Programmatic Options and Considerations.* Washington, DC: Center for Law and Social Policy, September 1989.

Skinner, Mary, Robert Greenstein, and Susan Steinmetz. "The Family Support Act: Accomplishments and Limitations from a Historical Perspective." In *The Family Support Act: Will It Work in Rural Areas?,* edited by Robert Hoppe. Washington, DC: U.S. Department of Agriculture, forthcoming.

Smith, Sheila, Susan Blank, and James T. Bond. *One Program, Two Generations: A Report of the Forum on Children and the Family Support Act.* New York: Foundation for Child Development, in partnership with the National Center for Children in Poverty, 1990.

Stewart, Denis. "Case Management." Paper prepared for the Pennsylvania Services Integration Consortium and the Pennsylvania Association of Public Assistance Executive Directors, Committee on Program Coordination, October 1989.

Strassburger, Heidi. "Implementing the Child Care Provisions of the Family Support Act of 1988: The Need for a Better Coordinated, More Child-Centered System for Providing Child Care to AFDC Recipients." Testimony Before the Joint Oversight Committee on GAIN Implementation, California State Legislature. San Francisco: Child Care Law Center, 1989.

Sussman, Richard A. "Case Management: Working Paper no. 1." Draft prepared for the Connecticut Commission on Children, Fall 1988.

Sylvester, Kathleen. "New Strategies To Save Children in Trouble." *Governing* (May 1990): 32–37.

Teen-Age Pregnancy and Parenting Project (TAPP), Family Services Agency, San Francisco, CA. Miscellaneous program documents and memoranda.

U.S. Bureau of the Census, Current Population Reports, series P-60, no. 175. *Poverty in the United States: 1990.* Washington, DC: U.S. Government Printing Office, 1991.

U.S. Congress. House. Committee on Ways and Means. *Overview of Entitlement Programs: 1991 Green Book. Background Material and Data on Programs within the Jurisdiction of the Committee on Ways and Means.* 102d Congress, 1st Session, 1991.

U.S. Department of Health and Human Services, Office of Human Development Services, Office of Policy, Planning, and Legislation. "Report on Progress and Status of Services Integration Pilot Projects: First Year Planning Phase." Washington, DC: February 1987.

U.S. Department of Labor, Employment and Training Administration. *Implementing Welfare-Employment Programs: An Institutional Analysis of the Work Incentive (WIN) Program.* R&D Monograph no. 78. Report prepared by John J. Mitchell, Mark L. Chadwin, and Demetra S. Nightingale. Washington, DC: U.S. Government Printing Office, 1980.

van Straalen, Catherine. "The Eligibility Specialist in Income Maintenance Centers: A Training Needs Analysis." Unpublished report submitted to Allen Kraus, Deputy Commissioner, New York City Human Resources Administration. New York, August 1988.

Wattenberg, Esther. "Mandatory Case Planning for Minnesota Minor Mothers and Their Children: A Report on Implementing Minnesota Statutes 1988, Section 257.33." Minneapolis: Center for Urban and Regional Affairs, December 1989.

Weil, Marie, James M. Karls, and Associates. *Case Management in Human Services Practice*. San Francisco: Jossey-Bass, 1985.

Weiss, Janet A. "Substance vs. Symbol in Administrative Reform: The Case of Human Services Coordination." *Policy Analysis* 7 (Winter 1981): 20–45.

Weissbourd, Bernice, and Carol Emig. "Early Childhood Programs for Children in Poverty: A Good Place To Start." In *Giving Children a Chance: The Case for More Effective National Policies*, edited by George Miller. Washington, DC: Center for National Policy Press, 1989.

Weissbourd, Rick. "Making the System Work for Poor Children." Working paper no. ES-91-4. Cambridge, MA: Wiener Center for Social Policy, Kennedy School of Government, Harvard University, 1991.

——. "Public Elementary Schools: A Ladder Out of Poverty?" Discussion paper no. H-89-3. Cambridge, MA: Wiener Center for Social Policy, Kennedy School of Government, Harvard University, December 1989.

Zill, Nicholas, Kristin Moore, and Thomas Stief. "Progress Report: Analysis of Employment-Related Characteristics of AFDC Mothers in National Survey Data Bases." Unpublished paper. Washington, DC: Child Trends, Inc., December 1989.

Index

About the Author

OLIVIA GOLDEN is Director of Programs and Policy at the Children's Defense Fund. She holds Master of Public Policy and Doctor of Philosophy degrees from Harvard University where she has also taught. She served as Budget Director for the Executive Office of Human Services, Commonwealth of Massachusetts.